RUN, RIVER, RUN

RUN, RIVER, RUN

A NATURALIST'S JOURNEY DOWN ONE OF THE GREAT RIVERS OF THE WEST

ANN ZWINGER

Illustrations and maps by the author

HARPER & ROW, PUBLISHERS

New York, Evanston, San Francisco,

London

RUN, RIVER, RUN.
Copyright © 1975 by Ann H. Zwinger.
All rights reserved.
Printed in the United States of America.
No part of this book may be used or reproduced
in any manner whatsoever without written permission
except in the case of brief quotations
embodied in critical articles and reviews.
For information address Harper & Row, Publishers, Inc.,
10 East 53rd Street, New York, N.Y. 10022.
Published simultaneously in Canada by
Fitzhenry & Whiteside Limited, Toronto.

FIRST EDITION

Designed by Dorothy Schmiderer

Library of Congress Cataloging in Publication Data

Zwinger, Ann.
Run, river, run.
   Includes bibliographical references and index.
   1. Natural history—Green River, Wyo.-Utah.
2. Green River, Wyo.-Utah.   I. Title.
QH105.W8Z87   1975   500.9'792'21   74-1874
ISBN: 0-06-014824-1

75 76 77 78 79 10 9 8 7 6 5 4 3 2 1

For Marie, with love

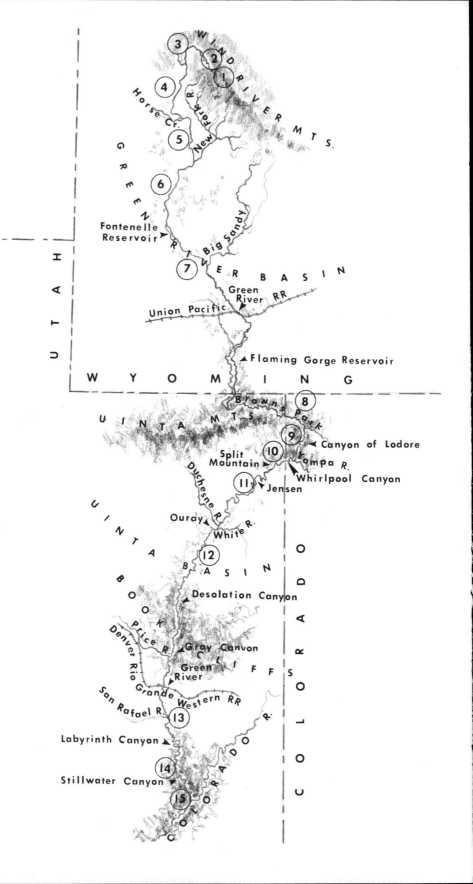

CONTENTS

Grateful acknowledgment is made for permission to reprint the following:

Excerpts from *The Ashley-Smith Explorations and the Discovery of a Central Route to the Pacific, 1822–1829* by Harrison C. Dale. Reprinted by permission of the Publishers, The Arthur H. Clarke Company.

Excerpts from *Beyond the Hundredth Meridian* by Wallace Stegner. Reprinted by permission of Houghton Mifflin Company.

Excerpts from "Down the Colorado in 1889" by Helen J. Stiles. Previously published in *The Colorado Magazine* 41 (Summer 1964). Reprinted by permission of the State Historical Society of Colorado, Denver.

Excerpts from *Exploration of the Colorado River and Its Canyons* by John W. Powell, published by Dover Publications, Inc.

Excerpts and illustrations from *Fluvial Processes in Geomorphology* by Luna B. Leopold, M. Gordon Wolman, and John P. Miller. Reprinted by permission of W. H. Freeman and Company. Copyright © 1964.

Excerpts from "George Bradley's Journal" edited by William C. Darrah. Previously published in the *Utah Historical Quarterly*, XV. Excerpts from "Pageant in the Wilderness" by Herbert E. Bolton. Previously published in the *Utah Historical Quarterly*, XVIII. Reprinted by permission of the Department of Development Services of the State of Utah.

Diagram adapted from *Glacial & Quaternary Geology* by R. F. Flint. Previously published by John Wiley & Sons, New York, 1971. Reprinted by permission of the author.

Diagram adapted from W. H. Bradley's illustrations in *Limnology in North America* edited by David Frey. Copyright © 1963 by the Regents of the University of Wisconsin. Reprinted by permission of The University of Wisconsin Press.

Excerpts from *Prairie and Mountain Sketches* by Matthew C. Field. Copyright 1957 by the University of Oklahoma Press. Reprinted by permission of the University of Oklahoma Press.

Diagrams from *Streams: Their Dynamics and Morphology* by Marie Morisawa. Copyright © 1968 by McGraw-Hill, Inc. Reprinted by permission of McGraw-Hill Book Company.

Excerpts from the tape interview with Ralph White, Clerk of the Moffat County Court at Craig, Colo., November 14, 1963, by Paul Ellis at the National Park Service. Reprinted by permission of Dinosaur National Monument.

Excerpts from *Through the Grand Canyon from Wyoming to Mexico* by Ellsworth L. Kolb. Copyright 1914 by Macmillan Publishing Co., Inc. Renewed 1942 by Ellsworth L. Kolb. Reprinted by permission of Macmillan Publishing Co., Inc.

Excerpts from *Trail to California: The Overland Journal of Vincent Geiger and Wakeman Bryarly* edited by David Morris Potter. Reprinted by permission of Yale University Press.

Excerpts from *W. A. Ferris—Life in the Rocky Mountains* by Paul C. Phillips. Reprinted by permission of Old West Publishing Company, Denver, Colo.

ACKNOWLEDGMENTS

No book of this kind can be written without the generous help of scholars and experts in the fields concerned. Those who read and commented upon the entire manuscript were Dr. Richard G. Beidleman, Dr. Luna B. Leopold, and G. E. Untermann. Dr. Beidleman, Professor of Biology, The Colorado College, also made available typescript material and made valuable suggestions on history. Dr. Leopold, Professor of Geology and Geophysics, University of California, was especially helpful in the area of fluvial dynamics, and gave gracious and appreciated encouragement; no book on any river would be complete without a thorough reading of his extensive research. Mr. Untermann personally showed me the Uintah County area with which he is so familiar, and provided much of its historical background as well as courtesy at the Utah Field House of Natural History in Vernal. Others read segments in their area of expertise and gave advice and criticism: Dr. N. Allen Binns, Wyoming Fish & Game Commission, commented in detail on the upper-river chapters and provided much local information. Dr. W. H. Bradley, retired Chief Geologist, U.S.G.S., read the section on the Green River Basin. Wallace R. Hansen, U.S.G.S., Denver, advised on the geology of the Flaming Gorge, Browns Park, and Dinosaur National Monument. Dr. Jesse E. Jennings, Professor of Anthropology, University of Utah, read the section on Fremont Indians. Dr. C. Gregory Crampton, American West Center, University of Utah, scrutinized the history, as did Marshall Sprague; their advice had added value as both are fine writers. O. Dock

Marston, the authoritative river historian, reviewed and expanded my material. Dr. Donald L. Baars, Professor of Geology, Fort Lewis College, checked the geology of the lower Green and updated geological nomenclature. Dr. William A. Weber, University of Colorado Museum, made plant identifications and commented on drawings. Donald J. Orth, Executive Secretary, Board on Domestic Names, U.S. Board on Geographic Names, pinpointed the source of the Green. I am also indebted to Robert Wiley, Wyoming Fish & Game Commission, for comment. I have observed their comments and corrections scrupulously; if there are any errors, they are entirely mine.

At The Colorado College, I would like to thank Dr. Jack Carter, Professor of Botany, and Dr. George Fagan of the Charles Leaming Tutt Library. The staff there were most helpful, especially Charlotte Tate, Donna M. Jones, Rosemae Campbell, Curator of the Colorado Room, and Reference Librarian Kee DeBoer, who could find anything, anywhere. Barbara Beers, University of California, gave extensive assistance on a working bibliography. At the University of Utah, I thank Dr. Jennings and Gardiner F. Dalley of the Department of Anthropology; Mr. Donald Hague, Curator of the Museum of Natural History, and Mrs. Edith Lamb; James Madsen, Jr., Research Professor, and Jim Howell, graduate student, of the Department of Geological and Geophysical Sciences. Bev Godec, Colorado Springs Utilities Department, and Jack Cartright, Bosworth & Sullivan, provided information about utilities and corporations that use water from the Green River. Finis Mitchell shared his unparalleled knowledge of the Wind River Range. I am also indebted to Joan Nice, editor of *High Country News,* Lander, Wyoming, for access to their files.

I have had the privilege of working with some of the best guides and boatmen on the river: Connie and Perry Binning of Pinedale, Wyoming; Paul Brown, Hatch River Expeditions; Patrick Conley; Kent Frost, Canyonlands Tours; Dan Lehman; "Moki-Mac" Ellingson, Bob and Clair Quist, Mark Davis, Moki-Mac Expeditions; Ken Sleight, Wonderland Expeditions. I also thank Don Hatch for river history, and Ron Smith, Grand Canyon Expeditions, for background on raft design.

Bill McCabe, Colorado Outward Bound, checked facts pertaining to their operation; along with Mark Leachman, I thank instructors Susie Rittenhouse, Jessie Morland, and John Pitman, who made it possible for me to go, plus a great crew: Jane Farrar, Hilo Gay, Helen Hilliard, Allie Jones, Lisa Nini, Stephanie Noyes, and Vickie Weitzel.

It is impossible for me to thank all the people who have added to my time on the river, and I hope I have thanked them personally. To some I am particularly grateful: Carroll Beek and her family, Nonie Boyce, Marge Elliott, Virginia Kaufmann, Dorothy Lirette, Jan Pilling, Bea Rizzolo, Lee Sayre, Mike and Dorothy Scorcz, Joyce and Vernon Smith, Janet Tibbetts, Sue Walton, Evangeline Witzeman, and most especially, Susan Conley and Pam Davis.

For help in preparation I thank Vivian and Sidney Novis, Dick and Judy Noyes of the Chinook Bookshop and their staff, and the staff of Copy Cat, Inc., especially Roberta Ring and Vicki Fulgenzi. For reading and comment I thank Anne Cross and Richard Rixon; for extended and detailed criticism, Timilou Rixon; for help in proof-reading, Marilyn Lewis.

I appreciate the kind understanding and firm editorial pencil of M. S. Wyeth, Jr., and the help of his assistant, Lynne McNabb. My appreciation of Marie Rodell, literary agent, is expressed in the dedication. And my special thanks to Dorothy Schmiderer.

I owe a great deal to a remarkable and resilient family, especially Sara, who kept house one summer so I could write, helped with the tedious jobs of card filing and proofreading, and who was Outward Bound companion. Jane read and commented on drawings and manuscript, sometimes ruthlessly, all the more valued; Susan, as a doctoral candidate in the fields of art, psychology, and education, and a writer herself, enriched my outlook tremendously. And most of all I thank Herman, who floated the Uinta Basin with me, flew me over the beautiful river many times, took me to all the places you can't get to from here, put up with a clacking typewriter, and without whom this book could never have been written.

Milkvetch
(*Astragalus* sp.)

INTRODUCTION

I GREW UP on a river. Not a very big river, across the street and down the bank, but it was always there, running downhill to the Wabash and the Ohio and the Mississippi. Even then it was rust red from a wire mill to the east of town. Long before white settlers came, the Munsee Indians settled along the White River. According to their legend, where the river made a horseshoe bend, as it did just half a mile west of our house, there would be no tornadoes. Whether they were right or not I don't know, but there were indeed no tornadoes.

In the summertime, with the windows open and the sycamore leaves silent and the cicadas still, you could hear it. Not very loud, but it was there. In the winter, when I was little, I could skate on it. I would slide down the bank, grabbing onto bushes to keep from going all the way down at once, put on skates, and half walk, half skate between the chunks of ice that buckled up with the cold. It was frightening because the ice boomed and cracked, and I was never sure but what it would open up in a great chasm and take me downstream forever. But I kept on skating, determined not to give up until it was too cold, and then I put on frosty shoes and struggled up the bank home for a cup of hot chocolate from a mother who used to skate on a river when she was a little girl.

In the fall there were "Indian trails," which were nothing more than hobo trails, but in those very young years Indian lore appealed more than the desperation of a recent and un-understood depression. One summer, when it had been terribly hot and drought conditions seared the Midwest and the river was down to a trickle, people came with bushel baskets and mallets; they went down the bank and hit the carp over the head and piled them into baskets and took them home. In the springtime there were violets, blooming in opulent purple-flowered drifts—of course there have never been such violets since. And then they cut down the trees along the river for flood control. My usually gentle father stood on the bank and fumed; cutting a tree was a sacrilege and he could not understand why cutting trees on a river bank provided flood control, especially when cement facings had to be built on the bank's steep side to hold the soil after the trees were gone.

I have been back since, and I suppose I always unconsciously checked the river. In later years there was too much traffic and probably the river couldn't be heard at all, but I opened the windows in the quiet hours before dawn and knelt there and listened, perhaps as much for childhood as for the river. Perhaps I did hear it, perhaps not. It doesn't matter. When there is a river in your growing up, you probably always hear it.

This is a book about a much larger river, the Green River, and how it relates to the landscape and how it goes and what it shows of rock and wind, how people have used it and how it has used people. Still wild in many reaches, it is a magnificent river. To me, it is the most beautiful river anywhere.

ANN HAYMOND ZWINGER

Goniobiasis shells,
Green River Formation

1

... while, almost at the captain's feet, the Green River, or Colorado of the West, set forth on its wandering pilgrimage to the Gulf of California; at first a mere mountain torrent, dashing northward over crag and precipice, in a succession of cascades, and tumbling into the plain, where, expanding into an ample river, it circled away to the south, and after alternately shining out and disappearing in the mazes of the vast landscape, was finally lost in a horizon of mountains. The day was calm and cloudless, and the atmosphere so pure that objects were discernible at an astonishing distance. The whole of this immense area was inclosed by an outer range of shadowy peaks, some of them faintly marked on the horizon, which seemed to wall it in from the rest of the earth.

WASHINGTON IRVING, 1859, *The Adventures of Captain Bonneville, U.S.A., in the Rocky Mountains and the Far West*

Rock ragwort
(*Senecio fremontii* var. *blitoides*)

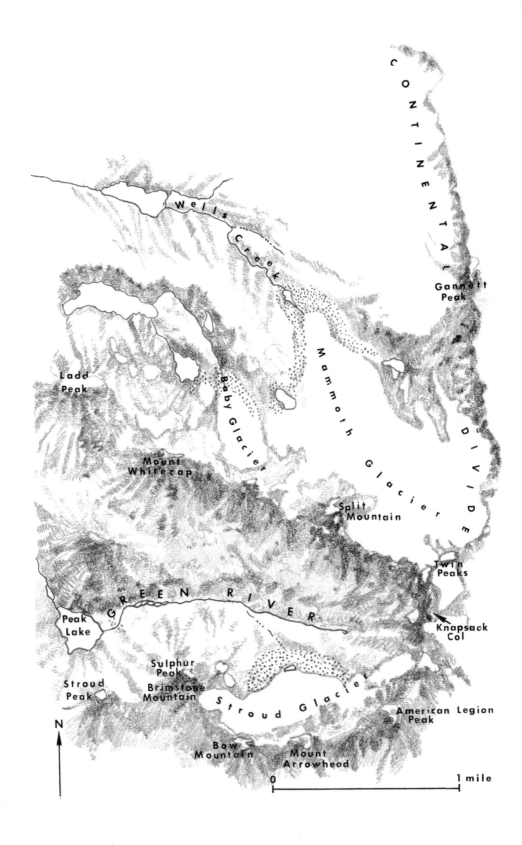

THE SOURCE TO PEAK LAKE

BENEATH THE BEATING of the wind I can hear the river beginning. Snow rounds into water, seeps and trickles, splashes and pours and clatters, burnishing the shattered gray rock, and carols downslope, light and sound interwoven with sunlight. The high saddle upon which we stand, here in the Wind River Mountains, is labeled Knapsack Col on the map, a rim left where two opposing cirques once enlarged toward each other. It defines the head of a rock-strewn valley less than a mile wide and some two miles long. This valley, hung like a hammock between twelve- and thirteen-thousand-foot peaks, is weighted down the middle with a lead-blue line: the first vein of the Green River. High altitude, intense blue sky, fresh wind, bone-warming August sun through the early-morning chill, panoramic view—I am bedazzled by this blazing landscape with its nascent river.

Part of my euphoria in standing here also comes, I suspect, from the fact that the only way to get here is on one's own two feet, and it has taken the three of us—Connie and Perry Binning and me—four days to do so. Connie is the only woman guide I know (and also the only woman I know to have a glacier named for her). When I am away from my family, she takes me into hers. Perry speaks to animals along the way, sometimes gravely, sometimes cheerfully, always courteously. I have long since stopped being amazed that, if they are within hearing distance, they answer in kind. Perry's walking stick is a basketless ski pole, and when Connie and I have lagged behind, we can tell we're on the right trail by the small neat perforations it makes in the dirt. We agree that this view of the headwaters of the Green River is an earned view, and the knowledge that not too many people have stood here as we do makes it all the more magnificent.

In fact, many people are not even aware of the Green River. I am abashed to admit that until a few years ago I was largely ignorant of its 730 miles of running—291 in Wyoming, 42 in Colorado, 397 in Utah—for it is a big river that has cut channels through mountain rock and canyon wilderness. It is a historic river, for it was the center of the beaver trade in the 1830s, its north-south course lay athwart westward migration, and heroic river runs were made through its canyons. In some ways, it is also a mysterious river, the derivation of its name lost in history, and its precise source, for one reason or another, until now only loosely defined.

Indians and mountain men had undoubtedly been traversing the Wind Rivers for years, but Captain Benjamin Louis Eulalie de Bonneville made the first recorded climb in 1833 and logged a vivid description, but no latitude and longitude. Major John Wesley Powell, the most famous river runner of all, did not enter the Wind River Range and only guessed at the coordinates; a party of the famous Hayden Survey of 1877 did climb the mountains, but their report also was vague. Ralf Woolley, whose definitive United States Geological Survey Water Supply Paper 618 on the Green River was printed in 1930, took refuge in saying the source lay in an "extremely rugged area" somewhere among the "glaciers and numerous small lakes on the western slope of the Wind River Range, near the Continental Divide." The U.S. Board on Geographic Names, the final authority on river sources, ruled in 1931 on the coordinates but was somewhat less specific about pinpointing the precise valley.

The U.S.G.S. topographic map—the Gannett Peak, Wyoming, quadrangle—was published just a few months ago. On my well-creased snow-dampened map we trace the stream that begins literally beneath our feet down to its first intersection, with Clark Creek, and then with Wells Creek in the valley below Stonehammer Lake; it is the master stream here and at every intersection down the line. In response to my request, final confirmation came in a letter from the U.S. Board on Geographic Names, which reviewed its 1931 decision, and

> concluded that the Green River heads in a large basin or cirque between Mount Arrowhead and Split Mountain in the Wind River Range, Wyoming . . . the geographical coordinates 43°09′N and 109°40′W for the

stream's heading falls within the basin of the northwest slope of American Legion Peak. It is also the longest unnamed head water branch of the Green River, and it probably receives more water because of its location below several small glaciers.

But even without that letter I would still feel a marrow conviction that I watch and inhale the beginnings of a magnificent river.

And the sense of riverness is so strong that I follow the river the rest of the way in my mind's eye: out of the Wind Rivers it meanders south across high hay meadows and sagebrush flats, and then snakes through the dry, alkali-splotched Green River Basin. When it snubs up against the Uinta Mountains at the Utah-Wyoming border, it is deflected to run east along their northern flank through Browns Park, a wintering place for traders and trappers and, later, outlaws, and still today isolated and remote. At the eastern end of Browns Park the river angles south and enters Lodore Canyon, incarcerated within its formidable red rock walls. Out of Lodore, it hooks around Steamboat Rock and charges sharp westward through Whirlpool Canyon, idles through Island Park, and dashes through Split Mountain, cleaving it nearly down the middle. It emerges and slows southward across the Uinta Basin. It begins to pare downward again as it bisects the Tavaputs Plateau, working through the pale sediments of Desolation Canyon and the craggy rock of Gray Canyon, bannered with its last white rapids. It crosses the arid Gunnison Valley, and then works its tortuous course through Labyrinth and Stillwater Canyons, through red rock and white rock, to its confluence with the Colorado River. There by Congressional proclamation, having fallen over 9,000 feet in 730 miles, the Green River ends.

THE ROCKY VALLEY below us runs nearly due east and west, and the morning sun spotlights it. The valley is narrow; the impervious rocks that floor and side it maintain a narrow drainage basin since they are very resistant to erosion, and since the river flows for such a short time each year. The drainage pattern that characterizes the length of the Green is laid out below like a topographical map, a dendritic drainage pattern in which small streams feed into larger, and finally into the main stream, as the twigs and branches of a tree feed into the trunk. Sometimes the channels run straight, sometimes in short looping meanders, sometimes braided around small slender islands, stating in miniature the configurations it will follow all the way downriver. In some places the channels are knotted into pools, and from here they resemble chunks of turquoise strung on a *hishi* of a stream, from which the pendant triangle of Peak Lake hangs.

This scooped-out valley is a cirque, the head of a glacier. Even on this sunny morning it is not hard to imagine the valley below as filled with snow, for we have crossed glistening and precipitous snowbanks on the way up, each still many feet deep and more or less permanent fixtures of the landscape. And even the lightest breeze, at this altitude, is on the sharp side.

Glacial periods existed in very ancient times, but little is known about them since evidence of early glaciation tends to be obliterated by later glacial advances. During the three million or so years of the Pleistocene Epoch (the geologic epoch characterized by widespread glaciation and preceding the Recent, in which we live), a series of glacial advances occurred, punctuated by warmer interruptions. And during that time the Wind River Range undoubtedly experienced some uplift, catching even more snow on the high peaks. Toward the end of the Pleistocene, there were several specific ice advances, alternating with retreat, marked by moraines—ridges of debris dropped as a glacier pauses in withdrawal.

The excavation of this upper Green River Valley probably also occurred then. It was first a stream-cut valley, its sloping walls of broken rock lying at a steep angle of repose, so that the valley cross-section was a V. The valley was then occupied by a glacier. During the next to last, or "Bull Lake," glacial stage, the ice extended about twenty miles west of the lower Green River Lake; during the last, "Pinedale" stage (named for moraines best seen near that town), a tongue of ice extended six miles. These names, based on morainal evidence in the Wind River Range, have come to be synonymous with glacial stages throughout the Rocky Mountains. Before the last ice withdrew some nine thousand years ago, Knapsack Col, where we stand, was smothered with a thousand feet of ice, and only the very highest peaks protruded.

When snow compacts into ice and becomes a glacier, an accumulation of 150 feet of ice is sufficient to start it moving downslope, grinding and plucking rocks out of valley walls. When glacier ice choked this valley, relatively rapid erosion of the whole cross-section took place. The result is a more straight-sided, round-based, U profile, a shape that has the minimum exposed area in proportion to the volume of ice forcing through the valley, and so offers the least resistance to the ice's passage. Although most glaciers move slowly, perhaps a few

River cut valley,
before glaciation

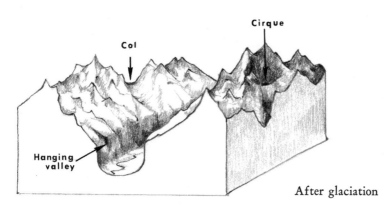

Cirque

Col

Hanging
valley

After glaciation

RIVER AND GLACIAL CUT VALLEYS
(Adapted from Flint, *Glacial and Pleistocene Geology*, 1957, p. 103)

hundred yards a year, the erosive power is tremendous, a more effective force than the narrow cutting edge of a stream. Although it is the river that animates the valley this morning, it drains an ice-formed trough: a stream knifes, a glacier reams.

To MY LEFT, hanging on the valley's north-facing wall, is the big white oval of Stroud Glacier. Mount Arrowhead and Bow Mountain, the peaks above Stroud Glacier, are gray rock shattered with sheer lines and cracks. Nineteenth-century travelers' accounts note much more snow than can be seen now, and although there have been minor advances, the general history of recent times is marked by glacial retreat, more snow melting in the summer than accumulates in the winter. The retreat of Stroud Glacier, like that of many others in the Wind Rivers, is marked by the withdrawal of the glacier from its terminal moraine. The hiatus between moraine and glacier is studded with a small lake.

We work down a thousand feet to the innermost moraine that dams the lake. This close, the glacier is no longer white. It pulls away from the mountain in a bergschrund, a sagging, crescent-shaped crevasse. The upper part of the glacier is grimy and puckered; the lower half is darker yet with blown dirt, thawing in thin steps of gray snow, hatched with streaming water, spattered with rocks and debris, splotched with rose and pink. Pure white shows but once: a desultory white line ends in a stubbed gray boulder that has tumbled partially downslope, leaving a wavering streak a hundred yards long like an awkward exclamation mark. But, in spite of the dirt-encrusted surface, the whole glacier is glazed with water and reflects resplendently in the morning sunshine.

Alpine sorrel and rock ragwort, both in bloom, and minute patches of moss cluster along the base of a few boulders in the moraine, watered by shaded snow wedges. Coin-sized cushions of snow draba grow where the sterile, gritty soil is stabilized, bearing a Lilliputian thicket of seed pods, hairy leaves blown gray with sand and silt. Except for these infinitesimal patches of green, it is a monotone moonscape, a study in neutrals, achromatic. The rivulets that run down the moraine's flanks are icy—the water runs at 34° F. I take a handful to drink and regret it: it is full of the finely ground debris spirited

Snow draba (*Draba nivalis*)

off the slope, with a faintly fishy smell and taste, and an unappetizing mousy color.

The right side of the glacier itself is partially separated from the main mass of ice by a rockslide. Water pours downslope, shoots slots in the ice, and sheets off an ice ledge overhanging the small lake at the base of the glacier. The constant hissing and gurgling of water penetrates the wind's continual pounding. The glacier's whole surface seems alive, bouncing, in constant motion. Although the slope looks impossibly steep and slippery, once on it, I find it surprisingly easy to walk across, albeit wet and puddled. Spumes wash the surface clear and clean, and I walk on gravels embedded in a diamond-clear matrix.

Near the base of the apron boulders remain elevated on snow pedestals three or four feet high; Perry says in some years they may even be elevated to ten or fifteen feet. The degree of slope in most places is insufficient to allow them to slide and so they stand like stone-capped mushrooms. Connie gives me a foot up onto a fifteen-foot-wide slab, disturbing a small sunning wolf spider that scurries into a crack. On top of these rocks are the only dry spots on this whole glistening glacier.

From this exalted perch I can see where the glacier abruptly changes slope. In that angle the water from the steeper gravel-and-rock-spattered face above collects and gathers into chutes. Four feet or so apart, they auger down the ice, piling up water on the outer curves of the short corkscrew meanders. Even when the channels are hidden, the surface of the ice erupts in quixotic fountains. The water runs at 32° F. and is crystalline. Flow energy, converted into heat energy, is sufficient to melt and cut the troughs even though the water itself is running just at freezing.

Near the base of this apron, the torque of one of the channels has cut a hole through twelve feet of ice, and fifteen feet below, in the shadows, lies the glacial lake. Another rivulet pours through a hole a few feet away, more heard than seen, hollow and sonorous and frightening. All the meltwater off the glacier funnels into this small celadon lake, caught between moraine and mountainside. Its basin is steep-sided and very deep; the lake is very cold—a classic tarn. The lines of the rivulets that gloss the glacier's face reflect thin pale jade on the lake's surface, shimmered with morning breeze.

This is a sterile lake. No green algae enliven its edge; no duckweeds form flotillas along the shore; no cattails, no rushes, no willows, no sedges stalk the bank. No fairy shrimp scull around the edges. Not only is the temperature forbiddingly cold, but a large amount of "glacial flour" is held in suspension. It is this that gives glacial lakes their particular opacity and color. The water has an odd porcelainlike appearance, a color that persists as far as the Green River Lakes, over ten miles downstream. Water is more viscous when it is so cold, and debris tends to remain in suspension almost indefinitely. Such silt clogs breathing gills and screens out light. Rooted plants, could they adapt to the temperature, would not receive enough light for photosynthesis.

The lake is always gelid. It absolutely congeals my hands, in the low forties even in the sunshine, and that only on the surface inches, warming little during the day. It is open only a few months of the year, for snow piles up to twenty-three feet deep in this headwater valley, and ice may be up to thirty feet deep in an alpine lake. Even now, as it lies sun-faced and breeze-shot, it remains remote, a cold, cold turquoise, difficult of access, numbing, emanating chilling vapors, empty of visible life, fatally cold, infinitely hostile, yet for all that a strangely lovely part of the beginning river.

WATER DOES NOT completely fill the lake's basin, but seeps out through interstices in the moraine, pouring down a rock slide on the other side in a wide, lathering cascade, draining across a bench into a quiet pool before it falls again into the valley. These seemingly bottomless boulder slides are a permanent feature of the landscape, continually replenished by rock falling from the over-steepened valley walls. Often water pouring off the snowbanks and glaciers runs beneath the boulders, sometimes a vagrant sparkle catches the eye, but most of the time one hears only a furtive commentary as each runnel works through the rocks. Even when temperatures are well below freezing, water may still run beneath the snow and ice, insulated from the extremes of temperature above, feeding the river, if only in a slipping film, all year long.

I rest on a stable rock platform part way down, while Perry and Connie go on ahead; it takes me hours over these teetering boulders while Perry and Connie cross them like gazelles. At my feet, water from an invisible snowbank above flares out into a shallow, glittering stream, and back against a warm rock, I am lulled by the gentle susurration of the water. The rocks sparkle with quartz and mica, veined and striped in arcane patterns, shot with dark dikes or laid with chunks of gleaming quartz. Some rocks are pale gray with large,

Gneiss fragments, Wind River Range

rough crystals, traced with spidery black veins. Some are ebony, subtly marbled. Others are putty colored, granular, streaked with black lines of the original sedimentary layers, cremated to granite, metamorphosed to gneiss.

Many of these rocks fell onto the valley glacier, let down as the ice support beneath melted away. More are recently riven and fallen, edges sharp and angular. Water seeping into surface cracks and freezing builds up pressures capable of splitting rock asunder. Such frost wedging is most effective in just such a climate as this, where daily temperatures often range back and forth through the freezing point. It is just this aspect of the Wind Rivers that General John C. Frémont noted in his journal on August 13, 1842:

> It is not by the splendor of far-off views, which have lent such a glory to the Alps, that these impress the mind; but by a gigantic disorder of enormous masses, and a savage sublimity of naked rock, in wonderful contrast with the innumerable green spots of a rich floral beauty, shut up in their stern recesses.

On the way down, I take a drink from the streamlet; the chemical composition of water running through this hard rock basin is almost identical to that of rainwater and tastes marvelous. Out of curiosity, I poke around the stream, turning over stones for signs of life. All I can find living in this 42° F. water are wormlike midge larvae, a quarter inch or less long, tapered at both ends, pale brown with a dark head. Two prolegs—unjointed appendages—protrude from the last segment; on each is a cluster of crotchets making a tiny circle of grappling hooks by which the larva anchors itself to the rock's surface. Only a change of sheen on the surface film betrays their presence; otherwise the larvae nestle so tightly and are so nearly the same color as the rocks that they are next to invisible.

Although this has been a long day of climbing and plodding across wet snowfields and treacherous boulder piles, I find that I am reluctant to go down. I would like to remain here, wind ruffling notebook paper, back against a sun-warmed rock, watching the Green River begin. It is an intensely practical wish: when it takes so much uphill effort to get here, it is disappointing not to be able to stay longer. Another part of my wish to remain is that sense of at-homeness I feel in the wilderness. I realize that, when I get myself together to walk "home," I am thinking not of a city house but of a small blue tent pitched behind a stand of wind timber a couple of miles downstream.

I walk downvalley as far as the falls that gush down the rocks below Stroud Glacier. The line of the rimming moraine is now high above me, as even and gray as unmixed cement, a contrast to the spiky cragginess of the mountains. The main valley glacier cut deeper than its tributary glaciers; when the ice disappeared, small side valleys were left hanging, and it is here that the water cascades as from a fire hose, shooting over the rock rim, splitting into loquacious spouts that can be heard clear across the valley. A thin spigot of water separates from the main fall and splashes on a rock step in an occult white circle. Into my mind flashes an image of Stillwater Canyon, the lowest canyon on the Green River, and of a pale circle chiseled by a Fremont Indian hundreds of years ago into a rose sandstone wall. I realize, at this moment of white circle on dark rock, that knowing what is below gives meaning to what I understand today, and it is the knowledge of a wide silt-laden, canyon-bound ending river that intensifies this steep, sharp beginning.

I have thought, so many times this August day, how I would like to begin here, magically set down at the source, and follow the length of the Green River in one continuous trip—although my narrative is geographically continuous, it perforce is not chronologically so. It is impossible to do because of weather. Late May through June, when the upper river is high, is too early to backpack safely into this high valley, where access is best in late July and August. And by August the upper river is too low for canoeing. So I have done the next best thing, gone whenever I could on the river, canoeing from the upper Green River Lake to the Gates of Lodore, rafting the rest of the way. I've been on every inch of the river at least once, and most of the river many times —except for one segment that is, as far as I'm concerned, no longer river: Flaming Gorge Reservoir.

I've followed the river in other ways too; it is possible to drive along some miles of it, and even better, to walk. Pacing alongside the river imprints the speed of the current, its purposeful going, the volume of thousands of gallons of water pouring past a single point. But best of all, other than being on the river itself, I've flown over its whole length many times, sitting next to my pilot-husband, Herman, as he counters the broad meanders below with a tilt of wing, turning as the river turns. I watch the river, flowing flat and even, green along its edges even in dry country, or bound between cliffs and streaked white with rapids, or see where it once was in a flood plain scribed with the oxbows of abandoned channels. Perhaps at these times, although farthest from the river physically, I have had the greatest understanding of how the river fits into and molds its landscape.

I continue downvalley through knee-high sedge turf, thick and shining, interspersed with drifts of lavender daisies, spatters of gold ragworts, and pure vermilion paintbrush. The water alternately ruffles and sheets over the rocks, swinging white triangles down from each boulder, or shallows out into smoky turquoise pools. Even in this quieting light of late afternoon the water sparkles and strikes fire.

When the path rises above the stream, water from high, unseen snowbanks chatters downslope, keeping the mountainside green and melodic. At the foot of the slope there are lush clumps of magenta monkeyflowers and thin-leafed chiming bells, blooming in splendid profusion. I walk to the low sun, a softening downvalley breeze at my back, in a thin end-of-day warmth, and I think the Elysian fields must be like this—redolent with blowing flowers beside quiet waters, clear, gentle air floating in a mountain valley, and a knowledge of beginnings. The wind stills and a squadron of mountain midges, backlit, comes out of the sun like sparks from a fire.

Turning, I look back to the moraine, to the glacier, to the high saddle at the valley head. The stern gray mountains dominate the river, and here it begins in rock, just below the sky. There is so much to remember here that I try to lock this green and blowing time forever in my mind. Only then can I turn and walk with the river.

BY THE TIME I get back to camp, late light bathes the whole valley head. Thin, high altocumulus clouds web the sky. After dinner, it is still too light to go to bed and I am still too elated to settle down. I prowl the dry meadow around camp. Our tents are pitched just behind a low moraine stalked with krummholz, timber flagged by the heavy winter westerlies that scour the valley and nip off all growth on the windward side of the trunks. (We fly over a month later and I am

Lewis monkeyflower
(*Mimulus lewisii*)

amazed at the smallness of the timbered swath; down here it seems so protective.) The branches swish in the early-evening gusts, papery gray bark and short needles identifying them as subalpine fir. The moraine is not very high, the remnant of a momentary pause in the valley glacier's retreat when incorporated rock and debris were simply dropped like a windrow of dirt awaiting a Brobdingnagian dustpan. The river ponded behind it, nudging at the loose rock, weakening it, finally bursting a notch through which it now pours and froths; the remaining rim gave enough shelter for the firs to root and grow.

At eight o'clock the light fades, the valley chills, the rocks dull. The sky pales, the clouds thin. The air cools quickly. We have cups of hot chocolate and talk quietly in a close sharing of time and mountains and the day's journey to the source of a river. Beyond the low-slung ridge that separates this part of the valley from the upper, the valley head turns pink in alpenglow, beginning and changing and deepening to a spectacular lavender-salmon, finally glowing like a hot coal. The color lasts only a moment or two, and then dims and dies to gray. And finally the sky congeals to navy blue behind a barque-shaped moon.

At midnight I clip back the tent fly to look out to a high scud across moonlit cliffs. At dawn I awake to a brief simmering of icy rain, spattering drops that sound like rice thrown at the tent. A gust of wind rattles the nylon. Thunder purrs in the distance. It grumbles and rolls closer, down the valley and across, sound swooping in and piling up, then fading away. A pika fusses, staccato, then stops.

In the suspended silence I wait for the rain to begin in earnest, for the wind, the lightning. Raindrops form tiny constellations on the tent wall. The rain quickens, accented with the sound of hail snapping and splatting. The lightning flares and flashes, blinding through the thin tent wall that quivers with the wind. I look out: rain shreds the mountain wall white. The storm seems somehow appropriate, near the beginning river: the potential energy of each raindrop matching each river drop in the stream outside, its energy, as the river's, determined by the height from which it falls and the elevation to which it goes, a raindrop microcosm of the river.

It is cold inside the tent and I slide back into the warmth of my sleeping bag. Lightning flutters, thunder bangs down the valley. I doze, to awake to brightness, blue sky, white clouds, and sun in a blinding platinum aureole that shatters on the ridgetop, a baldachino for the valley.

2

The air at sunrise is clear and pure, and the morning extremely cold, but beautiful. A lofty snowy peak of the mountain is glittering in the first rays of the sun, which have not yet reached us. The long mountain wall to the east, rising two thousand feet abruptly from the plain, behind which we see the peaks, is still dark, and cuts clear against the glowing sky. A fog, just risen from the river, lies along the base of the mountain. A little before sunrise, the thermometer was at 35°, and at sunrise 33°. Water froze last night, and fires are very comfortable. The scenery becomes hourly more interesting and grand, and the view here is truly magnificent; but, indeed, it needs something to repay the long prairie journey of a thousand miles. The sun has shot above the wall, and makes a magical change. The whole valley is glowing and bright, and all the mountain peaks are gleaming like silver. Though these snow mountains are not the Alps, they have their own character of grandeur and magnificence, and doubtless will find pens and pencils to do them justice.

JOHN C. FRÉMONT, August 10, 1842, *The Exploring Expedition to the Rocky Mountains, Oregon and California*

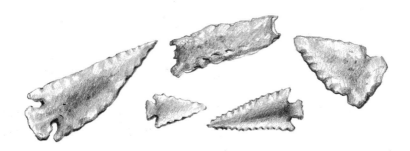

Points found in Wind River Range

Green River

Clear Cr.

Lakes

White Rock

G

R

E

E

Elbow Cr.

N

Squaretop
Mountain

Granite
Peak

Pixley Cr.

R

Marten Cr.

Tourist Cr.

I

Wells Creek

V

Clark Cr.

E

Trail Cr.

R

Stonehammer
Lake

Cube Rock Pass

Dale
Lake

Peak
Lake

N

0   1 mile

PEAK LAKE TO
LOWER GREEN RIVER LAKE

EVERYTHING NEEDS to be reasonably dry before being packed up. On the outside of the tent a dozen winged creatures alight, including some mayflies, small ones with enormous round eyes, fine-veined wings, and two long cerci streaming out behind. The nymphs undoubtedly live in the nearby streams since they are characteristic of cold streams nearly everywhere, and while I wait for the tent to dry, I search under the rocks of the stream. But I find only more midge larvae and gain nothing but congealed hands.

When we start down the moraine, it is all I can do to keep from looking back, looking back. A row of boulders makes stepping stones across the river, and the river drops over them and then courses back and forth through a sedge meadow until it reaches Peak Lake below. We follow the trail around the north side of Peak Lake, fording the river just above where the water tumbles out through a slide of huge rocks and drops three hundred feet to Stonehammer Lake. Chiming bells luxuriate on tiny rock islands in the middle of the torrent; their leaves are pale blue-green, set in the deeper green of the willows. Around them, the river splashes and pours. It goes with verve, completely energized into a frothing white spray, a dichotomy of air and water—although it is the hard pull of gravity that makes it crash in turbulence, the constant shooting spray seems to deny that gravity even exists and to affirm that it is an airborne, weightless river.

Since it is nearly impossible to work down through this boulder pile over which the river explodes, we keep with the trail that sensibly

Colorado columbine
(*Aquilegia caerulea*)

crosses over Cube Rock Pass to the head of the main Green River Valley. There we can look down to more rock slides below, and see as far northwest as the distant Green River Lakes, still shrouded in early-morning mists. A row of clouds strings out above the horizon line of the mountains. The colors of rock and sky are soft but the outline of the ridgetops is sharp, every view underlined by the placid sounds of the water conversing with itself around the rocks. A small stream coming off a snowbank and out of tiny Dale Lake drains down the trail, three feet or so wide, disappearing under the boulders to join, unseen, the water coming out from under a late pink snowbank remaining in the notch of the valley. The path works down against the cliff, embellished with blowzy clumps of columbines and compact patches of brilliant yellow ragwort and a few cushions of pink moss campion. A huge rock slide obscures part of the path, and within it nothing grows. The protected crannies are not soil-filled, but seem to open down into a dark, bottomless nowhere. On one of the boulders, facing the sun, an orange butterfly is imprinted like a triangle of orange tissue paper.

The trail, and the valley's drainage, come out into a high subalpine meadow. Here the stream larks through grassy banks and boulders piled like cairns. Just out of the snowbank, it runs an icy 36° F. It percolates through the rocks, backing up and pouring over, murmuring and guggling. Heavily mossed to the edge, it is a storybook stream, thick with flowers: brook saxifrage crowded in round shiny-leaved rosettes; fringed Parnassia with creamy white petals and small globular buds; star gentians inky-purple. In the pools between races, water striders skitter across the surface, more visible through their shadows on the bottom silt than they themselves are. The water is cold and

Star gentian
(*Swertia perennis*)

Brook saxifrage
(*Saxifraga odontoloma*)

hard, crystal made liquid. When I drop a pebble in, I almost expect the water to shatter with a faint glasslike tinkle.

From this subalpine meadow there are two ways to continue. One can fight down along two miles of river hemmed in with rocks and deadfall, a difficult-to-impassable two miles. And, until one has bushwhacked through one of these stretches, the word "impassable" has little meaning: ten-foot boulders, no way to get by without walking through an unwadable torrent, a quarter-mile walk upslope looking for a way past, vision always blocked ahead, a corner turned to find that a painstaking ascent leads nowhere and has to be backtracked, time and again beginning over, backpack snagging on deadfall, no view toward an ending.

The other way, via a trail that goes up and around an unnamed mountain and drops down into Three Forks Park, is much longer, but it is passable. This trail snakes down the mountainside through a snow-slide area. Some trees are bent, some snapped off a few feet above the ground, or even uprooted, whole carcasses strewn across the slope in jackstraws of deadfall. Snow piles up and slides down these steep slopes in more or less regular slide patterns, booming into the valley below. This trail, like so many others of the upper Green River Valley, was bossed out by an old trapper, Gottfried Rahm. He trapped marten and lived here most of the year, except in the spring during snow-slide season when the snow thunders down the mountainsides like locomotives under full steam.

Across the valley, the river bursts out of Stonehammer Lake and comes down the opposite valley flank in a torrential cascade. It is raining again, and through the peppering damp and the heavy atmosphere the marvelous rushing sound pulsates in the air between. The water tumbles and jets, all white water, sometimes woven into the dark evergreens, sometimes open, and then disappears into the valley below, hidden in a thick tangle of spruce and fir.

The peaks of Stroud and Brimstone steam with mists, like some Wagnerian stage set, as the storm sweeps in from the southeast. Most storms in the Wind Rivers come from the west and tend to open up promptly at four in the afternoon. An unusual weather pattern of morning showers, coming in from the southeast, has been engendered by the presence of a low to the southwest that changes the air flow and pulls in warmer moist air from the southeast. In my experience in the Wind Rivers, it inevitably rains sometime or another during the day, and a day without rain is a rare one; the afternoon showers usually mean setting up camp in the rain, the morning ones delay starting. But this incessant and reliable supply of moisture is basic to the Green, and at no place in its lower reaches is it replenished with a like amount of water. Even at the confluence, the supply of water from the Wind Rivers keeps the big river alive.

AFTER FLOUNCING some two miles downstream, glimpsed only through the woods like scraps of torn paper, the river emerges to meander across the flat, open meadow of Three Forks Park. Wells Creek, coming off Mammoth Glacier, forms one of the three forks for which the park is named; the Green River goes straight upvalley (and was once called Stroud Creek or Middle Fork); Trail Creek comes in from the right. These major streams occupy fracture zones, that provide natural troughs which the drainage follows.

Three Forks Park is filled with waist-high grasses and sedges and willows, caught in a heavy early-morning mist, a stationary world. Nothing moves. Mists hang thick, separate minuscule water drops suspended in saturated air, a sweet smoke. There is a curious sensation of arrested time; even the early-morning light seems unchanging for an hour after sunrise. The fume of the river far upstream is muted, no louder than its quiet chirruping around the grassy banks and gravel bars at my feet. A few isolated pines grow here, but mostly there are thick grasses and herbs. Not a leaf so much as quivers.

Water vapor condenses on everything, a fine glazing on flowering grass panicles, making even the thinnest stems seem frosted. Salsify leaves hold different-sized drops, from a millimeter up to twenty-carat cabochons. Meadow rue is glassy with finer drops that merge into each other at a touch, magnifying the veins beneath. Small chickweed flowers are submersed in a vitreous ball; a crystalline dot studs each impeccable notch on a strawberry leaf. The spikes of ladies' tresses orchids are picked out with a spiral of glass beads. Many of the grass leaves are gray-green to begin with, and now, all arched over and hazed with water, they turn the meadow silver.

First sun lights only the high cliffs, the upper phalanx of the mountains, bringing out their roughness in jagged shadows, picking up peaks far down canyon to the west. Then it lights the meadow only on this side; the other side remains enshrouded, mysterious. The mists pick themselves up and move out, swiftly, as if fleeing the light. A breeze motions across the meadow. The Indians who summered here believed that the Wind Rivers were the home of the spirits, and that here one could see the spirit land of afterlife. The mists sweep off the river, out of the meadow, invading the trees surrounding the knoll on which I sit. Their presence is so ephemeral that only the sparkle of sun in a once-quivered drop on a pine needle betrays their passage. Unthinking, I reach out my hand to delay, to ask—the sense of presence is so strong at this moment. This feeling comes so often on this river: I have felt it while standing in the doorway of an old homestead cabin, or rinsing off in the river, and at so many unexpected places that I nearly turn to see who stands near.

And at this moment, when the mists evanesce into daytime, there comes a fragment of rainbow, a rainbow of odd, hard pastels containing the same cold turquoise that the river runs. And then the whole park lightens and warms, the base of some golden bowl filled with gleaming.

THE RIVER BREAKS out of Three Forks Park and foams and fumes just out of sight, roaring through fallen timber and rock slides, guttering and pounding, always audible even if hidden. The path steepens downward through the woods. After a rain everything is soggy and spongy, a morass of puddles. Other hikers have made new paths to avoid the mud, creating parallel trails that infringe on the forest. Big patches of liverworts frost the ground; luxuriant mosses flourish in bouncy bolsters. Every leaf and needle has a drop or more of water. Heart-leafed arnica, that on the way up lined the trail with sunny yellow, now, after a hailstorm, is all stalks. Farther down they are untouched and blooming, a brightness in the dark woods, unusually abundant in the disturbed ground at the edge of the path.

This is my idea of the forest primeval: filled with deadfall, very still, ground soft and cushioned, a windrow of porcupine needles, big circles of dog lichen, trees festooned with old man's beard, wintergreens, bulbous yellow mushrooms like huge pats of butter, a touch of red in an already turned leaf, cinnamon-brown pine needles, streamers of twinflowers, a pale bluebell, ground pebbles grainy and lichen-spotted, scraps of bark and mats of pine needles. Although one has a sense of openness, vision is always blocked. In the quiet of the woods the river's sound is reduced to wistfulness. The river is not so hypnotic, placed in this arboreal frame of reference.

Then the path emerges from the trees and confronts the river.

Heart-leafed arnica
(*Arnica cordifolia*)

Twenty feet across, the water is totally turbulent, foaming ivory, carved jade, shot with pale-turquoise depths and ice colors, scarcely relatable to the calm river less than half a mile upstream. Its fall of some 240 feet in a distance of 4,000 feet makes it churn against the canyon walls and bound back in alternating sashes of white water. There is a total continuous boom, filling my ears, echoing off the rocks, reverberating through the woods. The vibration of the river comes right up through the soles of my boots. It seems irrational, incredibly powerful, a different stream from that fine, dashing filament below Stroud Glacier, a different stream from the quiet one meandering through Three Forks Park, a stream running so crashing and full that I would not even think of wading in it.

And, in the midst of the pouring and pounding, a robin-sized gray water ouzel flits onto a rock, bobs, drops to a lower boulder nearly awash with water, bobs again, skims to another, low over the water, in perfect control of air current and wave, indifferent to the cold, holding firmly to wet rocks with long muscular toes, completely at home, the embodiment of John Muir's description in *The Mountains of California*: "Find a fall, or cascade, or rushing rapid, anywhere upon a clear stream, and there you will surely find its complementary Ouzel, flitting about in the spray, diving in foaming eddies, whirling like a leaf among beaten foam-bells; ever vigorous and enthusiastic, yet self-contained, and neither seeking nor shunning your company."

The river is on our right. To the left, a snow-slide area, depleted of trees, and now in summer an open meadow, reaches two thousand feet up the mountain flank. Trees come down the protected drainage lines and provide cover, and plentiful grass grows in the meadow. Elk feed here at dawn and dusk, lying out the day in the high grass. Two females with calves and one bull graze as we watch, working across the slope in the dimming light. Most of the Wind River slopes are timbered; only where snow slides keep trees from growing is there a chance for meadows to develop, and these open slopes are prime summer feed grounds for elk, deer, antelope, and mountain sheep.

At the foot of this meadow slope the river quiets. Lodgepole pines dampen the upstream noise, spindly trees set in alleys of diminishing greenness, in a thick, closed stand. Old cones knot the empty branches; not until the heat of a forest fire opens them do the seeds fall out, sprouting to form again these dense stands. The needles are soft, a somber green padding on the ground; the rain-softened bark, beaded with amber pitch, is as pliable as leather.

At dusk the river turns a steely gray except for the center channel, and it retains its deep turquoise, laced with whitecaps as it bucks and pours over rocks. At the edge, tiny waves creep to the shore, lap into a little bay or slick over a rock and drop in a twelve-inch waterfall into a quiet harbor with a mica-sparkled sandy bottom. Swags of pine needles wash up on the lower edge of the bank, obscuring the shoreline; they do not decompose readily, festooning the beach until they eventually waterlog and sink to the bottom of the stream.

The main chute veers away from the shore. The current's speed is misleading; it looks much faster than it really is, and I am to remember this downstream, where the river in truth has more velocity but looks to be lazing. We throw sticks in upstream and time them between two points, trying to estimate the current's speed. If a stick comes down the slower edge of the channel it can be followed by comfortable but brisk walking. We estimate three feet per second. Although a modest velocity, it is, however, competent to move stones three inches in diameter, and the high turbulence of glacial streams makes them able to move larger materials at lower velocities than might be expected.

But, if a stick lands in the fast middle channel, I almost have to

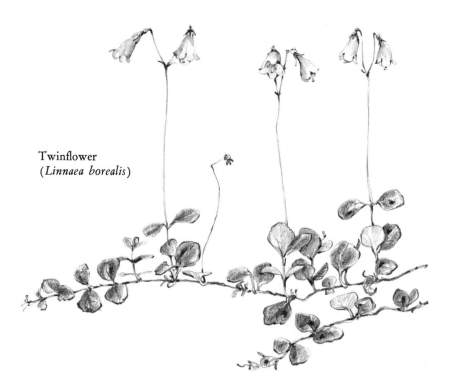

Twinflower
(*Linnaea borealis*)

run to keep up with it. At the top of a line of rocks just downstream, the velocity of the river flips it high into the air, over the edge, and it is gone. We do it over and over again, like children, and indeed I feel like Mole, in *Wind in the Willows*, who had never seen a river before, entranced and fascinated by this "sleek, sinuous, full-bodied animal, chasing and chuckling, gripping things with a gurgle and leaving them with a laugh, to fling itself on fresh playmates that shook themselves free, and were caught and held again. All was a-shake and a-shiver—glints and gleams and sparkles, rustle and swirl, chatter and bubble."

TOMORROW WE WILL be back to civilization—no matter how long I've been out, it is always a day, a week, a month too short. Dark clouds clot the night sky, but the soft rumbling I listen to all night is not a storm coming in but cavitation from the river, created by the tremendous velocity just upstream. When water is constricted into a small channel between rocks, an increase in velocity, a rise in energy, and a decrease in pressure occur. When the pressure decreases to the vapor pressure of water, bubbles form. As water streams through the constriction and spreads out again, the opposite occurs: velocity decreases, pressure increases again, and the bubbles collapse, giving off shock waves that travel outward. Building up in series, they make the peculiar soft booming, a Stygian rhythm that I feel through the ground as well as hear. And all night long the river murmurs and hums and shudders, but always beneath the louder rushing I hear the soft little waves at the shore.

I lie awake most of the night, sensitized to the river. Peace, contentment: these are programmed cultural words; what I feel is the infinity outside of culture, and although I sleep little, I awake rested. The dawn sky is pale and pearly, like a moonstone, webbed with a few clouds, the jagged skyline just beginning to pick up sunlight, that beautiful moment before full awakening when the world is fresh and clear and all is possible and good, a time of great expectations, and it is completely right, this gray rock canyon, this cold rock beginning, this beautiful river morning.

GOING DOWNTRAIL seems to take such a short time, not only because we are descending but because one remembers a rock, a tree, the way the river runs. We eat strawberries all the way down, a bumper crop just now coming ripe. We can find a handful at a time, fragrant and delicious, enhanced by a few grains of silt that grit in the teeth.

In the river big trees have fallen in; the current rocks them gently. The roots of one retain a clump of dirt and are massed with fireweeds in magenta bloom. The water swishes by, through more trees fallen across, making even canoe navigation impossible. The river runs fairly smooth and quiet, with ten-foot-deep pools at the shore and a twenty-five-foot-wide cobble bar built up in the middle. A big boulder at the shore lets the water swirl around it on either side, neat and precise, a diagram of water flow. It is a long, narrow rock, set at right angles to the current, and the water smooths over the top and curls back on the other side. As I watch the quiet, purposeful going, I still feel the power of the river pounding above, the white tumbling tamed here in a delta formed by the slowing of the river, filled in four miles back from the upper Green River Lake.

Clouds are building although the sun still shines; rain has come to be of no consequence to me—the mountains and the river are often even more beautiful in rain than in sunlight. But I do not relish a storm on the open lake ahead. The big fringed gentians and the more delicate lavender love gentians are beginning to close. By the time we reach where Perry cached the canoe on the way in, they are all furled against the coming storm, pollen safely protected.

After flowing so swiftly downhill, the river now uses much of its energy to meander across the thick sedge swale that carpets the delta. The current pulls chunks out of the bank on the outside, forms clear-water channels paddle deep or more, and tries to nose the canoe into the bank. Sometimes the channels are gravel-bottomed, other times sandy with shallow ripples, wide-spaced and discontinuous. The banks are two or three feet above the water, stuffed with grass and water sedge, daisies, avens, ragworts, and great clumps of gentians the color of Parma violets. We pass an abandoned beaver lodge, as forlorn as an old homestead cabin.

The current is no-nonsense. It is almost impossible to paddle against it (as we discovered on the way up), but running with it the canoe seems almost mystically propelled. We carom downstream, banging a bank with the bow, trading comments about various people's canoeing abilities or lack thereof, and I realize that I am just purely happy to be on the river again.

The stream flares out into the upper of the two Green River Lakes.

Three-flowered avens
or pink plume
(*Geum triflorum*)

The water is a dark and flinty turquoise, looped over with re-flection lines of pale blue and sage green. Smooth Vs string back from the bow and the paddle makes double vortices of passage that gurgle into lucid pipes of water, bringing back good memories: this is the kind of canoeing I grew up with, slipping across a summer lake. My first canoe was an Old Town canoe that my mother gave me, dark green canvas over a wooden frame, stabilized with air locks in the sides. It was broad and cumbersome, but nearly tip proof and ideal for a child. Perry's canoe is fiberglass, sleek and slender, eighteen feet long, strengthened with an aluminum shoe keel. The hull is trans-lucent, showing the white line of water surface split by the bow. This gives a deceptive sense of fragility: so one sees through an eggshell. But this sturdy canoe takes us through fast water and slow water, rock-garden rapids and chutes, all the way to the Gates of Lodore, and it comes to be an object for which I have a vast affection and trust.

Both Green River Lakes are impounded behind moraines dropped during recessional pauses within the last glacial retreat, which occurred with a warming interval between 4,000 and 6,500 years ago. The upper basin is probably shallower than the lower, its glacial silt main-tained in suspension by wind and wave action, giving it its distinctive deep color. Neither of the lakes is very productive; they may produce only a tenth as much trout or whitefish as lower-altitude lakes produce in perch, carp, bluegill, and bass. However, many fishermen consider the former superior fishing and rate the upper Green River and its lakes as excellent. We see several fishermen along the way; one stands on the moraine at the foot of the lake, pausing in his casting to wave us by.

The upper lake has channeled through its bounding moraine, and the river winds across a delta that separates the two lakes. Most of the material for this delta is brought in by Clear Creek, flowing down a fault separating White Rock and Osburn Mountain. In 1909 Clear Creek entered the Green River Lakes directly; now the delta is almost half a mile across. The river runs momentarily swift and shallow be-tween the two lakes; the cobbles on the bottom are gingerbread colored from a coating of algae, and dark gray granites lie blackened with moss or tufted with pale-green algae. A little two-inch boreal chorus frog, with a narrow cream stripe down its brown back, flies into the water and swims, childlike in configuration and concentrated effort.

The lower lake is deeper and clearer, and nearly double the size of the upper. In the darkening afternoon its surface sleeks to patent-leather black, swirled with navy blue, embroidered with drops falling off the paddle tip. Astern, clouds are beginning to roll in close. Stroud Peak is a smoky miter. The sky above is sooty blue with a dirty white line of clouds hanging beneath. Ahead, to the west, the sky is also blocked, shot with thin flashes of lightning, grumbled with thunder. Surrounded by storms, the limestone top of White Rock gleams pale, a long ramp pointing southeastward to summits now darkening in foreboding. White Rock, unlike the hard rock mountains of the interior, is formed of layers of sedimentary rock. These sedimentary layers once covered the whole range; now eroded away, they remain only on the periphery at lower elevation, striping the escarpments in tan and cream and rose.

The thunder sounds more ominous. Suddenly the canoe seems a vulnerable wisp of flotsam. The hull seems to adhere to the water, and no matter how hard we paddle, we seem no closer to shore. The wind kicks up a chop that splashes over the bow and gunwales. The lake turns an ugly, nasty, leaden green. It becomes a race to reach land before the storm hits. I feel as if I could swim faster than we are going. We sprint the last few hundred yards, and it is a great relief on my part to hear the prow crunch into the beach gravel.

And after all the shoulder-wrenching paddling and hasty unloading, the rains never come.

3

... what every man who has ever handled a boat on Green or Colorado or San Juan learns: how trivial a mistake can lead to trouble. The rivers are not "treacherous." They are only forever dangerous. One who has not tried it finds it hard to believe the instant and terrible force that such a current exerts on a broadside boat out of control on a sandbar or rock.

WALLACE STEGNER, 1954, *Beyond the Hundredth Meridian*

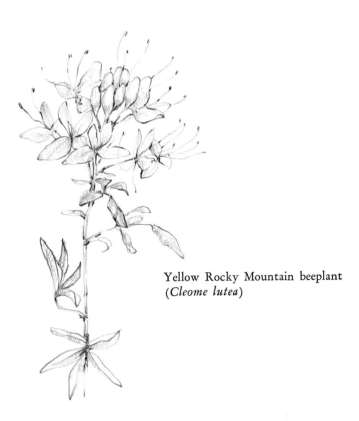

Yellow Rocky Mountain beeplant
(*Cleome lutea*)

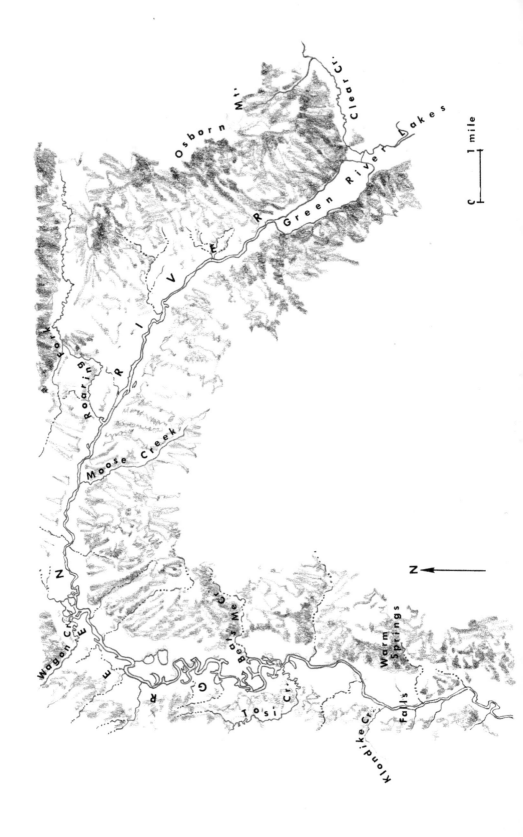

LOWER GREEN RIVER LAKE
TO KENDALL WARM SPRINGS

PERRY AND I have planned a canoe trip from Green River Lakes to Green River, Wyoming, for the third week in June to take advantage of peak runoff. Perry loads the last water jug into the canoe and I climb in and over the gear to the bow. Connie gives us a good shove, the keel grinds off the beach, and the canoe swings out into the pellucid water of the lake, scattering wind wrinkles. We slide easily beneath the footbridge at the outlet at the northwest end of the lake, but have to duck our heads down to our feet to scrape under an old bridle bridge.

Although the river was running fuller a week ago, a mid-June snowstorm and cool weather here (precisely what prevents backpacking to the headwaters any earlier than the end of July) have shut down the flow temporarily, closing the glacial runoff like slamming a headgate. Like all streams heading in glacial reaches, the upper Green River has high periods of runoff directly related to snow melt, and also daily fluctuations from night freezing and day thawing, and spasmodic changes caused by vagrant weather patterns. In typical years, the Green River peaks around the third week in June, and then declines through the summer to a base flow in September.

I enjoy the difference between lake and river canoeing. Lake canoeing is work, paddling against more or less dead water, often as not against a head wind or quartering against a chop. River canoeing is one-directional, and although it requires a prompt and intent awareness of the river, and although the wind may come directly upstream and often does, the current pulls sleekly downriver.

The river, just out of the lake, flows with untrammeled beauty here, and the canoe glides easily over the surface of the water. An eagle circles high above us. Fish dart through the water almost too fast to see. Red-winged blackbirds cross and recross the river in complicated quadrilles, epaulets flashing. Surface patterns reflect on the bottom in a precise golden fretwork, inner-patterned with thin lines pleated by the wind. It is the reality of the here and now that is so completely enchanting: the sound of water slipping off paddle tip in silken drops, birds exulting, grass and willows blowing, ripples shooting glints of sunlight.

The channel is narrow and deep. It is hard to judge the current because there is so little debris in the water to match the canoe against. The current is sufficient to give impetus to paddling, but not strong enough to tumble the grapefruit-sized rocks lying on the bottom. The water of the upper river is deficient in minerals and nutrients, as are many headwater streams. This section of the river is marginally productive during low water, deficient during high. Plankton washed out of the lake cannot withstand water speeds of this velocity and are swept unceremoniously downstream, with little opportunity to become established unless caught in a clump of moss or a quiet back eddy, and the severe cold and winter conditions of the Green River Lakes produce rather meager populations to begin with. Once water leaves the lake and enters the river channels, plankton populations decrease precipitately.

Rainbow and brown trout reproduce naturally in the tributaries

Rocky Mountain or Yellowstone phlox
(*Phlox multiflora*)

to this reach of river, but are also stocked. There are also some native brook and cutthroat, but the original trout of the Green River drainage, the Green River cutthroat, has nearly disappeared from a combination of competition and interbreeding with exotic introduced species (such as rainbow trout) and a deteriorating habitat. *Salmo clarki,* with its black-dotted flanks and scarlet throat slash, was discovered by and named after William Clark of the Lewis and Clark expedition, and at one time this species had the widest range of all native trout. Now the species as a whole has diminished sharply throughout the West, and the Green River cutthroat, S. *clarki pleuriticus,* has become a rare and endangered species.

Ahead, a view of mountains still glazed with winter snow is a reminder of the heavy snows and ice of yesteryear. A lateral Pinedale moraine flanks the river, formed around the convex side of the glacier that extended down the Green River Valley forty miles from its cirque. The surface of the moraine is rough and studded with boulders; pale, unenriched soil shows between well-spaced sagebrush and scattered cushions of white or brilliant lavender phlox. The plum-pudding arrangement of irregular rocks within the soil, characteristic of a moraine, shows when a road cut is visible from the river, revealing the loosely packed and porous substrate.

The immaturity of the soil also shows in the pale tan rims of white-tailed prairie-dog holes which abound along the bank. Locally called "gophers," they stand picket-pin fashion on their haunches, stationed at the edges of their burrows, chirruping like birds. Most of them watch the canoe slide by; the coats of those that duck for cover gleam in the sunlight. They are common to this high country, and in July, when the weather becomes too hot on these sagebrushed slopes, they will estivate—the summer version of hibernation—to appear again in late summer. True hibernation begins in October or November, and lasts until March, when mating occurs, with young born early in May. The prairie dogs supervise the river bank every quarter mile or so, sentinels that pass news of river travel downstream in a high chittering code.

THE RIVER BEGINS to spread and shallow. Many of the morainal boulders have rolled into the riverbed, pushing the smooth surface of the water up into pillows. If a rock broaches the surface, there is no problem (other than missing it), but if under the surface—a

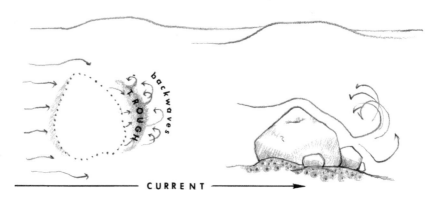

READING THE RIVER SURFACE FOR "SLEEPERS"
The deeper the rock the farther downstream the backwave.

"sleeper"—one must learn to read its depth by the bolster it makes. If close to the surface, the water slicks over the top and falls into a small hole on the downstream side, terminating in a brief standing tailwave or two that break upstream. Sometimes submerged rocks are nearly invisible from upstream, and one becomes attuned to the slightest convexity of surface. I watch for them and try to estimate the inches of clearance available, and whether we can slip over or must go around. That ominous presence, revealed only on the downstream side, is the responsibility of the bowman, since in white water someone seated in the stern often cannot see rocks ahead. I begin to feel very apprehensive about the white water we are due to run tomorrow.

With the river lower and the loaded canoe, no amount of vigilance can prevent contact with the rising streambed as we approach the entrance of the Roaring Fork. A tick on the keel is the first warning, followed by several louder knocks in rapid succession on the hull, and I fully expect to see a geyser at my feet. A moment's pause, then the current shoves the stern around and a firm abrasive grinding begins. It stops only when the hull hangs firmly snubbed into the streambed. The only solution is to get out and line the canoe by holding the bow and stern lines and leading it through the rocks. I put my feet in gingerly, remembering the untenable cold of the upper stream. Surprisingly, although the water is chill, it is pleasant. Little glacier water is feeding in from above, and here where the stream is shallow and sunny the afternoon sun warms it to 58° F. Turbulence over the rocks mixes the water and leads to uniform temperatures throughout, unlike the lake water, which is warm only on the surface.

The whole riverbed is filled with boulders, some brought in by the Roaring Fork during times of heavy runoff, some washed in from morainal debris hanging on the slopes above the river, most deposited by the glacier. The Roaring Fork enters five miles down from the lower Green River Lake, charging down from the mountains into a short flood plain, clear, cold, low in dissolved minerals, offering habitats for trout spawning in its quieter reaches. After this stream enters the Green, the combined waters fuss and fume over the rocks, pour in shining humps and pillows, chunk into foot-long channels, split and reunite and bounce up into the air with great verve and splash, navigable by nothing larger than a three-inch scrap of wood.

The rocks could not be more slippery and treacherous. I take an ill-advised step and slip in over my knees in the shoving current. My recovery is less than graceful and that takes care of being wet to the waist, and I feel as if wet jeans weigh twenty pounds per leg. Few of the rocks have flat tops big enough for a foot; most are as rounded as a basketball. My feet continually slip off and wedge between two rocks that hold the heel of my sneaker in a vise, and no matter how tightly tied on it is, my foot comes out, leaving a shoe to be fished for while I balance on one foot. Ankles crack and shins bark against unyielding stone. There is no such thing as caution; it is simply a headlong progression into disaster with every foot for itself.

At this time of year, larger plants are not yet well started. Smaller ones are more noticeable: mosses hanging over the bank or tufted between boulders in the stream, minute algae that coat the rocks and make them slippery. Water moss grows in tassels of small, fine-set leaves and firm holdfasts, well adapted to resist white-water turbulence, a characteristic moss of waterfalls and rocky chutes. Golden-brown algae are plentiful enough to give the rocks an amber tint visible through the clear water's magnification, their green chlorophyll masked by a pigment that gives them their tawny color. They survive in this current by being attached to good-sized stones; smaller ones are too easily rolled by the current, abrading off surface growth.

Whenever possible we climb back in and run a short spurt of white water. The thin prow cuts a narrow V of pale-olive lace foam. The canoe flies down the wave-corrugated channel, the water spanks against the bow, the bow lifts and knifes and lifts again, and I get my initiation to white-water canoeing. It lasts but a moment, and then the shallows come up and we climb out to coddle the canoe through another interminable stretch. The bow swings free of a boulder and bolts out into the current, tugging hard; the line burns out to the end of my hand and I can't go fast enough and end up lunging against the gunwales or simply sitting down in the stream. Even without passenger weight, the canoe catches on rock after rock and needs to be nursed through, pried, pushed, lifted, cajoled, and then suddenly the current catches it and it leaps downstream, shuddering to a halt again, locked between two rocks.

I now understand all those complaints of Major John Wesley Powell that lining required "excessive labor and much care."

ONCE IN A WHILE there is a respite and a chance to enjoy the landscape. Flanking the river is the most recent terrace it has cut, a remnant of a former flood plain. During the post-Pleistocene period, as the ice melted and glaciers retreated, large amounts of rock, sand, and silt were exposed to water action at the same time that large amounts of meltwater were available to act on them. As a result, rivers formed glacial outwash or flood plains, usually filling in and building

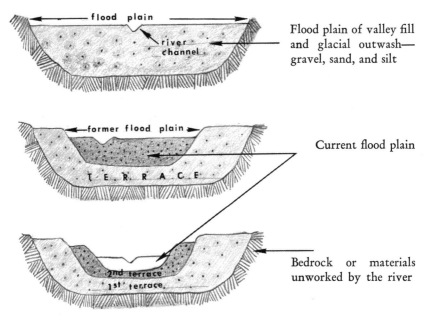

Flood plain of valley fill and glacial outwash—gravel, sand, and silt

Current flood plain

Bedrock or materials unworked by the river

RIVER FLOOD PLAINS AND TERRACES
(Adapted from Leopold, *Water, A Primer*, 1974, p. 96)

up the river valley by carrying in and depositing gravel, sand, and silt. With each climate change, the previous river level and its flood plain were abandoned, and a new flood plain built at a different level.

These abandoned and now dissected flood plains, called terraces, stand as remnants in the form of spurs or flat-topped benches. At least three terraces roll up from the right bank of the river, blending into each other, the lowest (and youngest) creased by vivid green drainage lines. Sometimes merely fragments remain, curled around a river curve like an oversized tadpole. River gravel mixed with sand underlies these terraces, and unlike morainal debris, these rocks and cobbles are relatively uniform in size and shape, smoothed toward perfect ovals. The soil is richer and therefore darker. On the oldest terraces in the region, river gravels may be ten to twenty feet thick. Although visibly different from moraines, terraces also are porous and well drained.

At the Big Bend, after flowing out of the mountains toward the northwest, the Green River now hooks to the south, and the rapids end for the time being. The absence of large rocks beyond the moraine's end is striking. The channel is less steep, the water runs quietly, and there are no more big boulders in the river until it crosses the terminus of the Bull Lake moraine farther downstream. Large boulders must remain near their source until they are fragmented enough for the river to carry them. Smaller rocks group into the alternating sand and cobble sequence that again begins to appear beneath the canoe. A thread of surface debris concentrates in a line down the center of the stream. Bits of flotsam roll just beneath the surface, following different tendrils of current from those on top. The water is so clear that each bottom pebble seems drawn separately— pale olive, mottled gray, pearl, buff.

Killdeer skim the river, and a pair of mallards wing off ahead, the male's head gleaming like the river. A sandhill crane beats across the river just above the horizon. We see it first as it stands in the marsh near its nest, serpentine tan neck extended above the band of green like an old bleached tree branch. It heaves itself into the air, neck extended straight out, a huge bird with wings beating so slowly that it seems never to catch sky. Recently an endangered species, the greater sandhill cranes are once again established along the Green River, their hollow calls once more part of the river sounds. That call, which carries so far, results from the length and size of a windpipe that extends into the keel of the breastbone, giving great resonating power.

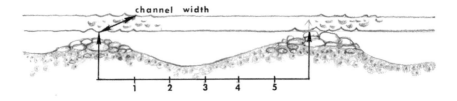

POOL-AND-RIFFLE SEQUENCE

Although the river channel holds fairly straight here, the streambed does not—it undulates between pools and shallows. Gravel-patched bars appear with fair regularity, distance apart varying between five and seven times the width of the stream. A similar ratio exists where the river meanders, suggesting that both are created in a similar way, the difference in pattern depending (among other things) upon stream velocity, the materials of which the bed and bank are formed, and the steepness of the channel. As sediments flow into the river, they gather into groups that form bars with pools between; the alternation of shallow and deep is an inherent part of the quasi-equilibrium of the river system, the workings of which are only dimly understood. Part of the enchantment of a river lies in these unanswered questions.

For pools and riffles to form there must be some disparity in the size of stream materials, which must be larger than coarse sand; pools and riffles rarely form in purely sandy reaches because sand tends to cave in at the sides, forming broad, shallow channels. At low water they pattern the river's surface with glassy streaks and broken water. Once formed, gravel bars tend to remain fairly stable, more force required to separate out and move gravels or cobbles already clustered. Although individual cobbles may migrate downstream to the next bar during a spate of high water, they are replaced by others from the seemingly endless source upstream.

The wind pushes through the grass and sedge along the bank and sweeps across the lush hay meadows glazed with buttercups and dandelions, meadows that turn pure bronze in the fall. The river is flanked with banks so verdant that it seems impossible to add another stem or leaf. Even when a chunk of bank drops away, the rich dark soil does not break up but is held solid by intermeshed roots.

The canoe cuts through swarms of caddisflies, that pucker the water, land on the thwarts, on my gloves, on my face, get caught behind my sunglasses, small fluttery mothlike creatures that struggle helplessly on the water surface. The larvae of most species build ingenious tubes or nets and are inhabitants of both slow and swift streams; they pupate under water and often hatch *en masse*. We must have come upon such a mass emergence, and many of them, caught on the surface film, disappear in widening circles of trout feeding.

Small creeks enter the upper Green River every mile or so, like road markers, cold, clear mountain streams that are important to the river and calibrate our passage downstream. Wagon Creek, entering right, brings in the first significant amounts of dissolved minerals, draining an area of sedimentary rocks to the west rather than the hard gneiss of the upstream reaches. Beats the Hell Out of Me Creek enters from the east through a beaver pond. Tosi Creek, named for a Shoshone medicine man, enters on the right. All the small streams along the upper Green River run steeply in their upper reaches, slowing when they reach the flood plain of the river; all provide spawning grounds in their quiet water—for rainbow trout in the spring, brook and brown trout in the fall.

Two huge beaver on the bank interrupt their evening feeding to scrutinize the canoe. One swims toward it as if checking us out, smacks its tail smartly and dives; the other one sidles in immediately. A coven of blackbirds chase a crow, deviling it into the horizon. The paddle dips into reflections of blue sky and late-afternoon clouds; the sound of the paddle mingles with the constant bird trilling. Drops off the tip of the paddle spatter into pinheads, skittering across the surface like motes of mercury. The cloud reflections in the water are simplified, darkened, their diaphanous quality calcified so that they seem more like some strange, linked vertebrae. The water is clear bottle green. Each paddle stroke forms double vortices into which I look as into the glass neck of a wine bottle. A coyote cries twice, a drawn-out wire-thin sound. A white duck feather floats across the water, mirrored to perfection.

THE BEACHING PROW cuts a thin wedge into the narrow shelf of dark silt at the river's edge, next to the seven-inch tracks of a sandhill crane and the ivy-leaf prints of a duck. There is something so familiar about the every-which-way patterns in the mud—then I remember: they remind me of a piece of Green River Formation shale, fifty million years old, imprinted in the same way with wandering shorebird tracks.

Sagebrush buttercup
(*Ranunculus glaberrimus*)

The overhanging grassy bank is a recent terrace, a four-foot scramble above the water. After unloading and unpacking, the first thing I do is put on dry hiking boots and thick wool socks, pure heaven to icy, battered feet and ankles. The second thing is to pull out my guide to white-water canoeing. Having had an afternoon of canoe and rocks, and having already seen Kendall Warm Springs rapids from the bank, I feel a vast uneasiness. When I leave to pitch my tent and return, Perry is earnestly reading the book. Upon my query as to why such an experienced guide as he should need to read such elementary instructions, he replies that he has not canoed these upper river rapids and has always wanted to do so, the main reason being that everyone said it couldn't be done, and now I was his excuse. I feel somewhat like the cartoon airline passenger when the pilot walks down the aisle with a *How to Fly* book tucked under his arm. My only revenge is that Perry has forgotten his boots and has to endure cold, wet feet.

Across the river are the cabins of the Gros Ventre Ranch, the first dude ranch in Wyoming, established by William Wells and run from 1894 until 1906, the same Wells after whom Wells Creek is named.

The buildings stand part way up the slope of a large moraine. A water-wheel was once installed in the small unnamed stream that falls half-hidden down its slope. The moraine is big and high, a smoother slope than that of the younger moraine we followed this afternoon. The sagebrush-covered slopes haze to blue-gray in the evening light. The white boulders, set in diaper pattern on the slope, turn lavender. The hill is dark toward the top, lodgepole pine and spruce in close-packed perpendiculars, with flares of aspen at the lower rim. Grasses and willows on the opposite bank reflect off the river. A muskrat swims along, trailing silver Vs, its head making a small pillowed wake, going downstream to its wickiup.

The first frogs begin simmering. Swarms of cliff swallows inter-weave like aerial maypole dancers, crossing and arcing in intricate arabesques. Nighthawks cross higher above, their wings making rapid fluttering, almost pulsating, sounds. A sandhill crane calls, far down-river, calls again, still farther, a lonesome warbling. The air chills. The opalescent sky to the west darkens and all the subtle night sounds seem easier to hear in the cold, clear air, underlaid by the silken run-ning of the river. The river still holds the light, a pewter thong binding the landscape across the river with this grassy bank.

I fall asleep to awake in the dark of night to such a stillness: the high mountain cold locks the night flow and even the river is silent. I lie and listen. A duck flies by and all that tells of its going is the soft wheeping of its wings.

I AWAKE again when sun hits the tent. A disk of ice a quarter inch thick clinks in my cup outside. The river shines clear and sharp. We eat breakfast sitting in a thatch of grass. So tentative is the morning breeze that only a single blade moves at a time. Overlaid green on top, at this altitude and latitude, the grass is still brown beneath, even in late June.

The river rises a couple of inches during breakfast, covering but not destroying the bird tracks. The silt, in which they are impressed, bubbles gently where ground water runs in. The sky is high overcast by the time we shove off. An upstream breeze brisk enough to tip foam off oncoming waves catches me in the face. In this light, the water turns tawny. The channel is reassuringly deep, showing rippled and wave-marked sands beneath. But within the hour, as we approach

Kendall Warm Springs, the river shallows and becomes ominously rocky.

The springs flow out, more or less in a line, about a quarter of a mile from the river, on a steep ridgeside of dolomite. Dolomite is a type of limestone containing a large proportion of magnesium, its hardness indicated by the prominent ridge it forms wherever it outcrops, a coarse-grained sugary rock that becomes pitted on the surface with weathering. Springs form when surface water flows through underground faults and fractures. Here the water circulates deep enough and close enough to hot rock at depth for it to become warmed. Discharged through a surface weakness, here on a hillside, the temperature of the water is unusually high and directly influences the solubility of the many minerals and gases that may be dissolved in it. This warm solution carries considerable amounts of calcium in the form of calcium carbonates and bicarbonates. The excess calcium carbonate precipitates in thin layers, building up basins and terraces of marl, stepped down to the river. The warm water descends through this series of basins, becoming cooler, finally dropping into the river and enriching it with dissolved minerals.

The characteristic plant of calcium-rich springs is stonewort, a large alga; its common name describes its hard, brittle, limy surface. Although it more resembles an ordinary herb in size, it has an alga's simple cell structure and no roots, simple branches springing out in whorls at nodes along the stem. The rough stems are the result of an unusually high calcium carbonate content. Animals (except for certain beetles) avoid eating it for this reason, although its tangled mats form prime protective habitats for the smaller creatures of the pools, tiny crustaceans and dragonfly nymphs, soldier-fly larvae, and minute snails and beetles. Stonewort is so brittle that it cannot endure much current, but otherwise seems able to grow abundantly in places that higher plants would find hostile. Stoneworts play a role in precipitating the insoluble calcium salts brought into the pools. The salts form minute crystals that so heavily encrust the plant with mineral matter that it can be both seen and felt. When the stonewort dies and cell walls decay and disintegrate, the residue of lime remains, layering into these marl terraces.

The first time I saw these springs was on an August day, when it was logical for the pools to be warm, for daisies, small fireweeds, yellow monkeyflowers, brook avens, and cinquefoils to be in bloom. One expects green horsetails, mosses, and water spring beauty. The next time was in January, when the air temperature was nearly zero.

These warm springs were a striking dichotomy, with snow and frost patterns juxtaposed with bubbling water and green plants. The snow looked freshly sugared from the hoarfrost that coated it. Every exposed dry grass blade near the pools stood like a motionless banner, half to three-quarters flagged with frost. The springs provided ample water vapor, that crystallized on surfaces cooled below the dew point. The air sparkled with ice crystals. It was physically and visually breathtaking, the radiant gleaming surfaces alternately revealed and obscured by floating mists. At the edges of the pools the snow surface was shaggy and imbricated, hanging over the water like white cockatoo feathers. The mists sifted aside, the sunlight unfurled, lighting all the snow and frost patterns with a blinding clarity. Where the stonewort grew above the water line it was frozen crisp and bleached nearly white; beneath, in the warmth of the water, it gleamed emerald. White patches of snow capped each rock island, looking like heaps of feather boas. A water ouzel pranced, dipping briskly, a slate-colored lagniappe for a winter day.

The water was pellucid. The small rocks on the bottom, patched with olive-green algae, looked like old Indian-head pennies. The water skimmed through small channels, wedged and scalloped on the surface. Inch-long fish slipped with the current, then swam back against it. Called Kendall dace, they are endemic to these pools, a species (or subspecies, depending upon definition) of the speckled dace that live in the river below, isolated by the rising terraces of marl that finally prevented a free exchange between the river and the warm-springs populations.

I followed the springs down to where they debouch into the river, sometimes breaking through the snow crust well over my knees. The water spread and fell as a shallow screen, tossing up fingers of spray that tipped off into flying balls, frothing down the spillway into a small black pool that the warm water kept open in the frozen river.

In June, from the river below, the runoff streams spread and pour over the edge in filaments, gathering together in curtains that flash across the ledge, over the marl-built caves beneath. Their rushing sound is lost in the roar and pound of the rapids. The upper Green is a vigorous river, dropping a thousand feet over the seventy-five-mile stretch below Green River Lakes, an average of thirteen feet per mile, such a gradient alone engendering swift flow. Here it is steeper yet, and we face a plethora of boulders, which very nearly form a breakwater across the width of the channel. And Kendall Warm Springs rapids are prophetically marked on the topographical map as "falls."

In smooth water the bowman is no more than a galley slave. But in rapids, to be in the bow is to be dripping wet, involved in more action than there is time to react to. In running rapids, the object is to keep the boat parallel with whatever current it runs in, and the only way to maintain control is to go faster or slower than that current. The first stroke *not* to learn for river rapids is the forward stroke, for this only impels the canoe into bigger trouble quicker, the rush of the current itself adding enough acceleration into disaster without helping it along. The most important strokes are the backstroke and two sideways ones called a draw and a pry. With a draw the paddle is put out directly to the side of the boat, blade parallel to the gunwales, and drawn in flat toward the canoe; it pulls water beneath the canoe and the bow slips toward the side upon which the draw is made. A pry accomplishes the opposite. Neither is a natural movement and in practice I add more water to the canoe than I do direction.

In a rock-garden rapid, such as we prepare to run, ideally the bow spots the rocks the stern often cannot see, draws or pries to avoid them with a nicety of judgment, for a vast displacement skews the canoe about, making it vulnerable to being caught sideways by the current, at which point the river makes the decisions. The stern patterns his strokes upon those he sees the bow make: if the bow pries, the stern draws to counteract the torque and keep the canoe aligned with the current—running rock-garden rapids has been described as sidestepping downstream. There is no time for verbal commands, and even if there were, they more than likely could not be heard over the roar of the rapids.

At this moment, the canoe looks very frangible and I wish I were back upstream reading about running rapids in a book. The penalty for hanging up on one of these rocks is a capsize. There have been times on the river when I have thought a good capsize was part of "writer's experience." But when I actually confront this white water, self-preservation comes first: these rocks look like bone breakers. I do not want to lose my duffel or drawing pads and notebook, or see paddles splinter or the canoe smashed. There are white-water canoes with a watertight apron, but we are running in a standard open canoe that can ship large amounts of water, immediately rendering it cumbersome and unmaneuverable. Mathematically, in a ten-mile-per-hour current (which is a good fast rapid) the force broadside on a canoe hung up on a rock can be up to ten thousand pounds. The swiftness of a flip is incredible, quicker than one's mind can react. No amount of intellectual awe at big figures prepares me for the emotional instantaneousness of that force and its power.

More apprehensive than experienced, more overreactive than precise, I miscalculate and draw too hard on the left. The bow barely ticks a monstrous rock but it is sufficient to break our controlled forward motion and the canoe swings broadside against it with a ferocity that nearly throws me out of the boat. Water piles against the boat from upstream. Pressure surges against the hull. The canoe hangs there, tilted, alternately wedging tighter and rocking loose, water rushing too fast and too deep for me to be able to step out into the stream. Why we do not capsize I will never know—perhaps it is because the canoe is loaded, giving it a stability that a lighter one does not have. But mostly it is because of Perry, who keeps his head and does precisely the right thing at precisely the right moment. Somehow he pivots the boat off and we slip free and ferry to shore. I am trembling so hard I can barely get out of the canoe.

But running white water is like riding a horse: if you fall off, you'd better get right back on. The water for the rest of the morning is fast moving but the rocks are neither so large nor so close together, the slope of the channel not so steep, and the water not too deep to stand in if need be. It is good running, great for confidence. I can see the rocks pillowing up in front of bouncing backwaves. The rhythm of manipulating the bow becomes an elation as the canoe skims by easily and safely, rock after rock.

As we swing close to the bank, a mallard hen springs out, followed by three golden-tan ducklings that rock and lurch downstream in an effort to keep up with their mother, and I don't know whether I am laughing at them or just for the relief of not having capsized, or the joy of being on this river, this glorious, beautiful river.

4

The Paches [Apaches] took my beaver—five pack of the prettiest in the mountain—an' two mules, but my traps was hid in the creek. Sez I, hyar's a gone coon ef they keep my gun, so I follers thar trail, an' at night, crawls into camp, an' socks my big knife up to the Green River, first dig.

Lewis H. Garrard, 1850, *Wah-to-Yah and the Taos Trail*

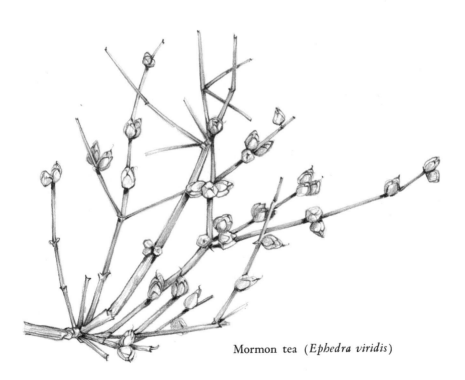

Mormon tea (*Ephedra viridis*)

Whiskey Cr.

Tie Camp

Cemetery Creek

Rock Cr.

Red Creek

Jim Creek

Wagonteur Cr.

Badger Cr.

Twin Cr.

Mud Creek

Black Butte

Spring Cr.

G R E E N   R I V E R

N

Proposed Kendall dam

The Narrows

0   1 mile

Warren Bridge

KENDALL WARM SPRINGS
TO WARREN BRIDGE

A FEW MILES downstream from Kendall Bridge a small cemetery marks the site of the tie cutters' camp once run by August Kendall. Ties were cut and trimmed for the railroad in the winter and floated downstream in the spring. A dense new growth of lodgepole pine on the hillside has sprung up; the original cutting was, in order to have straight ties, extremely selective.

A historical marker notes that the tie camp was open 1885–1905, and that seven lie buried here: Bert Glines was killed by a tree, Billy Williams was shot to death; the infant Barnhardt twins, cause of death not stated; and three others, unknown. The large grave in the center is heaped with chunks of white dolomite and ringed with the dark circles of animal burrows. The twins' graves, on the edge of the cemetery toward the river, are so small, outlined with stones and sprigged with rabbitbrush and gilia. There are no headstones. The hard rock ground must have been nearly impossible to excavate for a grave. It was a hard life that ended in hard ground, and only the river runs easy.

Gravel derived from the glacial-outwash terrace continues to dominate the river-channel material. When the canoe has to be walked, the rocks are still treacherously slippery, but being a little larger and laid more evenly in the streambed, are a little less difficult to traverse. But the water is much colder, just out of the morning mountains. All along the river willows form dense screens, almost impenetrable; from the air they look like green candlewicking. Part of the time it is possible to walk on the edge of the bank, working the line through the willow tangle, and then the thicket closes in and there is only one place to walk and that is back in the frigid river. I begin to have some empathy for the trappers, who worked waist deep in the bone-congealing water of early spring and late fall to trap beaver.

Sometimes there is enough water to coast along a narrow channel under the willows, almost hand-pulling along by the branches. Without the sound of the paddle heralding our approach, ducks tend to stay longer on the water before leaping off with stentorian calls and much flapping and spray. Mallards and mergansers are the most common, in groups of eight or ten, sometimes mixed. Mallards arrive on the northern Green in March and leave in November, sometimes the last to go. Now toward the end of June most of the eggs have hatched and nearly every duck has a string of ducklings; the young are able to swim and walk almost as soon as they are dry, feeding chiefly on vegetation alongside the river.

Mergansers are fish-eating ducks and swim underwater after food. When disturbed, mallards almost spring straight up, while mergansers make a long taxi on the water. Mergansers are long bodied, somewhat loonlike in aspect; both red-breasted and American mergansers frequent the upper river. The females of both are so boldly marked with a crested rusty-brown head that it is some time before I can identify one as a female American merganser rather than a male of some species that simply does not exist in the bird book. One problem of canoeing is getting identification books in and out of complicated waterproof sacks; by the time the book is out, the bird is gone. We slip around a bend where a large flock of mergansers is feeding. They spring off into a long serpentine line, looping like a huge Möbius strip, banking into a figure eight, going back to land only when we are far downstream.

The big rivers not only offer clear landmarks for migrating birds, but also food and shelter. The upper Green lies along one of the major flyways of the West. Since the rivers are often open when lakes are not, plants and small animals emerge first along the riverside and are likely to be out later in the fall, so rivers insure feeding grounds for birds that are early and late migrators. Birds have been observed following a winding river course faithfully, even though shortcuts were easily visible across the narrow neck of a horseshoe curve.

Bankside willows are well pruned by beavers, fresh cuts light against darker bark. There are alleyways between the high shrubs, but within ten feet one can, for all intents and purposes, disappear. Protection for large and small animals is perfect. Beneath the shrubs, summer flowers are thick and in full bloom, vermilion Indian paintbrush, blue chiming bells, purple violets and lavender-blue veronica, pink wild geraniums, yellow avens and cinquefoils, tiny white chickweeds almost buried in deep green sedges, and drifts of wild strawberries. Overhanging willows provide cover for trout pools. Since only rainbow and brown trout are stocked, brook and cutthroat and other fish retain their populations by spawning in the quiet backwaters of the river's tributaries.

The downriver view is framed by willows, a stream a hundred feet wide and widening, gleaming and sweeping. Probably it is still technically a stream, navigable only by canoe or kayak or rowboat, but to me it is beginning to look like "river."

THE BED beneath the canoe is sandy bottomed. The bed not only looks homogeneous, it is: channel sands are composed of nearly all similar-sized sand grains. Once in a while a long, narrow triangle of sand streams out on the downriver side of a tiny embedded pebble. Deeper than the paddle in most places, the water remains clear enough for me to see the ripple patterns on the bottom. Sometimes the ripples lie close and even, but most of the time they are piecemeal, falcate, arranged in echelon. They scallop the bed for a few feet, then fade away, only to rise to sharp-capped complex ripples again, all facing downstream like miniature cuestas.

Ripples form only in sand, not in loose gravels or cohesive muds. At low velocities the current cannot move the particles making up its bed, but when velocity increases, as it does during spring runoff, the bed surface blurs as sand particles begin to move, and ripples form almost immediately, often around some nucleus—perhaps no more than a bit of gravel, a pebble, or an embedded twig. The current, flowing over the protuberance, causes a minute eddy on the downstream side. The rising vortex of this eddy checks the forward motion of oncoming grains and they drop down the lee side of the forming ripple, building it downstream; simultaneously currents eat away at the upstream side. The result is that ripples tend to travel downstream at right angles to the current. They are asymmetrical, steeper on the lee side, that tends to be the angle of repose of the sand grains, gentler on the upstream side. (By contrast, ocean-beach ripples, formed by oscillating waves, are symmetrical.) The crests are sharp, and even through four to six feet of water their crisp contours show clearly. As long as they are less than approximately two inches high, they are classified as "ripples."

But what I am watching beneath the prow look larger, perhaps five or six inches, and these are technically termed "dunes." Dunes are merely larger sand waves, formed in the same way, with the same asymmetrical profile. Both form under the low-flow regimen that characterizes this part of the river most of the year.

The complexity of ripples and dunes grows, caused by secondary currents, the dominant downstream impulse elaborated by smaller errant currents springing from changes in bed or channel or minor obstructions. However, leaning over the gunwale to watch the bottom is not a very effective way to paddle a canoe—or so I gather by comments from the stern.

THE MAIN RIVER current fetches back and forth across the river, and the canoe follows, crossing to catch the swifter flow just along the outside banks of the meander. Seen from an airplane, a river's course may be straight, meandering, or braided, the patterns constantly intergrading. Meanders constitute the most common pattern. The convex inner bends often contain small sand bars. The concave outer bends offer spirited currents that send the canoe flying.

A meandering river weaves an elegant, sinuous serpentine across the landscape, a form that depends on many variable factors—the steepness of slope, the kind of material through which the river flows, its velocity, the amount of discharge and the load it carries, its width and depth, and the roughness of its bed. If meanders from different-sized rivers are converted to the same scale, the proportion of the wave lengths is extraordinarily similar, predominantly five to seven times the channel width, as in a pool-and-riffle sequence. Laid on the land with the geometric purity and economy of nature, meanders pose the quintessential question of the river: what is around the next bend?

The shallow crossover points in a meander correspond closely to the gravel-bar intervals in a pool-and-riffle sequence, and lie slightly downstream from the center point of the meander bend. This becomes of immediate practical importance when canoeing, and we become

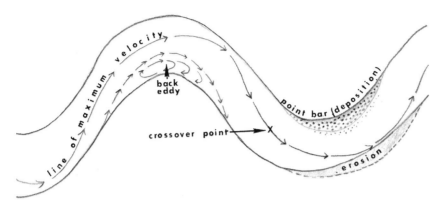

FLOW IN A MEANDER
(Adapted from Morisawa, *Streams: Their Dynamics and Morphology*, 1968,
pp. 83 and 139)

practiced in estimating just where this is. Otherwise the canoe may hang up on the intervening gravel bar or miss some of the lilt of running through the happy water against the outer bank. When the bow catches the crossover point just right, it flies into a curving chute where the river's velocity is highest. The water peaks up, centrifugal force actually causing it to pile up against the bank and break into small peaked waves. Just before the canoe collides with the shore, I lean as far out as possible to draw away; otherwise the shooting force bangs the bow into the bank with a jarring thud and swings the canoe around; strenuous paddling then is required to get it back into control again, and lots of comments from the stern about the bow's responsibility. (The trouble with paddling bow is that without eyes in the back of your head, you never catch the stern in error.)

One problem with running under the outer bank is that the shearing stress of the water claws away at sod and bares tree roots, undermines big shrubs and trees that then lean out over the water, branches extended with intent to snag. Most of the time the boat brushes the overhanging branches, since a complete miss is usually beyond my strength and calculation, and as a consequence, the canoe picks up all kinds of freeloaders: caterpillars, leaves full of leaf miners, a weft of discommoded mosquitoes, a huge female stonefly loaded with eggs. She clings to my gloves with grappling-hook feet. I remove her and she stalks the gunwale, walks the thwart, even clings to the highly varnished paddle shaft.

Her wings are large and heavily veined, and remain firmly closed. The long antennae probe every step of the way. She absolutely refuses to fly. It may be that it is too cool or that she is simply too heavy and not a flyer to begin with. She was obviously interrupted in the task of dropping her eggs and the extruded egg mass still clings to her abdomen. A fiberglass canoe is not the appropriate site for egg laying, but trying to dispossess her is like trying to get rid of a piece of fly paper. I finally take my gloves off, get a firm grasp on her thorax, and pull her off my jeans to which she sticks as if with adhesive tape. As we pass close to the bank I toss her to shore and we leave her—a large, ponderously pregnant insect—teetering precipitously on a stalk of grass.

THE SILT at the edge of the wet bank where Jim Creek enters the Green River is full of moose tracks, paired teardrop shapes deeply impressed. The banks are a solid thicket of willows, tops so even that they look as if they had been mowed. Primary moose wintering grounds lie between Black Butte and Kendall, a secondary range from Kendall to the Green River Lakes. High on a hillside above the river are two grazing females, resembling nothing more than big ungainly horses. The herds in this area have shown an increase for the last decade, and their population is estimated to be near fifteen hundred. Their winter range is small compared to their summer range, and these willowed bottomlands along the river are vitally essential for their survival since moose are not amenable to artificial winter feeding.

The wind freshens, making paddling hard work. The best solution is to run under a windscreen of willows, but when this is impossible the only solution is to lean in and paddle against the chop. Above a stand of unleafed aspen a hawk is harassed by two blackbirds, that hang right on its tail. A little farther, a bald eagle surveys the mouse-populated meadow from a "beaver slide" hayrack. The white head and ample profile are unmistakable. At the canoe's approach it launches into the air, taking deep strokes to gain altitude, then coasts in vast, flat circles, a magnificent creature, easy and high. On the skyline ridge two antelope graze, nibbling sagebrush beside cattle who jerk their heads as they pull at grasses. They are slender, elegant creatures compared to the four-legged-box cows. At the sound of voices they spring across the rough terrain, oversized windpipe, lungs, and larger heart giving them marvelous running power. Most antelope winter below the confluence of the Green and New Fork Rivers, migrating long distances to summer range in the mountains.

Wash snaps on the line by a group of ranch houses that overlook a series of hay meadows, irrigated by water from the Green—hay is the only crop that can be grown in the short season at this altitude. Boulder Creek enters. Irrigation ditches come off the stream like snakes, even width, compared to the natural widening and narrowing of the river's channel, irrigation being the primary use of water from the upper river.

The old wooden Carney bridge spans the widening river, now nearly two hundred feet across. The bridge piers provide a hiatus in the current, and trout and whitefish lurk in their shadow. In spite of the barren look of the sand bottom here, there are ample midge larvae, many snails, and several species of mayfly nymphs, food necessary to support good fishing streams. Sawed-off pilings stand next to the present bridge supports like new shoots around an old lilac bush. Repair work is done on these bridges when the river freezes over; the top decking is removed, new pilings are driven in, boards replaced, and rotted pilings sawed off at ice level. As we slide beneath, I glimpse the original twelve-by-twelve beams. These old bridges must be a maintenance nightmare, but aesthetically they are a pleasure, weathering to gray, vastly more attractive than modern sharp-angled harsh-painted metal bridges.

The river continues to rise. Thumb-sized twigs bob in the current, a signal of rising water as the river picks up debris, leaves, and branches off the bank. Wind converts the willow leaves to silver. The river turns west and the Wyoming Range lies dead ahead, snow-patched, footed with rolling bluffs. I am so entranced with the view that we are nearly upon a beaver before I see him. A stack of fresh-cut willow twigs lies near the lodge entrance. He is a big armful of an animal, poised halfway between dinner and surprise. About four feet long in all, tail about a third of this, he must easily weigh fifty pounds. He freezes for a split second, then makes a flying leap from the bank practically over the bow.

A beaver's pelt is well oiled from highly active oil and wax glands in order to retain body heat when in contact with cold water. The pelt consists of an outer layer of somewhat stiff red-brown guard hairs, and a soft underfur of gray hair that is the commercially valuable growth of fur. When a beaver dives, the guard hairs form an oil-insulated cover to which no air clings. There are other adaptations for a semi-aquatic life: a beaver's nostrils are positioned back on the head, and both eye and nose openings can be closed by a valve to prevent water from entering. In spite of a portly appearance, they are streamlined for easy passage through the water: consolidation of the neck and shortening of the skull give compactness to the forebody, while the rear portion is elongated into a paddle tail. A beaver's tail is an appendage of many uses: as a rudder, as a balance when running or sitting, as a tocsin. The beaver surfaces, takes one look at the canoe, and whacks his tail. He arches his body and tail upward at the same instant that he dives, and when about halfway under, whips the tail forward and then back flat down on the water with a resounding smack.

In this area a beaver's first food preference is aspen; after that, succulent roots, cottonwoods, and willows: spring willows, summer willows, silvery willows, green willows, divine willows. Larger trees are felled by being gnawed in a deep circular wedge around the trunk about a foot up from the ground; many extremely large cottonwoods still standing along the river downstream are so girdled, where ambition exceeded ability. It is a myth that a beaver plans where the tree will fall—Washington Irving quotes Captain Bonneville, who had often

> seen trees measuring eighteen inches in diameter, at the places where they had been cut through by the beaver, but they lay in all directions, and often very inconveniently for the after purposes of the animal. In fact, so little ingenuity do they at times display in this particular, that at one of our camps on Snake River, a beaver was found with his head wedged into the cut which he had made, the tree having fallen upon him and held him prisoner until he died.

Beaver are so frequent along this reach of upper river that I find it difficult to realize that, because of the caprice of London dandies for beaver hats, beaver were once nearly trapped out of this whole drainage. Beaver pelts were a basis of trade, a symbol of nationalistic ambition, and the foundation for a unique life style of a particular group of independent and adventurous men whose names remain imprinted on the Green River landscape: Ashley, Bridger, Fontenelle, Henry, Ham, Jackson, Sublette, and others. As accessible streams became trapped out, trappers explored further into the recesses of the wilderness until they had an understanding, as no other white men of their time, of the geography of thousands of back country acres.

When the beaver market collapsed, the mountain man, skilled in this most demanding of professions, became proficient in others: Jim Bridger was guide, trading-post operator, advisor to emigrants, and route maker (the Pony Express and Overland trails followed Bridger routes); Kit Carson rode the Pony Express and guided for General John Frémont; others ran ferries and posts. It is ironic that these supreme practitioners of solitude made possible the influx of settlers to the West, and that men who lived in such close harmony with the land nevertheless nearly deleted an entire animal species.

IN THE EARLY 1820s many small fur companies operated in southeastern Wyoming; by 1830 the locus of the fur trade moved to the Green River Valley. The American Fur Company, backed by J. J. Astor, and the Rocky Mountain Fur Company, founded by General William Ashley and Major Andrew Henry in 1822, dominated the scene, competing with each other and the British Hudson's Bay Company. Competition became increasingly intense and bitter as the amount of beaver dwindled and the amount of national ambition grew.

The beaver trade peaked between 1830 and 1832, with a price for skins between $4 and $6 a pound, and a trapper could take 400–500 pounds a year. Exportation probably reached 200,000 skins annually during peak years, and at this rate the supply of beaver began to dwindle. By 1833 the price of beaver had weakened. Machinery was invented that produced a good wool felt for hats, and silk hats began to replace beaver in fashion. By 1840, the price for pelts was $1 to $2 a pound, and 150 pounds was a good year's harvest.

In its heyday, much of the beaver trade was carried on by "free trappers" who worked alone, or with a few others of their kind, and sold pelts to whomever they wished. Those who worked directly for a specific fur company received their supplies as well as sold their pelts only to that company. The best pelts were to be taken in early spring and late fall; wading waist deep in mountain streams, a mountain man's occupational disease was rheumatism. Beaver traps were simple spring-loaded devices; a line of five or six were usually set at one time, at dusk and dawn, trap jaws hidden about four inches below the water surface. Castor, a beaver secretion, was rubbed on a bait stick. When the swimming beaver raised its head to sniff it, one or both feet touched the pan of the trap, releasing the springs. In panic, the beaver dove for deep water, where the weight of the trap held it down.

If a trapper worked alone, he did his own sets, skinning, and stretching. The tail, one of the delicacies of the trapper's mess, and the castor, used for bait, were kept; the remainder was usually discarded. The pelt was removed and scraped clean, then stretched. W. A. Ferris, a trapper for the American Fur Company, described a trappers' camp of 1832, when

> we found a party of trappers, headed by Bridger, one of the partners in the R. M. F. Company. Their encampment was decked with hundreds of beaver skins, now drying in the sun. These valuable skins are always stretched in willow hoops, varying from eighteen inches, to three feet in diameter, according to the size of the skins, and have a reddish appearance on the flesh side, which is exposed to the sun. Our camps are always dotted with these red circles, in the trapping season, when the weather is fair.

The individual trapper packed little in the way of gear. His personal articles, such as flints, bullet mold, and lead or bullets, and powder, were tucked into a "possible sack"; four to six traps were folded up into a trapsack. He carried a knife and rifle and often a handgun. The Hawken rifle, made in St. Louis, was a favorite; it weighed nearly twelve pounds and had a large bore—.53 caliber—which took nearly a half-ounce ball that, needless to say, did massive damage. A mountain man was skilled in making the first shot count; since the rifle was a muzzleloader, the time necessary to reload was often sufficient for game to get out of range or an Indian within range with bow and arrow.

Green River knife

A trapper's other prized possession was his Green River knife. In 1824 John Russell established a small company in Green River, Massachusetts, and began the manufacture of a knife that soon became coveted in the West. Russell instituted the first water-powered trip hammer and stamping machines, and his knives competed in quality with those produced in England. His major items were heavy utilitarian knives, upon the blades of which were stamped "J. Russell & Co." and, below, "Green River Works." The Green River knife was a handy, hefty tool, not only for skinning game and carving meat, but for the less culinary activities of dispatching and scalping an Indian. It had a short, sturdy blade, and when it went in up to the trademark, the deed was accomplished, usually irrevocably so. Hence, "up to Green River" became a popular expression in the West for something first rate, a job totally done, a metaphor matching "up to the hilt." Since the western Green River was the domain of the mountain man, and carried the connotation of self-reliance in the wilderness, the "Green River" on the knife blade became associated with this Green River rather than the one in the East, and the knife gained a reputation far beyond that of good design and utility.

During the height of the fur trade, five thousand dozen Green River knives were sent West for trade and sale, and many still exist. Perry has an original one: the handle is comfortable and well-balanced, its grain worn, impregnated with the grease and oil and dirt of years of use. The blade, honed down narrow from the original shape, still holds a keen edge. And on the darkened metal are the words "Green River Works" that came to mean "all the way."

EVEN IN SUMMER, evenings on the upper Green River are chill. I have paddled all day without sunglasses, thinking them unnecessary with the overcast. Nevertheless, the glare off the water is sufficient to make my head ache. It has been a long day on the river. I go to take a high-energy bar and a sweater out of my waterproof bag and fumble the buckles, clumsiness indexing the extent of fatigue and the recognition that, were I alone, such overtiredness would be both foolish and dangerous, leading to errors in judgment that have an unnerving way of becoming serious. To have lived alone in this country was no small accomplishment.

I am thankful when we pull off river. I walk around on the sagebrush terrace and find that there is not enough room to pitch my

Sagebrush with galls
(*Artemisia tridentata*)

tent without implanting it on either a very large thistle or a fresh
cow pat or over a yawning badger hole, and I am no match for an
ill-tempered badger. Down nearer the river, where it is flatter and
more grassy, it is also more mosquitoed. The night fire, built both for
smoke and warmth, reminds me of the nineteenth-century western
chronicler who, listening to someone rhapsodize about the romance
of a campfire, acidly remarked that it only emphasized how cold his
backside was.

The wind remains up. Gusts of sparks fly from the fire. The river
world is still restless. Cows complain in the distance. A goose close
by barks for a long time, riled up about something. The wind goes up
my jacket sleeve and chills my hands and makes me drop my spoon
and trip over a log. I mind neither rain nor cold, but wind makes
me edgy. Noises become too sharp and continuing noises annoy,
exasperate. The silly goose still spasmodically broadcasts her uneasiness, and a beaver that scents strangers continually smacks the water
with its tail. Smoke blows in my eyes. The wind frets all evening,

ruffling ashes from the fire, blowing the coals to glowing, plaiting and knotting the smoke and stretching it into thin whispers.

The tent rustles and luffs in an irregular, annoying way. I know that there is a hairline crack in one of the back tent-pole sleeves, and now I worry about that along with the white water coming up tomorrow above Warren Bridge. In the middle of the night there is a soft "ping" and I know exactly what it is. My first impulse is to bury myself deeper in the warm sleeping bag and ignore it. But there is really no choice; care of equipment comes first, and a torn tent is precious little shelter. I pull on jeans, jacket, boots, find the package of emergency sleeves in the tent sack, crawl out, stumble over my bootlaces, tie them, unstake the back stake, pull out the tubing, tape it firmly, holding the flashlight in my teeth. Back inside I pile most of my duffel in the back end for stability. I lie awake watching the tent quiver and shudder, wishing fervently to be anywhere unwindy, feeling out of phase, ill at ease, the object of some personal Aeolian vendetta. And then the wind stops, and in the respite I fall asleep on the instant.

I LOOK OUT in the morning to see a huge moose come swimming downriver. He swims so silently that only the ponderous rack marks his approach. He climbs ashore directly across the river and prances off, neck extended, a big chocolate-brown mélange of an animal, heavy head out of place on graceful racehorse legs, surprisingly light-footed and fleet.

The river still rises. By the time we have the canoe packed, the water is up five inches and still rising. Knowing that there are rough rock-garden rapids ahead, I view this as a mixed blessing. On one hand, deeper water covers the rocks better, but on the other, it will also increase the current's velocity. If there is insufficient water, all I have to worry about is wet feet and walking, not missing rocks with a bow that in fast water seems hellbent on destruction.

A diversion channel marks the Canyon Ditch, where irrigation water is taken out of the river. A homestead cabin sits high on the small sedged terrace forming the left bank. The grasses and sedges are knee high, hiding puddles of water in the marshy ground. The cabin is about twenty by twenty feet, built with the log notches on the underside, so that when it rains water does not collect to rot them. The heavy door stands ajar. It is still in good repair, opening to a room with a dirt floor, no windows. Outside, under the apex of the roof, a cliff swallow has daubed its nest and the young mew and squeak. A robin nests under the eaves and three small wide yellow Vs are the gaping mouths of the eternally hungry.

The cabin was undoubtedly built to fulfill residence requirements for the Homestead Act of 1862. The act, passed ostensibly to open western lands for settlement and provide a solution for the over-crowding and economic conditions of eastern cities, was· an ironic failure in the arid country west of the ninety-seventh meridian. The starry-eyed homesteader was generally unaware of the brief growing season and the aridity, and many, in addition, lacked capital or labor or know-how.

The philosophy of John Wesley Powell, then head of the Geographical and Geological Survey of the Rocky Mountain Region, was summed up in the New York *Tribune*, April 28, 1877:

> The present land system of the country is not at all suitable for the area of the arid region. In the whole region, land as mere land, is of no value. What is really valuable is the water privilege. Rich men and stock companies have appropriated all of the streams and they charge for the use of the water. Government sections of 160 acres that do not contain water are practically worthless. . . . All the good public lands fit for settlement are sold.

Powell published his *Report on the Lands of the Arid Region of the United States* in 1878. He insisted that beyond the hundredth meridian there needed to be a new approach to settlement, socially, agriculturally, and politically. Instead of checkerboard plots, parcels should be defined by their relation to the drainage basin and topography, and the basin should also provide the natural limits for political boundaries. To this purpose, the entire United States should be sur-

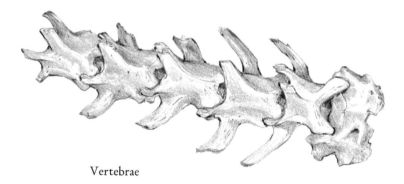

Vertebrae

veyed, producing a series of seventeen-by-twenty-inch maps, such as the ones with which we travel the river today. Powell saw in the eastern point of view, based on riparian rights, ample water, and a long growing season, a totally unrealistic approach to land use when applied to the arid and semiarid West.

Powell's judgment was all too realistic. By 1880 only one-seventh of the available lands in Wyoming had been surveyed and homesteaded. By 1890, when Powell's report again appeared, in magazine form, only one in three homesteaders had managed to survive. Failure to live up to the requirements of the act resulted in forfeiture; in this way many speculators acquired large acreages without ever becoming homesteaders. In spite of these failures, many politicians were infected with the belief that "rain follows the plow" and all that any good and ambitious man had to do was to cultivate his land and there would be sufficient moisture coming out of the sky to water all his crops and provide for all his needs—and that simple, tragic misconception ruined many well-intentioned, hard-working, hopeful people, as well as those less prepared. The Homestead Act, as it was written, was simply not feasible in the West.

One comes to have a certain feeling about these homestead cabins; some are falling down, others so well built that the corners are still plumb. But doorways are always empty, saying whoever lived here is gone, and it is sobering to think of the problems of living in this isolated cabin for five years without respite. These dark cabins on the upper Green, above the area of cottonwood shelter, stand out under the summer sun, a poignant reminder that you cannot cultivate eastern thinking in the high western basins.

FARTHER DOWNSTREAM we pass a proposed dam site for a reservoir that would back water up to Kendall Bridge, a reservoir that would cover acres of productive rangeland, change the kind of fishing now enjoyed on the upper river, inundate critical winter range for moose, degrade nesting, breeding, and brooding areas for waterfowl, block the migration path of deer and antelope herds to their winter ranges farther south, and irrevocably alter the life style of the people who live here. Cost estimates are unrealistic, as is its placement in a substrate of morainal debris and permeable sandstone that would permit copious leakage. One proposal will send water from the reservoir out of the Green River Basin, via canal and pipeline, for industrial use in eastern Wyoming. In return, the reservoir would provide commonly available "reservoir-based recreation opportunities," scarcely a replacement for one of Wyoming's four blue-ribbon trout streams, high ranches, and unique green wilderness. It would destroy the nesting site of the mallard that flops downstream alongside the canoe as if her wing were broken, trying to distract us from her five ducklings. She finally veers to the shore, and after we pass, I look back to see her, clustered with ducklings, paddling busily upstream. I wish I were doing the same.

The sky is overcast, making rock spotting more difficult. But the rocks are scattered, and some of the confidence of running fast water comes back. Then rocks begin to fill the channel and the white line of dancing water ahead indicates rock gardens coming up. The sound of water piling up, corkscrewing through slots, bounding over boulders, choking through gaps and around and over rocks becomes more insistent, a single melding sound that makes conversation impossible—reverberating sound, challenging, defiant. We have to get out and walk the canoe a short way and I feel the current nudge my legs. On the downstream side of a boulder there is a sizable hole that curls up into a backwave that looks higher than the bow to me, and I feel a firm and fearful sense of respect.

These noisy chutes are only preliminaries. The rocks now begin to line up like an obstacle course. We beach the canoe and hike downstream to seek a passageway, since none can be seen from water level. I register the landmarks that identify the turnings, trying to get into my mind the channels through which the canoe can pass. The roar of the water pounds in my ears. It is the sound, even more than the sight of the white water, that beats into brain and focuses in the knotted muscles of my stomach.

And then it is time to run. We climb in, backferry into position and go—no time to think, no time for apprehension, no time for fear, a half mile passing in minutes, so quickly over. We automatically pull the canoe off into a back eddy, run the bow up in the shallows, and lift it onto the bank. It needs to be bailed and checked, gear fastenings tugged and tightened, and for a suspended moment there is absorption in the necessities. I have no feelings, no reaction, hands work without the mind. And then, all of a sudden, standing ankle deep in the water and drenched to the shoulders from the spray, water still streaming down my face, ears still full of the rushing sound of the river, I am overwhelmed with a sense of soaring joy, of fragile invincibility, of having come through, of having flown with the river. Then there is the necessity to talk it through, in a rush of words, looking back upriver, seeing where it seemed impossible to come through but we did, the malevolence of those rocks gleaming under an inch of icy water, the downstream side of the peaking waves, bringing back with words what was thought and felt and what was done wrong and what right, what was learned and what to do better next time, and trying to describe sheer elation.

I am amazed to discover how quickly reactions have become ingrained, recognition of rock and response the same, mind and arm and canoe one movement, the feel of current penetrating through paddle to spine. And there is the pleasure of a good canoe that responds, that, given its head and managed properly, seems to go of itself and flies over the water. It is heady business, to anticipate the marginal inch necessary to miss a rock, to feel rather than to think of how to go with the current, to realize that it is your understanding that locks the canoe into the river's running, but that it is pure river that guides you through, pure beautiful river.

The canoe tugs beneath my hand. It seems animate, eager to move, listening just as I do to the sound of more rapids jubilating downstream. I feel honed to the essence of sunlight on water. A hawk cries overhead, a high, eerie cry that ricochets off the backbone rock, and I look down on a river streaming air and water. I shake the water out of my sneakers and climb into the canoe. I brace my knee and hip against the gunwale and settle into the configuration of going. Once more we push off and backferry into position, lining up with the current. The canoe poises for that same instant that precedes the hawk's stoop. A tiny corkscrew of foam shows on either side of the hull.

The rapids begin with the rushing sound of wind through wings. Then the bow lifts and we soar with the river.

Henbane
(*Hyocyanus niger*)

5

This establishment [Fort Bonneville] was doubtless intended for a permanent trading post, by its projector, who has, however, since changed his mind, and quite abandoned it.—From the circumstance of a great deal of labor having been expended in its construction, and the works shortly after their completion deserted, it is frequently called "Fort Nonsense." It is situated in a fine open plain, on a rising spot of ground, about three hundred yards from Green river on the west side, commanding a view of the plains for several miles up and down that stream. On the opposite side of the fort about two miles distant, there is a fine willowed creek, called "Horse creek," flowing parallel with Green river, and emptying into it about five miles below the fortification. The river from the fort, in one direction, is terminated by a bold hill rising to the height of several hundred feet on the opposite side of the creek, and extending in a line parallel with it.—Again on the east side of the river, an abrupt bank appears rising from the water's edge, and extending several miles above and below, till the hills, jutting in on the opposite side of the river; finally conceal it from the sight. The fort presents a square enclosure, surrounded by posts or pickets firmly set in the ground, of a foot or more in diameter, planted close to each other, and about fifteen feet in length. At two of the corners, diagonally opposite to each other, block houses of unhewn logs are so constructed and situated, as to defend the square outside of the pickets, and hinder the approach of an enemy from any quarter. The prairie in the vicinity of the fort is covered with fine grass, and the whole together seems well calculated for the security both of men and horses.

W. A. FERRIS, *Life in the Rocky Mountains: A Diary of Wanderings on the Sources of the Rivers Missouri, Columbia, and Colorado from February, 1830, to November, 1835*

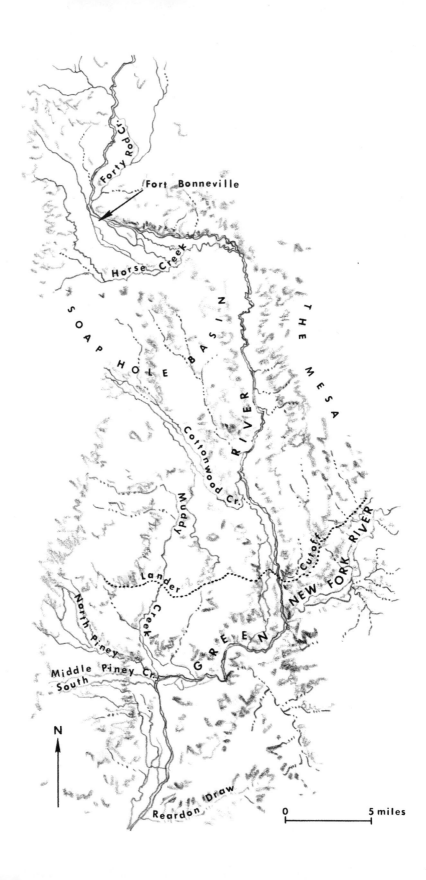

Forty Rod Cr.

Fort Bonneville

Horse Creek

S O A P   H O L E   B A S I N

T H E   M E S A

R I V E R

Cottonwood Cr.

Muddy

Lander

Creek

Cutoff

N E W   F O R K   R I V E R

North Piney

G R E E N

Middle Piney Cr.

South

N

Reardon Draw

0   5 miles

WARREN BRIDGE
TO REARDON DRAW

ROCK-GARDEN RAPIDS, a small weir or two, water pounding down chutes, quiet eddies to bail out in and from which to look over the next rapid, and always the continuum of the river: it seems like days but my watch says little over an hour. As we approach Warren Bridge I can see Connie's bright orange shirt, and then Darin and Holly waving. Connie's sisters and brother and their families, and her parents, meet us for a picnic. Their warmth and welcome make me feel more like a cherished cousin than an outsider. When we get back into the canoe after a satiety of good food and good talk, I am so relaxed that I immediately get us into trouble. After gloriously running the part of the river that "couldn't be run" in a canoe, there is one last short, simple stretch of white water below the bridge. With all the kids watching, I miss seeing a submerged rock and the canoe hangs up as if on a fulcrum. We have to disembark into calf-deep water and work it loose, receiving much unneeded, irreverent, and most certainly unasked-for advice. So much for expertise.

The river loops and swings into sweeping meanders. Sunspun currents cross from bank to bank in golden serpentines. A mink sleeks along the shore, seeming to flow over root and branch. A merganser with nine ducklings herds them downriver and corrals them under some overhanging roots. A doe watches us for a second and then bounds off on pogo-stick legs. Sometimes the banks are packed with river cobbles, at other times grassed to the edge. Narrowleaf cottonwood groves are a viridian green. Now the river's commentary is louder than it is dangerous, but it keeps one alert, careful, listening to catch the swish of water strained through willow branches caught in the current, or the gentler sound of inch-high waterfalls off cobble bars, embellishing the melodious running of the river with mordents. I relish the being on river, the sunlight, the skimming across the water and catching the spray, the lilt of happy water. The afternoon larks by in catching currents and watching ducklings and listening to willow leaves and turning clear around in the current like a top, out of sheer exuberance.

After flowing generally southwest, the river angles east and parallels Horse Creek, its name supposedly commemorating the theft of horses from trapper Thomas Fitzpatrick in 1820. Just above the confluence lies the site of Fort Bonneville, two blockhouses and a stockade, built in late summer of 1832 by Captain Benjamin Bonneville. He was given leave of absence from the army from August, 1831, to October, 1833, to, as he put it,

> establish prominent points of that country, ascertain the general courses &c of the principal rivers, the location of the indian tribes and their habits, visit the American and British establishments, make myself acquainted with their manner of trade and intercourse with the Indians, finally, endevour to develop every advantage the country affords and by what means they may most readily be opened to the enterprise of our citisens.

To carry all his equipment and goods, Bonneville needed twenty wagons, the first to be brought across the Divide. He arrived too late to do much trapping and barely got enough furs to cover his men's wages. The trip west was undoubtedly more time consuming than anticipated; like many Easterners, he understood little of the aridity or the problems of mountain travel. Either he had to build roads as he went, or put cables on the wagons and let them down difficult passes. And in the dry climate, as happened to all emigrants who came out of the humid Midwest and East, wooden parts shrank and separated, and Bonneville complained that "the wheels were incessantly falling to pieces."

I stand here, as Captain Bonneville once must have, turning 360 degrees to see big cottonwoods and willows screening the river, summer flowers blooming beneath the rabbitbrush, the long terrace across the river from which one can see for miles. This segment of land provides good pasture. The river provides ample water. There are cottonwoods for building and fuel. Situated at an unmarked crossroads, this site commands routes from nearly all directions. Anyone going to Oregon from the East, anyone crossing South Pass, any expedition out of the Southwest would have to pass through or near here. Only one problem existed: because of the high altitude it could not be used for wintering, so the less strategic-minded called it "Bonneville's Folly" or "Fort Nonsense."

Competitors hijacked his men and pelts with indiscriminate ease. He used up more of the trade goods than he could pay for. He lost many of his horses, leaving his outfit rundown and ill-equipped. The scientific aspects of the expedition were in no better shape. Astronomical observations for latitude and longitude were haphazard, and his maps were better than they deserved to be. Gannett, the surveyor with the Hayden Survey over forty years later, criticized the map as being "extremely faulty in geographical positions, many of them being one, two, or more degrees out of place."

In 1833 Bonneville sent a party to California under the command of Captain Joseph Walker, who attempted, among other business, to find if there was indeed a water route all the way from the Rocky Mountains to the Pacific. The myth existed partly because of the lack of accurate maps, but perhaps equally because people wanted so much to believe that it was so. Walker found neither route nor beaver. That September, Bonneville made the first recorded climb of a major Wyoming mountain, later named Gannett Peak, the highest of the Wind River Range although not as high as the 25,000 feet Bonneville estimated. In 1835, two years late, he went back East.

At this place, where the dust settles slowly and the sagebrush is fragrant, a plaque marks the fort's site. In this vicinity of the Green River, six trappers' rendezvous were held, more than in any other part of the Wyoming wilderness. And there is a strangely evocative quality in the late-afternoon light—the site looks, in certain directions, as it looked 140 years ago. I find myself listening for the rataplan of horses' hooves and the murmur of approaching voices, anticipating the cacophony of rendezvous.

THE ESTABLISHMENT of the rendezvous system is generally credited to General William Ashley. In 1822, Ashley and his partner in the Rocky Mountain Fur Company, Major Andrew Henry, advertised in the St. Louis newspaper for a hundred young men to go into the Yellowstone area and erect a fortified trading post. Answering the ad were men whose names became synonymous with the fur trade, among them Thomas Fitzpatrick, Hugh Glass, Milton and William Sublette, James Bridger, and Jedediah Smith. Smith and William Sublette, in an advance party, reached the Green River March 19, 1823, in the vicinity of the Big Sandy. After a season of trapping, Henry and Fitzpatrick took news back to Ashley in St. Louis that fall: the whole upper Green River drainage was rich with furs. Ashley set out in November, 1824, reaching the Green in the area of Fontenelle Creek in April, 1825.

There he organized four parties: three of them went out to trap. Ashley captained the fourth brigade and prepared to set off down the Green River. All arranged to meet July 10 on the Henrys Fork of the Green. Ashley's group built a bullboat, made of buffalo skins stretched over a willow frame, waterproofed with pitch and tallow, in aspect and configuration not entirely unlike the shallow-draft modern rafts used commercially on the river today, but essentially fragile and not adapted to white-water running. Passing through the unnamed canyons of Flaming Gorge and Lodore, capsizing in the latter and making numerous laborious portages, they continued past Split Mountain, down to the mouth of either the Uinta or Duchesne River. On June 7, Ashley met trapper Étienne Provost and his men. Provost told Ashley of the experience of four of his men in a canoe down through what are now called Gray and Desolation Canyons. Ashley himself continued south by canoe, but came off the river before the rapids and high walls of Desolation. He returned overland with Provost to the July rendezvous he had designated to be held on the Henrys Fork.

Running the river, Ashley discovered several important facts. There were fewer beaver as he went downriver, and the Green at high runoff was not the same as a placid Missouri stream and not likely to improve at low water for a bullboat. Rapids that capsized boats would also ruin pelts, and this river could not be relied upon for transporting either furs or supplies. He also surmised that it was probably part of the Colorado River drainage system, and was not, as sketched on contemporary maps, a river that ran all the way to the Pacific. (One of his trappers, Jedediah Smith, followed the California coast northward, looking for the mythical river two years later and seven years before Captain Walker did, and could not find it.) Ashley's knowledge, considering the vacuum that then existed, was considerable. It seems quite likely that trappers coming up from the south had traveled as far as the Uinta Mountains and knew the middle Green's connection with the Colorado River, but this is the first documentation of a connection made between the middle and the upper river.

ASHLEY HAS BEEN credited with giving the Green River its name, and it does fit in with others he gave—short, descriptive, unsentimental: Henrys Fork, Hams Fork, New Fork, Big Sandy. But naming the river, as one historian suggests, after a convenient Ashley partner named Green is too pat. Still, its actual naming is lost in history, for like many rivers it had different names for different reaches, and in addition was tied up with that hope of a water passage from the Rockies to the Pacific.

The Indian name Seedskadee was in general use for the upper river until 1840, spelled in all the various ways an Indian word passed along by word of mouth could be, even to a French trapper's "Quesquidi." To the south in Utah, where the Old Spanish Trail crossed it, the Spanish called it Río Verde. In its middle reach, a Spanish expedition coming into the Uinta Basin from the south in 1776 called it Río San Buenaventura, and did not connect it with the Río Verde below, mapping it as if it ran all the way to the Pacific. Jefferson's instructions to Meriwether Lewis speak of "the North River or Rio Colorado, which runs into the Gulf of California," and it is included in their maps, Lewis calling it "River Colorado" and Clark, "Río del Norte." The first documented crossing of the upper Green was on October 18, 1811, the Astorians going west, calling it the Colorado or Spanish River, as did Robert Stuart on the return journey, perhaps simply a recognition that this was a river of Mexican territory that lay south of the forty-second parallel, or inferring that the connection might already have been made with the lower river.

Describing the river as he saw it in the 1840s, General John Frémont wrote: "The refreshing appearance of the broad river, with its timbered shores and green wooded islands, in contrast to its dry sandy plains, probably obtained for it the name Green River (Río Verde), which was bestowed by the Spaniards, who first came into this country about 1818." Another poetic fancy averred that the green soapstones of the upper river colored the water—Gannett thought the "Green River was so called from the green shale through which it flows."

After all the speculation, it appears most likely that the pragmatic traders and settlers, as they had often done elsewhere, merely translated "Río Verde," a name that had been in existence for at least a century if not longer, into its English equivalent. Green River is a name with a certain spare simplicity that frames the complexity of the river itself, a shorthand notation for all its different facets. Green is the color that unifies sky and sand, a pivotal color underlaid with warm and cool, a color that is the basis for being.

If Ashley is not credited with naming the Green, he is with the establishment of the trappers' rendezvous. Hitherto, trade went on principally at established posts, with no particular time pattern. Indians and trappers brought in pelts when they had some or needed supplies. The trading posts, built on navigable streams, then shipped pelts piecemeal to St. Louis, through hostile, and becoming more so, territory. Perhaps with the example of periodic Indian fairs in the back of his mind, and certainly prompted by the inconvenience of the trading-post system for the far West, Ashley began an annual meeting at which trade was conducted for the whole year. Pelts of the entire spring and fall hunts were packed and taken overland to St. Louis. Location for next year's rendezvous was set before the present one dissolved. After 1825, they were held every year but one until 1840, and of these, six were held along the Green River, between Horse Creek and the New Fork River —those of 1833, 1835, 1836, 1837, 1839, and 1840.

The first rendezvous was a small gathering; Ashley recorded only 120 men present. But the returns were generous, netting Ashley nearly $50,000 for 8,829 pounds of beaver skins, a price never again matched. After the second rendezvous, Ashley sold out and retired, a wealthy man. Beaver continued plentiful, and the new partners of the Rocky Mountain Fur Company made enough to pay off their debts; 1827 was not as good, and competition, in the form of the American Fur Company, invaded a field which, in spite of the vast distances involved, was beginning to become a little crowded. But in 1828 the Rocky Mountain Fur Company grossed even more and enjoyed the fact that their rivals had had a less than successful year.

Rendezvous of 1829 and 1830 were held farther north; in 1831 no official rendezvous was held because no supply wagons arrived in time. By 1833 Bonneville had built his fort and rendezvous moved there. By then, too, it had burgeoned into a full-scale institution with a life of its own. Word was out, and in summer, trappers and Indians began filtering in like iron filings to a magnet. Besides the business of selling pelts and buying supplies, it was a medieval fair, a gambling spree, a squaw exchange and courting, an Indian trade fair, a time to refurbish worn-out buckskins and to show off marksmanship, and for many, one long hangover. As Washington Irving, through Bonneville's eyes, described it:

> The arrival of the supplies gave the regular finish to the annual revel. A grand outbreak of wild debauch ensued among the mountaineers; drinking, dancing, swaggering, gambling, quarrelling, and fighting. Alcohol, which, from its portable qualities, containing the greatest quantity of fiery spirit in the smallest compass, is the only liquor carried across the mountains, is the inflammatory beverage at these carousals, and is dealt out to the trappers at four dollars a pint. When inflamed by this fiery beverage, they cut all kinds of mad pranks and gambols, and sometimes burn all their clothes in their drunken bravadoes. A camp, recovering from one of these riotous revels, presents a serio-comic spectacle; black eyes, broken heads, lacklustre visages.

The selection of goods was more varied and exotic than any single trading post stocked, and consisted of a long list of necessaries spiced by eye-catching luxuries, and sounds like the inventory of any remote country store even today: coffee, sugar, bright cloth, awls, ribbons, sleigh bells, needles, buttons, combs, scissors, earrings, gun flints, fish hooks, liquor, and much more. There were blankets and light, strong steel traps from England, beads from Italy, powder from the Du Ponts in Delaware and lead from the mines in Missouri, Green River knives from the Russell Mills in Massachusetts and venomous whiskey from Turley's Mill near Taos. Wholesale prices in St. Louis were 15 cents a pound for coffee, 9-10 cents for sugar; at rendezvous the standard price was $2 a pound. Gross profits were calculated at 2,000 percent. As many as 200 whites and 2,000 Indians bargained and bartered, and tipped up the scales on one side and pushed them down on the other, shortened whiskey measure by putting their thumbs in their cups, and washed it all down with Green River water.

The rendezvous of 1833 was one of the most congenial; the two big rival fur companies put aside their antagonisms and divided up the territory, the American Fur Company going west, the Rocky Mountain Fur Company remaining in the Green River Valley. But cooperation was only stopgap. Ruthless price cutting and vindictive piracy were making trapping more difficult and less profitable, and even the furthermost headwaters were becoming noticeably empty of beaver.

Rendezvous in 1834 on the Green was attended by two notable

scientists, Thomas Nuttall and John Townsend, the latter minus his journals lost in crossing the Green on horseback. But, if the beaver trade was dying, it was as if rendezvous had a life of its own, and the 1835 meeting was one of the most colorful. Bankrupt Bonneville was there, along with all the free trappers and hundreds of Indians. It began in late June and went on for five rowdy weeks, until the caravans came in August. Reverend Samuel Parker records how Dr. Marcus Whitman, the first reliable doctor to come, removed a three-inch Blackfoot arrow from Jim Bridger's shoulder that had lodged there during a battle at an earlier rendezvous. The doctor expressed considerable surprise that Bridger had been able to carry on for so long without discomfort; the reported laconic reply is pure Bridgerism: "In the mountains, Doc, meat don't spoil."

Dr. Whitman brought his wife, Narcissa, to rendezvous in 1836, she and Eliza Spalding being the first white women in the area. Since mountain men were more used to Indian squaws and many prided themselves on being taken for Indians, the advent of white women and all that they implied in the way of lace curtains and sober Saturday nights and churchly Sundays must have made many of them extremely uneasy as to the future. Times were changing, and the shift was underlined by an ominous scarcity of beaver.

The rendezvous of 1837 is the best recorded because Alfred Jacob Miller, an artist, came with the party of Captain William Stewart, a wealthy Englishman who had been in Wyoming between 1833 and 1836, and returned with a retinue for the rendezvous of 1837. He brought a suit of armor for Jim Bridger, and Miller portrayed Bridger in it. He drew and painted insatiably—camp along the Green, a "surround" of buffalo, trappers cavorting around the campfire, the red circles of drying beaver skins that Ferris described—and his perceptive eye and accurate drawings and paintings fill in much of the detail of life in that time and place. Stewart also brought his own horses to race against native ones, and interest ran high enough to put together the first, last, and only Green River Sweepstakes, run on August 15, 1837. Matthew C. Field, assistant editor of the New Orleans *Picayune,* was a member of Stewart's party and kept a diary which he later worked up into a series of sketches for the newspaper. His entry reads:

Purse—1 doz champagne, 1 Doz Hock, 6 leather shirts, 1 pair pistols, Indian trinkets *ad lib.* and 2 mules—value, at Rocky Mountain prices $500.

Entries 1/2 mile
Sir Wᵐ's spotted bay horse, Chieftain—125
Col. Sublettes, Sor[rel] h.   Tom—125
Graham's B.m.—Bess—120
Jack Robbertson's S.h.   Suskeedee—150
Miles Goodyear's g.m.—130

The nags started off finely—Indian Tom yelling—all arms flying—
whipping, yelling and dust flying—at the judges stand it looked limbo
broke loose—spirits bursting from smoke—Tom, the half-breed, rode naked
(or three cornered breeches, made out of a red handkerchief) and bare-
backed, coming in 30 yards ahead, like a bronze mercury in a state of
supernatural animation! Never saw a more beautiful picture—a loud roar
of admiration burst from all present. Brown Bess fell on passing the pole,
and broke her rider's collar bone (technically speaking, *fractured his clavi-
cle*), so Dr. Tilghman was compelled to leave the ground and operate for
the injury.

Several quarter heats followed, which I can fill up *ad lib*—But to the
summing up of this mornings first gallant contest—
Result—
J. Robbertsons Suskeedee—ridden by naked Tom. "Poor Tom's a-cold!"
No. 1

But the price of sugar was up and the price of beaver was down, and
by 1838 the beaver trade was washed up. Silk hats were in vogue and
there was no place for a trapper in the mulberry-leaf business. Robert
Newell was a trapper who did an unusual thing for a man on the go:
he kept a journal. It is economically written and records only the
facts, and there is underlying pessimism in his entry for the following year.

1839 on to Blacks fork   Green River   one of the best places for wintering
in Rocky mountains except Game that Generly Scarse   we arived there
on the 10th of march and now the 21 our horses are mending fast but poor
yet   we had a verry hard winter   lost Several horses and mules   Snow
2 & 3 feet   verry cold   Tedious   from Blacks fork on to Bear River
left walker   on to hams fork to Green River   met Drips with 4 Carts
of Supplies from below   held rendezvous

This rendezvous of 1839 was the next to the last; only four wagons
came with trade goods and supplies. It was almost as sparsely attended
as the first one, in 1825. The last rendezvous is remembered for the
appearance of a Jesuit, Father Pierre de Smet, who, on July 5, 1840,

held mass on a dry, bony rib of land that looks down a hundred feet to the cool flood plain of the Green River. But to Newell it was a tame affair, and he noted that "times was certainly hard to beaver and everything dull."

Perhaps the unkindest cut of all was that a red-calico and Indian-beaded, horse-racing, whiskey-swilling, gambling, bragging, squaw-chasing, beaver-based frontier institution should be—of all things—dull.

WE WALK a short way downriver from Fort Bonneville to a stand of narrowleaf cottonwoods in which a heron rookery is ensconced. The nests are well hidden in the eight-foot-high trees, and considering their bulk and general dishevelment, this is no small accomplishment. A parent comes in to land, signaling arrival by a loud, drawn-out screech, somewhere between tearing metal and screaming brakes. The bird is a package of uncoordinated wings and legs hung behind an outlandish bill. The legs dangle while it maneuvers against the wind, trailing edge feathers fringing a six-foot wingspan like a curtain. It is a long, nearly interminable moment before the legs touch the nest platform and stiffen to bear weight.

Now, at the end of June, the nests are full of young. They are fed by regurgitation, and the heron pokes its long beak into each waiting gullet. The young grow very rapidly the first year but do not develop the long black crest and white forehead of adult plumage until the second. They are able to fly by the time the river begins to freeze, and migrate with their parents. Besides the general diet of fish and frogs, heron also eat small rodents; a family may toss down a dozen gophers, ground squirrels, or meadow voles a day before leaving the nesting site. The young learn to fly with a great crashing and smashing. Their first efforts are accompanied by flailing wings that cause showers of twigs and leaves, an ear-shattering commentary, and a rain of excrement from the nerve-shattered fledglings—one ornithologist suggests that observers of this scene might do well to wear rain slickers and hats. There must be a dozen nests here, and there is an incessant flying in and out, the general caterwauling of feeding time making the grove seem wired for sound.

I remember the great blue herons of the lowest canyons of the Green, usually solitary birds, walking with stately grace and dignity along the river edge. Or one of those sentinels standing on a dead limb

at the very top of the tree, haughty on its precarious perch, taking off
with unhurried wing beats, neck pulled back into an elegant S, back
legs trailing gracefully. Life in the garrulous heron nursery is quite
different.

FROM THE HIGH terrace across the river and above Fort Bonneville
and the rookery, one can look down on the islands that pattern the
channel. The terrace is bony and dry, sagebrush and rabbitbrush, a
little lupine, a few asters. Clover smells sweet in the afternoon sun.
Below, the river runs cheerfully. It bubbles and murmurs over the
cobbles, one of the most reassuring and comforting sounds in the
world, serene yet busy, soothing yet animated.

What cannot be seen when on the river is that this is a double, in
some places triple terrace, laid with river rocks on top, many heavily
scabbed with crusts of alkali. Some have tumbled down the slope,
catching and piling up into small heaps behind the sagebrush bushes.
This upper terrace level was developed by an ancestral river, probably
in pre-Pleistocene time. Then a plain of vast extent was traversed by
one or more rivers draining from the north northwest. Much later, in
Pleistocene times, the sequence of glacial and interglacial periods
created the present drainage basin of the Green River. Since the flow of
water in a meandering channel is rotary, like a helix augering downstream, meanders migrate both downstream and downvalley, sweeping out a wide area and depositing alluvium, so that over the centuries
the river forms a flood plain. During the period of ice melt, as glaciers
retreated, the large volume of water built wide gravel-floored flats,
which now can be seen as the terraces above the present river. The
present flood plain of the river is, in proportion to the wide green
valley, very narrow.

This is a historic segment of river for reasons other than Bonneville's fort: it is the type locality of a "braided stream." On the 1877–78
Hayden Survey, the Green River Basin was divided into regional
districts. Orestes St. John led the group in charge of the Green River
environs; with him was mineralogist-geologist Dr. A. C. Peale. The
team surveyed 116 miles of the Green River. Each survey station was
marked by a five-foot cairn, established for the purposes of triangulation. Beginning from a baseline determined by astronomical observation, using a transit and triangulation tables, they laid out common-
sided triangles in series, a fast and accurate method of plotting a basic

map, and advantageous in open country like this where long sight lines were possible from different stations, thus providing ease in back checking—Station #12 lies just upstream on the west bank of the river; Station #13 is on a limestone cliff three miles away.

Horse Creek, in Dr. Peale's words, "flows out into a broad valley in which it is side by side with the Green, and finally, to use an anatomical term which exactly describes it, joins the latter by anastomosis. There are at least five islands formed by the two streams in the lower end of the broad valley." "Anastomosis" refers to the separating and joining of different branches originating in a common vessel, as in the capillary system of the human body. On the map, this is precisely how the river looks.

Here the Green River snakes through dry country, and the alluvium of the flood plain—the nondissolved sediment load of the river—provides the ideal material within which the river can adjust, working its channel patterns in the loose sediments according to the amount of discharge and velocity. Both braided and meander patterns begin when bank materials can be eroded and transported downstream, and then deposited. Here the tight-woven meadows of upstream are replaced with open sagebrush flats, the lush water sedges and grasses with sparser ones, and the fine dark soil of upriver with the dry, granular soil recently weathered out of the Wasatch Formation flanking the river. Braiding usually occurs with a higher slope; just below Daniel, in a divided reach, the river drops, in a horizontal distance of five hundred feet, six times more steeply than in the unbraided portion.

The islands that separate the braided channels were formed of cobbles and gravels carried during periods of high runoff, materials that ordinarily cannot be carried during periods of lower flow. Any decrease in velocity, however brief, allows some of these larger particles to come to rest and form a locus for continued deposits. Eddies form around them, still places in which additional stones are dropped. Once at rest, these cobbles and pebbles tend to remain so, building up and catching silt, over a period of time rising above water level as an island. The Hayden map of 1877 is almost identical to classic channel pattern studies made on this same reach below Fort Bonneville by Luna Leopold and Gordon Wolman in 1953. Now, almost a hundred years after the Hayden Survey, the large island, cut at its upper end by the highway bridge, remains, although today the southerly channel carries very little water.

Back on the river, we take the deeper, left-hand channel. Evening time is beaver time and tonight is no exception: at high water I am eye to eye with a big old beaver on the island. He has firmly subdued a succulent willow branch under his left front paw and looks as if he cannot decide whether to keep eating or to betake himself to the safety of the river. Wisdom is the better part of hunger, and he catapults into the water with a stupendous belly whopper.

A FIFTY-FOOT sandstone cliff defines the left bank, pale sandy gray, studded with huge splotches of red concretions that look like dusty stoplights. Concretions are masses of mineral matter found in sandstones and other rocks, often round because they form around a nucleus. When the cliff breaks back from the river, the view of the countryside opens out, low and undulating, with buttes and bluffs. Patches of white alkali stain the ground, and prickly-pear cactuses sprawl in big patches. The only trees are those that string along the river. This landscape marks the next four days on the river, the landscape of the Green River Basin.

The basin is roughly triangular, its apex formed by the Wyoming and Wind River ranges. It spreads southward some 170 miles to a base described by the Uinta Mountains at the Wyoming-Utah border. It encompasses some 21,000 square miles, sinking from mountain meadows in the north to dry desert and scrub and badlands in the south. When the Rocky Mountains were raised, basins contiguous to these ranges—such as the Green River and Uinta basins—subsided, covering a much vaster area than that of the mountains themselves.

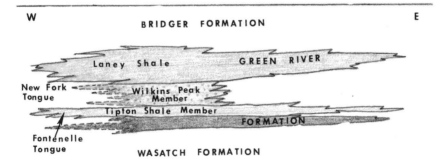

CROSS SECTION OF THE GREEN RIVER BASIN
(From Bradley, "Paleolimnology," in Frey, *Limnology in North America,*
1963, p. 630)

Wild iris (*Iris missouriensis*)

The Green River Basin lowered more or less continuously, and also more or less uniformly, at the same time filling in with sediments brought in by rivers and streams coming down off the adjacent mountains. As a consequence, the layers of sedimentary rock within it are unusually level, and the beds are extraordinarily even in thickness. The seven-hundred- to two-thousand-foot-thick accumulation of sediments that hardened into rock records the history of the mountains from which they came in three different rock formations, the Wasatch, Green River, and Bridger formations; the first two formations characterize the landscape along the river. F. V. Hayden named both the Wasatch Formation and the Green River Formation in 1869, the former for its exposure in the Wasatch Mountains of Utah, the latter for exposures along the river near Green River, Wyoming. Such sites are "type locations," specific stratigraphic sections that form a standard of reference. These formations flank the river with distinctive colors and shapes that become part of the knowledge of the river itself: the farther one goes down the river, the more the understanding of rock becomes the understanding of river.

RANCH LAND now lies on either side of the river, and the river is often channeled mechanically, bulldozed into breakwaters to back water up and shoot it into irrigation ditches. We run alongside one of these dikes; the water streaming over it is swift and there seems no place for the canoe to go through until we see a chute piled with white breakers against the far bank. With a little maneuvering the canoe sails through, almost as if picked up and thrown like a paper airplane.

A row of sacks hang between two trees; cows brush up against the insect repellent contained in them and are relieved of some of the torment of the incessant flies. We flush two Canada geese with ten goslings, the adults honking frantically. The goslings keep so close to the boat that I am afraid I'll hit one with my paddle. When they go as fast as they can, they almost run on the water, rocking back and forth with the effort. Tonight is a bird-world evening: an owl wafts out across the river and into a cottonwood grove and the grove's residents set up a clatter. A merganser with but one leg stands on a gravel bar, takes off a little lopsidedly, but flies straight and true. A huge raven's nest is tucked up under a tiny overhang of cliff, a scramble of sticks and twigs that looks too precarious for the large bird that swoops out of it like a bad omen.

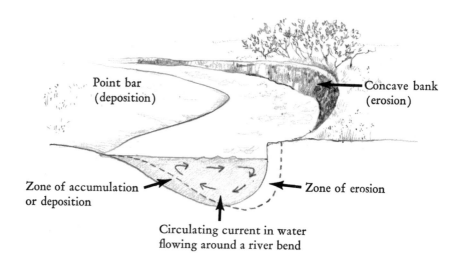

Point bar
(deposition)

Concave bank
(erosion)

Zone of accumulation
or deposition

Zone of erosion

Circulating current in water
flowing around a river bend

DEPOSITION AND EROSION IN A MEANDER
(Adapted from Leopold, 1974, p. 82)

The cliffs of the Wasatch Formation flank the river a mile or so, a yellow buff, capped by a harder thin red sandstone layer. Sometimes fingers stand out from the cliff, casting warped shadows. Ledges seem alive with swarming cliff swallows. In some places the layers are swirled and distorted; these were saturated delta sands that slumped down upon themselves before they solidified into sandstone. The neat layers of tan and rust red blur, twist, and then the cliffs retreat and disappear.

We run through a stretch of meadows, grassed to the edge, sod oftentimes rolled over the rim like a bolster. Broken-off chunks, still sodded and green with grass, are sometimes stalked with wild iris. The current slows again, sand and gravel point bars appearing on the inside of the curves. As the current eats away debris from the outer bank, it carries the debris and deposits it on the opposite side downstream. The rotary motion of the current on the outside of a meander is downward, with increasing velocity, able to carry particles out into the stream; on the inner side, the rotary motion is upward, with a lessening of both current and turbulence that allows these sinuous curved beaches called point bars to be deposited.

Up or down the river, given my choice, I would rather camp on a good point bar than anywhere else: flat, dry, backed with grass and trees on the upper river, cliffs on the lower, close to the soft night sounds of the river. River sand is soft and fine because of the large amount of fine silt and clay it contains. Dune and ocean-beach sands usually have these very fine particles winnowed out by wind or waves and are consequently generally coarser. Flat river cobbles pave the sand in a single layer, pulled from the outer banks, where they are embedded in the soil like raisins in a cake, and deposited on the inner banks by larger and more powerful flows. They disappear on the downstream end of the bar, leaving sand succeeded by silt where the bar slips beneath the surface. This progressive fining is characteristic both of island and point-bar deposits, formed now as in epochs past, preserved in the shallow-angle crossbedded sandstones of old river and stream beds.

It is late as we pull off river and the brilliant pink sunset flushes deep and lurid, color washing the underside of the clouds, glazing the river surface like a sheet of Tiffany glass, turning the sand an indescribable mauve. A thin, high whimpering floats across the river from a den of baby coyotes as I pitch the tent. Around it cobbles tile the beach. As far as I am concerned, no stones are more elegant than those worked by a river. There is general agreement that river stones are flatter than those worked by the ocean, and that abrasion and rock type have something to do with final shape, but there is no agreement as to the precise way in which they are formed.

No matter: river rocks are perfect. They fit firm and smooth in the hand and are part of what the river does to my sense of time. In the cooling air, the cobbles still retain a noontime heat. I hold in one hand the warm remnant of a mountain.

6

But Col. Lander, at the head of a U.S. exploring and pioneer party, has just marked and nearly opened a new road through the canyon aforesaid, which makes a northern cutoff, and strikes the old Oregon Trail some fourteen miles south of Fort Hall, saving sixty miles on the journey to Oregon.... I cannot, of course, say that this is better than the old route, but it can hardly be more destitute of grass, while the naked fact that it divides the travel affords cheering hope of a mitigation of the sufferings and hardships of the long journey.

HORACE GREELEY, *An Overland Journey from New York to San Francisco in the Summer of 1859*

From the Big Sandy to Green river, a distance of thirty-five miles, there is not a drop of water. By starting from the Sandy at the cool of the day, you can get across easily by morning. Cattle can travel as far again by night as they can during the day, from the fact that the air is cool, and consequently they do not need water. Recollect, do not attempt to cross during the day.... By referring to the large map, you can see that you save nearly five days travel by following what I have taken the liberty to call Sublette's Cut Off.

JOSEPH E. WARE, 1849
The Emigrant's Guide to California

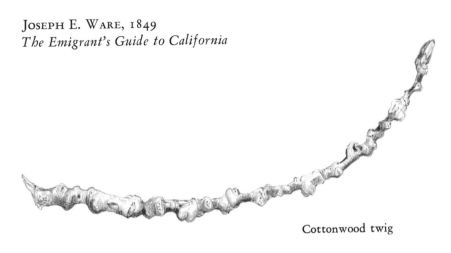

Cottonwood twig

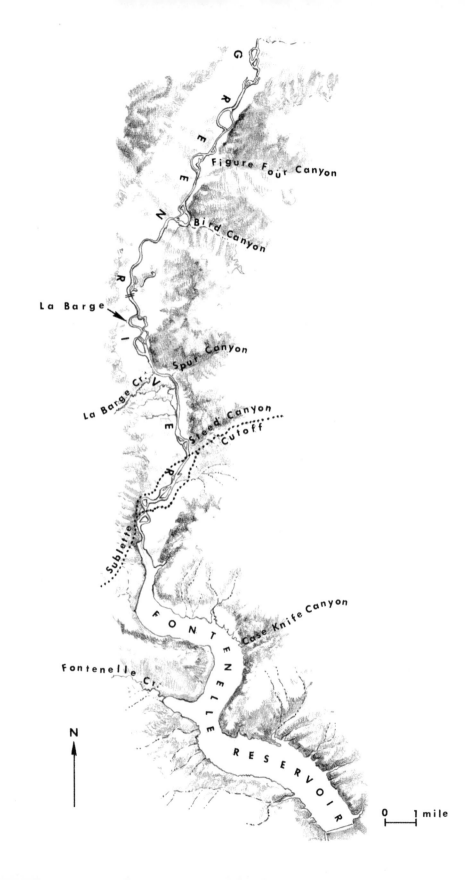

G
R
E
E
N
R
I
V
E
R

Figure Four Canyon

Bird Canyon

La Barge

Spur Canyon

La Barge Cr.

Steed Canyon

Cutoff

Sublette

Case Knife Canyon

Fontenelle Cr.

F O N T E N E L L E   R E S E R V O I R

N

0   1 mile

REARDON DRAW
TO FONTENELLE DAM

PERRY HAS FRIENDS all along the river, and since the canoe provides limited storage space, we stop at a ranch to pick up fresh water. I stay in the canoe while Perry takes the jugs up to be filled.

There is a great deal of minute debris in the river, hundreds of black-and-white-striped mosquito pupal cases hanging in the water like minute candy canes, the occupants gone to add to the already considerable mosquito population along the river. Out of curiosity I scoop out a cupful of water. In it there are a dozen pupae, all empty but one, and I notice it because it moves whereas the other cases are lifeless. I fish it out and put it in the palm of my hand in a teaspoonful of water and watch with a hand lens. The abdomen pulsates and straightens. The pupal skin opens and the pumping intensifies; the forelegs rest upon the water surface as the back legs work free. The antennae are not feathered so it is a female. She hesitates at the edge of the water, a tiny construction of teetering hairline legs and narrow scaled wings. She cannot bite for at least a day, until her mouthparts harden. I put her carefully in a shaded spot beneath a thatch of mint and refocus my eyes to the larger world of the river.

Across the river a mink flows along the bank. It carries a small limp prairie dog in its mouth, firmly clasping it around the middle so that it dangles like an Order of the Golden Fleece—avaricious eaters, mink feed on a variety of reptiles, frogs, trout, crayfish, eggs, and water insects. It is difficult to explain the pleasure I feel at seeing this feral animal; it is more than just unexpected surprise. Even as I child, I mistrusted Thornton Burgess's *Mother West Wind* stories, in which weasels and minks were always villains. Mink are not common along the river, and there have been two now. Long-bodied, dark brown, elegant of shape and movement, they are exquisite creatures.

ONE OF THE HAZARDS of paddling through privately owned land is that barbed-wire fences may occasionally be strung across the river. At low water level they may be far enough above the water not to be dangerous, but at high water they can be lethal. When fence posts appear on either side of the river it pays to look carefully into the future. Accepted procedure is to hold the paddle up vertically in front of your face, letting the wire slide up the shaft as your head goes under. Being a craven coward, I simply get out of the canoe and crawl under on hands and knees, in a foot of water, following the same procedure that I would were I on land, enduring much ridicule.

A pair of red-tailed hawks take exception to our invasion of their territory. They spin around the pylon of trees in which their nest is built, scolding with hoarse, wheezing squeaks. They circle quite close but retreat as soon as the canoe passes. The sun shining through their tails shows a beautiful Indian red. Their flight control is almost hummingbird-like: one stands on its tail and back sculls, then peels off into a steeply banked turn and pivots on a wing tip.

The river is wide and shallow, paved with huge cobbles between which masses of lime-green algae stream out downriver. I try to fish out some of the slimy strands but they are too slippery and slither off the paddle blade. In deeper reaches tufts float free just beneath the surface. Although algae may be well secured to rocks by rhizoid-like structures at the base, they are scoured loose by ice and flood and whole populations are whisked away, but are quickly restored from upstream sources. In quieter reaches scattered tufts of pondweed stretch out, leaves thin and threadlike, drawing lines in the current.

A dead cow is stranded on a gravel bar, unnoticed until downwind. The corpse lies like some beached hull, misted with flies. And more dead cows—whether from infection, accident, or stupidity we can only guess. The aroma downriver of various states of decomposition ranges from unpleasant to pungent to nauseating. I can now well imagine the summer of 1887. The previous summer was a drought year, followed by an extremely severe winter. Cattle died by the thousands and it is said that the stench on the plains and along the river was unbearable. In this dry climate it may take more than one

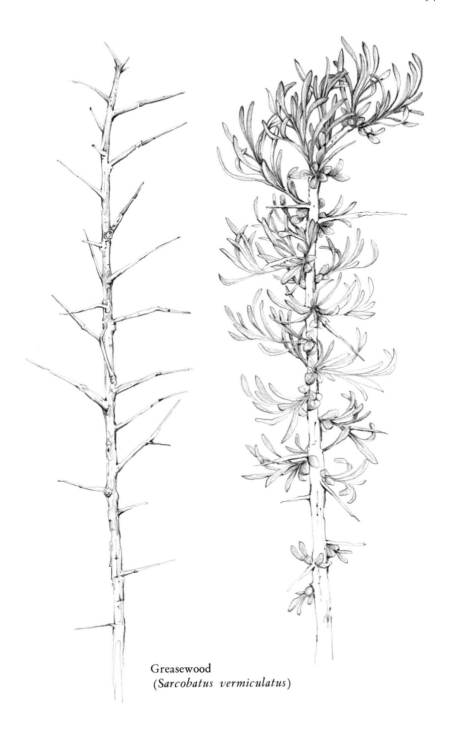

Greasewood
(*Sarcobatus vermiculatus*)

summer to decompose a carcass and hides may not disintegrate for years. Crows, magpies, and golden eagles work the carrion, but many corpses, bloated and stiff-legged, remain posted on the sand bars like sentries from some forgotten war. In contrast to the clear upper river, where one can still dip a cup and drink, the river's purity is now very suspect.

A flock of lesser nighthawks appears, wheeling low overhead, white wing bars flashing on black wings angled almost like an M. Unlike common nighthawks, these appear in the middle of the day, swinging back and forth in short arcs as they sieve insects out of the air. Whereas the former prefer mountains and dimmer light, these are birds of the lowlands, laying eggs on the open ground of graveled desert or dry wash. They remain in the sky, off and on, most of the day.

The Soaphole Cliffs come toward the river from the west. This area was valued by Crow Indians, whose winter encampments stretched from La Barge to Kendall all along the Green River. Now in June the land is bleached to a sun-shot desolation. It is too alkaline for crops to grow in it; only greasewood bushes flourished. It cannot be irrigated because it contains too much alkali to be dumped back into the river—it is this alkali that makes reservoirs notably unsuccessful here. After irrigation water has leached through this soil, it re-enters the river and renders it unfit for other uses. Nevertheless this land is much valued as prime wintering range for deer, herds of which migrate considerable distances to gather on both sides of the river. With open lands becoming more limited each year, these infertile alkaline flats take on significance in the preservation of abundant game on the upper river. Without these lands, the large game populations on the upper Green would decrease precipitously.

Narrowleaf cottonwoods stalk almost every bank. Even though there may be several trunks to one tree, their aspect is much more slender than that of broad-leafed cottonwoods at lower altitudes. There are often many small dead branches that form picturesque tangles at the base of the main branching, sometimes within the foliage. We pull off at midafternoon beneath a cluster of five big trees on a terrace above the river—Perry's blend of cereal that he calls "mush" is so substantial that one cupful lasts well past noon. Fingers of marsh mark where the river creeps in during high water, abandoned channels marked by rows of willows and deep green slashes of sedge and damp mud. The terrace is on the outside of the curve where the water comes piling into the bank, lopping off big lunettes of sod, making a great

Narrowleaf or Mountain cottonwood
(*Populus angustifolia*)

swishing and rushing, and the river, peaked up into foaming waves, smells like summer.

We lay out the day's maps on the grass, weight them down with cobbles and notebook and pan lid and calculate the morning's progress to average four miles an hour, which includes rest stops, watching goslings, paddling, stopping for fresh water, more paddling, dodging willows, talking and not paddling, taking notes, paddling, and breathing river.

The river becomes a way of thinking, ingrained, a way of looking at the world. I listen to its commentary on the rocks and willows that block its way, feel cooled by the touch of spray, and smell all the odors that emanate from it. Judgment and recognition of odors depend so much on familiar reference smells that it is difficult to describe a new smell without recourse to them. The river, of course, often smells of off-river odors: the sweet, heavy aroma of an acre of sand verbena, a dead cow on a gravel bar, wet stones, cold muck. But it also smells of itself, an aloof and elusive smell, soft, faintly like clean clay or like wet wash hanging out on a windy day. It is neither sweet nor sharp, acrid nor aromatic, nor distinctly anything ever smelled before or elsewhere unless one has had a river in his or her childhood. It is a smooth, tentative smell. It is light and deep, cool, it comes in curling tendrils and sometimes it is difficult to pick out from other smells. But it is there. And, once smelled, it becomes easier to recognize and soon there is almost a sense of river in the landscape even when it cannot be seen.

"THE MESA" is a long low ridge, scrubby and pale, forming a low skyline on the east, prime winter range for antelope. The cliffs break back to gray scrub; a narrow line of meadow, full of dried grass, lines the bank. It is an arid breathless basin, bleached out, saved from utter desolation by the arabesques of the river and the green cottonwoods stalking it. Not being able to see the mountains any more somehow makes this June afternoon more like August. Because of the sun and reflection, I wear hat, gloves, and long sleeves, just like a proper turn-of-the-century lady, although my disreputable appearance hardly qualifies me for polite society. Everyone on the river eventually comes to wearing a hat, and through repeated wettings and dryings it soon becomes an object of unique and individual apparel. Perry's is of indefinite shape although it might have had a high crown in its youth.

Color? Hardly. It is bound with a cotton band that probably was red; a trout fly is stuck in the amply perforated brim. Its lineage may be suspect, but it is long. I might chide Perry about his splash paddling in the stern, insult his cooking, denigrate his trout fishing, but never would I ever impugn his hat.

The Lander Cutoff, one of the two main shortcuts on the Overland Trail, comes to the river at the southern end of The Mesa. The Oregon Trail, in good use by 1842 as far as South Pass, was fairly standardized although there was great variation in the path itself: a spring gone bad, a muddy campsite, one train trying to avoid the dust of another could make wagons spread out over a lateral distance of many miles. At the junction of the North and South Platte rivers, the Oregon Trail continued west; the Overland Trail angled southwest across barren alkali-patched country to Jim Bridger's trading post on the Blacks Fork of the Green River. In 1841, one hundred emigrants had crossed South Pass; by 1845 thirty times that many had come, and by 1851 there was practically a traffic jam on the trail. Two "cutoffs," the Lander and the Sublette, both crossed north of Fort Bridger to reach the Snake River. The Lander Cutoff was plotted in 1857–58 by General F. W. Lander and R. H. Wagner, sent west by the government to survey and improve, to "look out" and construct wagon roads. In the spring of 1858 Lander paid Shoshone chief Washakie for a right of way through Shoshone lands in order to establish this trail that shortened the trip by some two hundred miles. The cutoffs became more and more heavily used, for at an average rate of ten miles a day for a train (oxen averaged two miles an hour), even a short cutoff saved precious time.

I am beginning to feel that the cows are ubiquitous; they watch the canoe, sometimes stolid and unmoving, sometimes crashing back into the shoreline brush with the grace of a herd of hippopotamuses. The cliffs on the west turn back toward the river; game trails string on the bias to the top. Foam on the water is from alkali leached out of the soil. Large white patches of it on the ground are visible even from the air. In this dry climate, when there is a rare downpour, rain water carries soluble mineral salts down into the soil, dissolving lime and redepositing it in a deeper layer. Lime appears both as a subsurface layer of white and as splotches on top of the ground. Unlike the creeks flowing in from the Wind Rivers, which are clear and low in dissolved minerals, the streams bearing into the Green from the west now contain large amounts of minerals and salts, in some cases enough to interfere with crop plants if used for irrigation.

The New Fork River, springing in the Wind Rivers just south of the Green, enters on the left. Collecting smaller streams along the way, it is the upper Green's largest tributary. With the addition of the New Fork, the Green River settles down to a more phlegmatic flow and becomes an exceedingly circuitous river. Cutting down into the surrounding country rock, it knifes through sedimentary rocks laid during the last and largest transgression of an ancient lake. This is the type location for the New Fork Tongue ("tongue" designates a formation of limited extent) of the Wasatch Formation. Forming the buttes overlooking the junction of the rivers, it is gaudy and striking, gray mudstone banded with pink, dark red, gray, and green, shaded with ochre and maroon. The Wasatch sediments here are derived mostly from the Wind Rivers, carried down during the shrinking of the former lake. When the lake again expanded, it terminated the deposition of this tongue.

The ghostly bluffs of the Green River Formation rise in benches and mesas back from the river, weathered to pale oyster white, contrasting with the more brightly colored Wasatch. It is difficult to imagine that some fifty million years ago this sterile landscape, rolling dry to the horizon, once held an immense freshwater lake, accumulating sediments that compacted to between fifteen hundred and two thousand feet thick, covering several thousand square miles. The lake remained some four million years, such a quiet lake that even the seasons are recorded in the sedimentary layers. The Green River Formation is a classic in interpretive geology. Dr. W. H. Bradley, retired Chief Geologist, U.S.G.S., once said, "As long as I can remember, I have loved lakes. I count this one among my favorites." Lake Gosiute, as he called it, provided material for a wide-ranging scholarly interpretation that ran the gamut from description of square miles of sediment to "probably the most trivial thing in the world, for what can be more trivial than a few microscopic scales from the wing of a mosquito that has been dead some 30 or 40 million years?"

Lake Gosiute's shoreline was long; plants grew profusely and luxuriantly in and around it, fertilized by runoff waters heavy with lime and phosphate. Aquatic creatures were plentiful; turtles and crocodiles crawled along the shore. Fish fossils from the Green River Formation are famous not only for their place in evolutionary history but for their exquisite preservation. Small camels and tiny four-toed horses grazed the meadows. Birds stalked the mud flats and left tined footprints of sandpiper-like wanderings. There were cypress swamps and relatives of japonica and fig, palm and grape, that gave way to forests of oak and maple and other hardwoods, and pine, spruce, and fir in the higher elevations, identified from fossil pollen blown into the wet muds. The climate resembled that of the present-day Gulf Coast states, warm and humid with an annual rainfall between thirty and forty-three inches—today it is less than ten.

At the beginning the lake was large. With an outlet, it remained fairly stable, and the basin itself remained remarkably undisturbed by the uplifts occurring in surrounding mountains. During the second stage the lake shrank to a third of its former size. Since it had no outlet, stagnation occurred, and many layers of salts evaporated

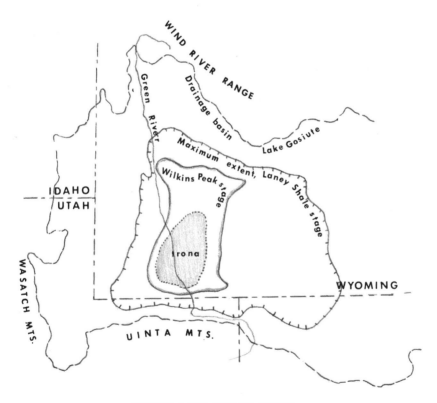

GOSIUTE LAKE AND ITS STAGES
(Adapted from Bradley, 1963, p. 632, and "The Green River and Associated Tertiary Formations," 1964, in *Geology of Green River Formation and Associated Eocene Rocks in Southwestern Wyoming and Adjacent Parts of Colorado and Utah*, U.S.G.S. Prof. Paper, 1964, 496-A, p. 36)

Fossil fish, Green River Formation (*Priscacara liops*)

out. Up to 1,350 feet thick, it is this middle layer that forms the prominent pale palisades at Green River, Wyoming, from which many industrial minerals, especially trona, are mined. In its third phase the lake expanded to maximum size, some 15,000 square miles, united with its counterpart to the south in the Uinta Basin. Oil shales, for which the Green River Formation is well known, were laid during the first and last periods of the lake and lie mostly in the central parts of the Green River, Uinta, and adjacent smaller basins.

We pass under Wardell's Bridge, built with wedge-shaped cribs filled with big boulders ballasting the uprights. The momentary shade is welcome for it is hot and dry. The greenswards are gone. Stark cliffs and scrubby mesas reiterate the definition of arid. Evaporation exceeds precipitation, and I feel it in my skin as well as see its evidence on the banks. The river bank on the right is ten feet high, a bare cut of soil with no horizons at all; it is undefined, unproductive, as streaked with alkali as if buckets of whitewash had been poured over it. We slide under Five Mile Bridge, so newly painted aphid green that I can smell the paint. The timbers from the original bridge are piled on the left bank, washed out in 1972 by the unusually high spring runoff.

Then the wind hits. Late-afternoon sunlight glares off the water. The flat surface seems to form a suction on the bottom of the canoe and it is difficult to paddle. Not only does the wind catch the canoe, but when the wind is against the current, the main velocity of the river is deeper beneath the surface and therefore of less help just when needed most. My eyes feel like two burnt holes in a blanket. I wear

Platanus leaf,
Green River Formation

my hat at an angle Maurice Chevalier would have envied, in order to
block the low, slanting sun rays, but I cannot keep the sun off my
face, which is beginning to feel like raw hamburger. My hat keeps
blowing off in spite of being tied on as tight as a garrote. In the shade
of the overhanging willows under which we take shelter are mosquitoes. Disturbed from virtuous rest they emerge screaming like
viragos and take immediate vengeance. They infiltrate sleeve plackets,
bite through my shirt, and get under my life jacket, where I can
neither swat nor scratch. The life jacket binds across the back of
my neck. The muscles across my shoulders burn with fatigue.

The river swings right to flow beneath thirty-foot-high sandstone
cliffs. On the cliff's shaded face are hundreds of cliff-swallow nests,
looking like short-necked jugs, pointing down at an angle, all full of
young. Along this bluff, at the outer curve of the meander, the water
is light and golden green. The suction on the hull breaks, the bow
springs up, and in the cool shadow it could be the beginning of morning.

A CHOICE of sand bar, cottonwood grove, or grassy terrace for tent
space is idyllic except for one thing: mosquitoes. Ample and perfect
breeding places abound: a backed-up finger of river, plashes formed
in the imprint of hooves in the muck, quiet eddies. The mosquitoes
are vindictive, ingenious, and dedicated to motherhood: as everyone
knows by now, *nur die Weiber beisen*—only the females bite. One
is spared the whine because they're too busy feeding even to talk with
their mouths full. I discipline myself not to swat: local tradition has
it that when one mosquito dies a thousand more come to the funeral.

The bottomlands back from the river bear evidence of old channels
in the curving grassed-over troughs and sand patches, an area of
corrugated curves. Cattle keep the grass so clipped that the only
surviving flowering plants are those that spread by stolons, tiny buttercups and cinquefoils. Some two hundred yards back from the
river the alluvial soil ends, bordered by a hard alkaline soil supporting
only greasewood, which recedes into the distance like an exercise in
aerial perspective.

In the beginning twilight I feel as if I am accompanied by the
entire female population of mosquitoes in a diaphanous cloud. I am
most sympathetic to the protestations of mountain men about mosquitoes; when they are so voracious that they spoil the aim of a man's
rifle or drive a horse to skin and bones, they are more than a nuisance.

The only solution that I have is to slather on repellent, a solution that can't be too different from that of a hundred years ago, other than the use of a chemical rather than a homemade one. In 1849, one beleaguered emigrant wrote that "one of the boys made an amateur chafing dish and lamp out of a little tin bucket, a tea cup of fat, with a taper, and a tin plate for the dish, on which we burnt tobacco, oil peppermint, oil aniseed, camphor, red precipitate, and in fact, some of everything that our medicine chest contained."

Many mosquitoes are attracted by a combination of carbon dioxide and nitrous oxide along with warmth and moisture that characterize warm-blooded breathing. Perhaps because of the focus of breathing, they bite more around my face, or perhaps that is all that is available when the rest of me is immersed in protective clothing. At any rate, I awake in the morning puffy-eyed and swollen-faced, having lost my ten rounds with *enceinte* mosquitoes.

WE PASS an old homestead cabin with cottonwood-planked walls; it looks made out of the landscape. Newer buildings spread out around, a ranch that just grew as needed. Tanks and small metal sheds of oil and gas wells appear, fresh-painted, shiny and geometric, in the rough countryside. Whereas a century ago oil seeps were used to grease wagon axles and shine gun barrels, today there are working fields, producing gas and crude oil, and occasionally there are oil spills in the small tributary streams along the west side of the Green. These streams, within the original range of the Green River cutthroat trout,

Shore buttercup
(*Ranunculus cymbalaria*)

are among the last holdouts of this endangered species. A few years ago the Wyoming Fish & Game Department obtained some eggs from a pure stock of cutthroat, hatched them, and transferred the young to Pinegrove Creek, west of La Barge. The fish flourished until an oil spill killed them all.

The roofs of La Barge appear among the trees on the west bank. General Ashley named the creek downriver for his friend Captain Joseph La Barge, pilot of the steamboat *Omega* that plied the upper Missouri. The original post office on the creek also took the name of La Barge. The present town farther north, founded during the oil boom of the 1920s, was once called Tulsa; it became La Barge in 1935.

I feel like a female Rip Van Winkle when we disembark for lunch, having heard no news, seen no newspapers, for five days. After meals eaten in competition with mosquitoes, the shiny closed cleanness of a small café and the friendly curiosity of its members require some adjusting to. The counter chairs are desk chairs mounted on swivels, well oiled and turning quietly; a slant-cut log oval with a mountain scene hangs behind the pine-paneled counter, flanked by a handsome antelope head and a huge stuffed trout. The owner is a lively, outgoing woman and takes our order and asks where we're from and where we're going in the same breath. She and Perry discover mutual acquaintances, and since the clientele is evidently a perennial one, instructions and directions are soon being offered on how far it is to Fontenelle Reservoir, how best to cross it, watch out for the whirlpool, and didn't know anybody canoed the river any more!

Perry asks for fresh water for the canoe and she volunteers that all La Barge water is trucked in by tank car as local water is "stout." Perry takes a swallow and his expression assures me that this is a euphemism for sulfur water strong enough to make your teeth hurt. As we leave she hands me two candy bars "for the road." It is an hour of talk and listen and I crawl back into the canoe with no sense of river progression having been broken and a nice feeling of reassurance. And the candy bars get me across Fontenelle Reservoir.

When the goal for the day is traversing a reservoir it takes some of the joy out of the afternoon. The land between the river and the western ridges is high and dry, a plateau shredded by dry washes and dry creek beds, extending nearly down to the river, where it cuts off in a three-hundred-foot bluff called Names Hill. La Barge Creek trickles in on the right, heading out of the west, barely trickling. At the time of the King Survey in June, 1863, when the Green River was "a stream of pale beryl, much too swift for an easy crossing,"

La Barge Creek was described as having a lively flow. Shortly below La Barge Creek the colorful striped beds of the Wasatch Formation disappear into the river, and from here south to Green River, Wyoming, the river runs in the pale, subdued Green River Formation.

Names Hill parallels the river, named from one of the rock faces used as a register for travelers using the Sublette Cutoff. The cutoff saved more than forty miles but led through a dangerous waterless stretch. Some sources say that it was used by the Sublette brothers in the 1820s; Ashley, in whose employ they were at the time, pushed off on his 1825 river trip somewhere in this area. Another trapper-guide, Caleb Greenwood, was credited with leading the first party by this route in 1844, and it was briefly known as the Greenwood Cutoff until it was attributed to Sublette in the publication of Ware's *Emigrants' Guide* in 1849.

Emigrants had a choice of two crossings; coming out just south of Steed Canyon, they could ford the river there or follow the river south about two and a half miles to just above what is now the entrance to Fontenelle Reservoir. Here the trails reunited on the west bank. Major wagon trains were usually composed of fifty wagons, and if two or three trains converged on the river at the same time, there was a massive jam of flapping canvas, lowing oxen, and fretful children. Although fords and ferries were established at the most stable places on the river, the banks of the Green in this area tend to be soft, and a few milling oxen could churn them into a morass. A long wagon train could take days to cross, hence double fords and ferries on the same trail were a necessity. Wakeman Bryarly, a member of the Charleston Company from Virginia, reached Sublette's crossing July 2, 1849, and recorded:

> We found many wagons waiting for their turn at the ferry. This ferry is owned by a Frenchman who had started for "The Promised Land" with two small pontoon beds and came to the conclusion he would stop here & establish a ferry, not so much for the accomodation of the emigrants as for the desire of monopoly. He charges $8 a load, & it takes three loads to one wagon. However, they *must* go across, & consequently the ferry is engaged for 4 days ahead, . . . The Green River is about 150 yds. wide, with a strong current, & 10 ft. deep.

Still, many emigrants became impatient, caulked their wagons, and tried to float them across, a practice that often lost both goods and lives.

For some the crossing was a time of meeting other trains and ex-

changing advice, and sometimes celebration, such as the Charleston
Company enjoyed on Independence Day:

> The next day was the Fourth of July, and there were a great many
> emigrants there resting. Up and down the stream they were camped about,
> three thousand strong. We rested all that day engaged in cooking, sewing,
> and washing. Tom Moore, from Harper's Ferry, Virginia, was selected as
> orator of the day. . . . Being the Fourth of July, our quartermaster issued
> whisky rations. Some had more or less, and some didn't have any. Those
> are the ones that didn't drink. We hadn't had our little cannon out of the
> wagon since we started, and we concluded that we would take it out that
> day and chain it to the stump. Moore felt pretty good, feeling the effects
> of his whisky, and everytime that he would say anything patriotic would
> touch the little cannon off, and the echo would bellow up and down the
> valley.

Needless to say, the morning of the 5th "was rather a blue morning."
The dugway on which they continued on the right side of the river
is still visible, beveled into the shale cliff, up off the flats that could
be marshy in high water, a narrow shelf that must have rutted deeper
with every gully washer. The trail crosses a narrow draw, no bridge,
just a short, steep descent that lunged wagon against oxen, and a stiff
ascent that took urging and pushing and patience and hard work and
maybe an extra team hitched on. And nothing but a sunbaked
monotony ahead.

NAMES HILL lies at the entrance to Fontenelle Reservoir; the Seedskadee Project, of which Fontenelle Reservoir is a part, encompasses
a thirty-five-mile strip flanking the river between La Barge and Green
River, Wyoming, including the Seedskadee National Wildlife Refuge.
Named after an outfitter for the American Fur Company, Lucien
Fontenelle, the dam was built in 1963–64 to contain 345,000 acre-
feet of water for irrigation and recreation, and to operate a 10,000-
kilowatt power plant.

The change in the river is surprisingly abrupt. After a running
river, the water drags. The only trees are one or two straggly cottonwoods that do not look as if they would last a hard winter. Land
along the bank that is submerged when the reservoir is high has been
cleared of trees, and there is precious little else growing. The littoral
is hummocky and ugly; here, where the gradient is low, a minor
fluctuation vertically makes a major transgression horizontally, baring

a wide area of shoreline (up to 60 percent of the bottom surface of
the proposed Kendall Reservoir could be exposed in this manner).
Dead algae clot the edge of the river and reek. Unbroken by trees, the
drone and whine of heavy trucks beats across the mud flats.

A dam raises the river's profile and this shallowing renders the
river less competent to carry the sands and silts that it usually trans-
ports. Some of the sediment load is deposited where the river slows
upon entering the reservoir, destroying the habitat of those animals
needing clear, open rock surfaces and well-oxygenated water, such
as stonefly and mayfly nymphs and trout. But underflow takes most
of the sediment down to the lowest part of the reservoir, against the
dam. Storage dams may ensnare from 95 to 99 percent of the sediment
that, before the dam was built, flowed downstream. As Luna B. Leopold, M. Gordon Wolman, and John P. Miller wrote in *Fluvial Processes in Geomorphology,* an authoritative book that deals with rivers
and their workings, "These changes in regimen associated with construction of dams are certainly heroic. It is difficult to conceive of a
climatic change producing a change in vegetation on the watershed
such that 95% of the sediment would no longer be delivered to the
stream system."

It does not take four hours of laborious paddling to convince me
that a reservoir is not a river. The untrammeled wind blows across
the open miles. It kicks up a wave system that is dangerous for a small
boat, and increases surface evaporation far above that which would
evaporate from the river. With no stable vegetation along the shore,
we see little wildlife, only a couple of gulls at the entrance. The
Hayden Expedition described broad river bottoms richly carpeted
with good grass and big cottonwood groves. Now there is no shade
whatsoever. Heat shimmers off the clustered metal trail roofs in the
small campground. The last miles must be across open water, quartering against the wind. It is an unpleasant, uneasy hour, and I am vastly
relieved to touch shore.

After the pleasure of clean point bars, I deplore this beach of rough
jagged sandstone slabs that scrape the hull, hard to walk on, un-
gentled by years of river. We unfold the maps to see how far we
actually came and how well we made our landfalls. In color, the map
looks just as the reservoir looks from the air, an elongated light blue
triangle impressed on a white field of barren countryside. The triangle
spreads over darker blue dashed lines that delineate a once-flowing
river, now buried beneath heavy water, silt, and beer cans.

7

The buttes around Green River are wonderful in size, shape, and color, and variety; there are towers, castles, and cathedrals, bulbous knobs and excrescences, colossal mushrooms, "giant's clubs" and "giant's teapots," forts, temples, tombs, and shapes of things unknown, possibly, in the heavens above and certainly in the earth beneath; all carved out of rich red and brown and cream-colored limestone, strata upon strata of varying color. The river sweeps in great curves, washing a white sandy beach with its clear emerald-green waters—the brightest, richest green that ever flashed in sunlight, caught from the color of the shale over which it runs. Every foot of ground for miles around is rich with fossil flowers, ferns, fishes, and even insects, buried in every layer of shale, waiting for the treasure-seeker's hammer.

FRANK LESLIE, 1877, dispatch to *Frank Leslie's Illustrated Newspaper*

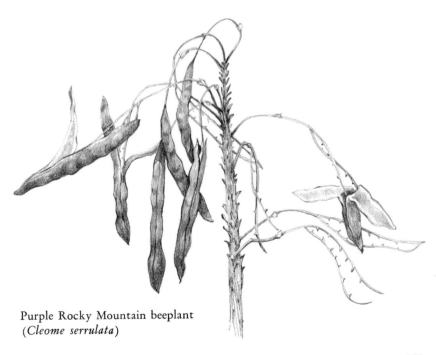

Purple Rocky Mountain beeplant
(*Cleome serrulata*)

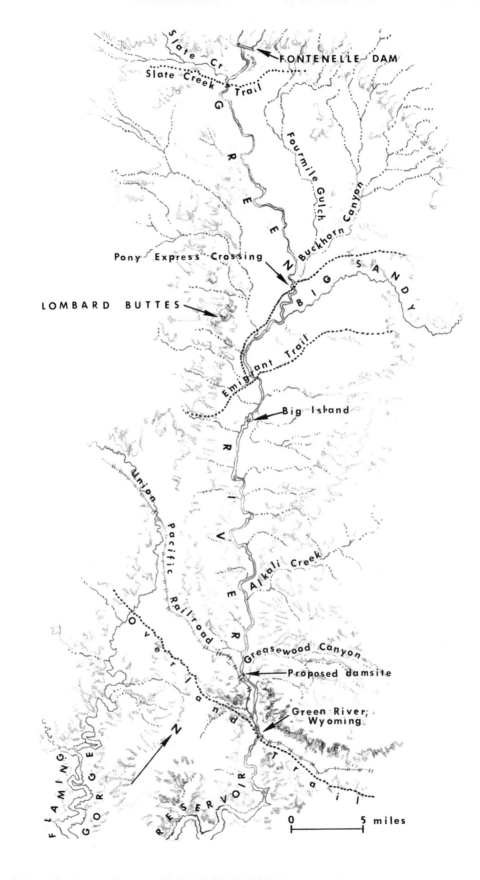

FONTENELLE DAM

Slate Cr

Slate Creek Trail

G R E E N

Fourmile Gulch

Buckhorn Canyon

Pony Express Crossing

BIG SANDY

LOMBARD BUTTES

Emigrant Trail

Big Island

R I V E R

Union Pacific Railroad

Alkali Creek

Greasewood Canyon

Proposed damsite

Overland

Green River, Wyoming

N

Trail

FLAMING GORGE

RESERVOIR

0   5 miles

FONTENELLE DAM
TO GREEN RIVER, WYOMING

THERE IS only one way to get around a dam and that is to be ignominiously ferried. Connie meets us with the truck and we trundle the canoe down to the base of the dam, decorated with the bright lights of the power plant. On the left an emasculated river slithers down a long straight spillway. I feel the same as I do at the foot of a glacier, primed by the illogical suspicion that it may let go at any minute. Which, in this case, is not too illogical. In September, 1965, when the reservoir first filled, leakage from the dam became so massive that the reservoir was hurriedly drained, ranches along the river below were evacuated, while water rose in basements as far downstream as Green River, Wyoming. Newspaper accounts warned of possible dam failure. The embankment and dam were repaired, but there is still leakage through the abutments adjacent to the dam, what the Bureau of Reclamation says "is considered normal for an earth filled dam." Leakage from around the reservoir has created a new stream (called Flume Creek) near the base of the dam and the shale cliffs on the east. About a mile downstream, a fifty-foot cliff of these shales streams with water. Fontenelle Reservoir has also raised the water table, and water seeps, trickles, and runs through these permeable shales.

On the right bank a small metal enclosure marks U.S.G.S. Gage 2112, one of eleven thousand stations in the hydrologic network of the United States. Gaging stations are installed at comparatively stable and uniform reaches. A cross-section of the channel area is calculated, and this, multiplied by the velocity of the river, gives the river's discharge in cubic feet per second, abbreviated to "second-feet" or "cfs." Calculations result in a "rating curve" for each station that relates the amount of discharge to each particular stage of the river; at any river level, the amount of water flowing through that point can be read off the rating curve, providing necessary information for flood control, irrigation, water supply, pollution control, and fish management. Measured by the U.S.G.S. over a forty-two-year period prior to the closure of Fontenelle Dam, the maximum monthly mean flow of the Green for June and July was 13,430 to 14,450 cfs; minimum monthly mean flow, November through March, was 250-300 cfs.

In September, 1973, release from the dam was withheld. The State of Wyoming presently buys 60,000 acre-feet per year from the Bureau of Reclamation (under whose jurisdiction the reservoir is) that it sells to industry. The state is contemplating buying an additional 60,000 acre-feet, so flow was reduced in increments to 1,600, 800, 500, and 300 cfs in order to study the effect of such further withdrawals on the river. The state's follow-up study was conducted by the federal Bureau of Sport Fisheries and Wildlife in conjunction with the Wyoming Game and Fish Commission. Although concerned primarily with fishing below the dam, the implication is that if the river is qualitatively and quantitatively unsuitable for fish, then it is unsuitable for other uses also. Prior to the dam, the river was relatively warm and turbid, supporting carp, catfish, and other nongame fish. The original ecosystem no longer exists. The dam, by holding back silt, now maintains a trout fishery that provides a tourist attraction. The study recommended various flows, depending upon the time of year, in order to maintain this fishery: 800 cfs provides "the most balanced habitat diversity"; a short-term sediment flushing flow of 1,600 cfs; and a winter survival flow of 500 cfs with "an emergency short-term winter survival" flow of 300 cfs. At 300 cfs the Green is, as local newspapers pointed out, a trickle across mud flats, with dead fish in stagnant ponds, irrigation intake pipes above water level, plus the specter of endangered water supply to cities dependent on the river. There is no written contractual agreement that these flows will be maintained; only a minimum flow of 50 cfs at the U.S.G.S. gaging station at Green River is mentioned, a flow too low for any purposes.

Below Fontenelle, the Green's flood plain narrows, jigsawed with the fragmentary curving oxbows, one often lying inside the other, that are remnants of old meander channels and a bigger river. Fewer clumps of sod break away from the bank since seasonal flood spates are controlled by the dam; fluctuations are now more frequent and irregular, depending upon the demand for electricity. A one-lane steel bridge, built by the CCC in the 1930s, spans the river above the old ferry crossing of the Slate Creek Trail. Evidence of the trail remains in patches of bare ground or intermittent gaps in the sagebrush, invisible unless one is really looking for it. But from the air the old trails are clear; they circumvent even slight obstacles, while modern roads are straight as a die, cutting imperiously through hill and mesa.

A whirling cloud of gnats is fed on by torpedo-shaped swallows, joined by lesser nighthawks. We see a few ducks, many blackbirds, some killdeer, but so far no beaver and no geese, and the only beaver lodge we pass is abandoned. Water plants stalk the shore, and each bottom rock is tufted or encrusted or streaming with algae. Many fishermen stand along the shore and we exchange the time of day. A peculiar situation exists in the Fontenelle tailwaters, one of the not-unexpected by-products of an artificially maintained habitat: the alternation of pools and riffles, necessary to trout survival in providing shelter and food organisms, are distorted here where long stretches of so-called "flat" water exist between pools. The flat water reaches are less suited for trout because of their shallow water depth and faster water currents (small fish need quieter water, and the swift runs are too shallow for larger fish that would ordinarily find good habitat here).

Huge electric pumps on the right bank lift water for irrigation on the experimental Seedskadee Development Farm, now leased to an individual rancher. Fontenelle Dam was originally planned to supply irrigation water to 70,000–80,000 acres; this was reduced to 58,000 in 1959, and latest studies indicate only 34,000 acres could be feasibly irrigated. Irrigating the original acreage would have involved construction of expensive canals, and much of the land is too alkaline. Now *no* water at all is used for irrigation out of Fontenelle Reservoir; all withdrawals are for "consumptive industrial uses."

AFTER NEARLY four hours of steady paddling, we take time for a dehydration stop. Through these arid lands, perspiration evaporates almost immediately, and without replenishment of body liquids the unpleasant symptoms of light-headedness and flushed face that presage dehydration quickly become uncomfortably evident. Good water was always one of the limiting and determining factors in crossing this dry land on foot. Even a century ago, a stream did not mean drinkable water; many journals report symptoms typical of contaminated water, and on Bonneville's crossing, "the suffering of both men and horses had been excessive, and it was with almost frantic eagerness that they hurried to allay their burning thirst in the limpid current" of the Green River.

With the canoe stabilized against the bank, Perry opens the water jug and I mix up cupfuls of orange drink, and between us, we imbibe a quart. Beside the boat, the river is about a foot deep. A twelve-inch whitefish (they are abundant in the river) works the water just beside the canoe, picking up insect larvae and nymphs off the bottom. With an imperceptible flick of its tail it swims upstream four feet or so, then drifts back, materializing like magic, not there and then there in the same flick of time. It lies so close to the bow that I can see the streamlined configuration of its body like a diagram. Like most river fish, it maintains its position heading into the current to facilitate feeding and respiration and take advantage of the current's push. Position in the river is maintained in relation to a fixed object, such as a strong bottom pattern or a large rock.

The whitefish dissolves out of sight, then reassembles, a pearly gray, mottled with tawny spots, precisely the same color as the rocks over which it feeds. Each time it forms out of the colors and shapes and patterns of the river bottom, the marrow of the river given life.

A SKEIN of tangled cables lies rusting at the old Lombard Ferry site. On shore, a rusted ratchet lies buried in the dirt. Cables were strung across the river to aid heavy wagons to cross without being swept downstream by the current. The map shows that to the east the emigrant trail branched to two crossings; Lombard Ferry is the northernmost. A hiatus in the willows reveals the old wagon path.

The willows along the river are heavily infested with galls; entangled with sticky-podded New Mexican locust bushes and henbane, they form a miserable thicket. Back from the river the soil is hard-packed, supporting mostly greasewood and tumbleweed, a small yellow Rocky Mountain bee plant or two, impoverished sage, tufts of rice grass, an assortment of thorny, prickly weeds. Heat radiates up from the ground. Flies and mosquitoes blacken my jeans and shirt.

New Mexican locust
(*Robinia neomexicana*)

From the air the terrain appears spatter-painted with scrub, dotted with bare circles; on the ground these circles turn out to be the hills of vicious ants, empty spots up to a yard across encircled with a slightly heavier growth of vegetation. I can scarcely walk across this

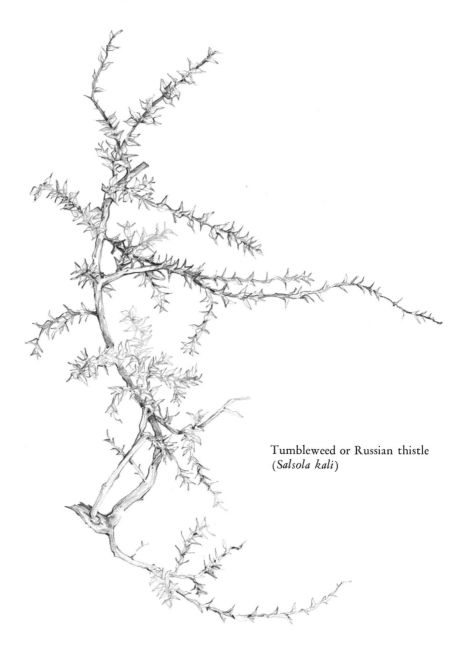

Tumbleweed or Russian thistle
(*Salsola kali*)

ground without turning an ankle. Riding in a wagon must have been
bone wrenching. For emigrants unloading stubborn mules and unyok-
ing oxen and putting them out to graze and rounding them up again

and reloading, day after day, the dream of a river passage from the Rockies to the Pacific seems understandable. The tediousness of this journey is caught in the laconic entry of nineteen-year-old John Boardman. The train with which he traveled reached the Green on August 10, 1843. He wrote: "Pleasant. 10 miles. We crossed Green River. Country sand and sage and has been since we left Laramie."

To someone coming from the lush greens of Ohio and Kentucky, this lumpy, sun-whitened landscape must have seemed both bleak and hostile. But this crossing has one essential: Lombard Buttes, just to the west of the river, ghostly white mastabas of the Green River Formation, are superb landmarks.

A pair of avocets swim upstream, bobbing reddish brown heads, still in their courtship plumage. They pass without taking off, ignoring the canoe, long beaks curved a little upward as if in disdain. I have the curious sensation that it is we who go upstream and they who go with the current. Four unsheared sheep huddle beneath a willow. They look miserable and forgotten, herds in this area having been sheared for weeks.

The Pony Express route crosses the Green River just below Lombard Ferry, following a route laid out by Jim Bridger in 1849 at the request of the Corps of Topographical Engineers. The route was used both by the Pony Express and the Overland Stage until Indian pressures forced traffic south to another Bridger route, just below present Green River, Wyoming. Officially called The Central Overland, California, and Pikes Peak Express Company, it was unofficially known as the Clean Out of Luck and Poor Pay. The stage service between Salt Lake City and western Kansas took ten days, carrying eleven passengers. Primitive accommodations were available en route; meals consisted largely of beans and bacon; coffee was considered fresh if made within the week. About the only thing that can be said for passenger amenities is that, at an average speed of eight miles an hour, it beat walking.

Established in 1860, the Pony Express covered its 1,960-mile route nonstop in ten days, using riders in relay. A rider could unsaddle, throw saddle and mail pouch on a fresh horse, and remount in two minutes; mount changes were made every 15 to 20 miles, rider changes every 75 miles, although William Cody once made 320 miles on a continuous ride of 21 hours and 40 minutes. Rates varied between $2 and $10 an ounce (this in a day when Overland Stage drivers made between $40 and $75 a month, Pony Express riders, $125) but even that was insufficient to support expenses. After eighteen un-profitable months, all assets were sold at public sale.

Today, a dugway in the soft sand angles up out of the river, and a dust devil scurries a cloud of dust, such as a rider might have made, carrying the mail west.

BIG SANDY, named by General Ashley for the character of the country-side, is the only perennial stream to enter the Green River on the east between Fontenelle Dam and Flaming Gorge. Like the New Fork, it rises in the Wind Rivers, and was the route by which many travelers on the Oregon Trail reached the Green River from South Pass. On March 19, 1824, Ashley's advance party reached the Green here, and on July 20, 1846, the Donner party, already running late, crossed on their way to Fort Bridger. In 1869 Hayden reported pleasant bottomlands with abundant grass. Now Big Sandy is polluted with irrigation runoff from the Eden-Farson irrigation project. At its best it is not a large stream, and today it is just a few feet wide; I am concentrating so hard on paddling against the wind that I almost miss it. What a ten- to fifteen-knot wind, head on, can do to a hundred-pound canoe, loaded with four hundred pounds, is depressing.

We stop on a small gravel spit where there is no shade in hopes of avoiding mosquitoes. Away from the river, flowing sand is interrupted only with scattered brush. Nevertheless this desert country is con-sidered to be excellent sheep country and the herds we pass are legion. On the nearest spit upstream six sheared rams cluster at the riverside, feet in the water, watching, loppy-eared, as we beach. From down-stream their rumps all line up together; if one pulls out, the rest close ranks and the odd man out has to push in. They turn and watch me balefully, shuffling sideways, keeping their feet in the water. I under-stand: cool feet feel very good.

The river cobbles on the spit catch silt and sand, and as the water level fluctuates, threads of algae dry into gray tangles. Dust and dirt encrusted, the usually elegant river-washed ovals are intermixed with chunks of shattered green shale. Also called soapstone, it is given as one of the reasons that the Green River is green. These soapstones record volcanic activity in the Uinta Mountains to the south, the color possibly caused by their formation in a shallow, fluctuating lake where oxidation was incomplete or very slow. The sand between stones is alive with minute black beetles and frenzied flies that pop like jumping beans, too swift to catch, or to be more honest, I am too lethargic to try to do so. Although the wind dries the top layer of sand to a hard crust, the bar has been so recently inundated that moisture pools beneath every cobble.

The wind persists, the hot breath of some marauding dragon searing the countryside to pale breathlessness. After an hour of paddling, an empty house appears on the east bank. Built of neatly notched square logs, it is a big house of six rooms, with truly fine proportions, windows and doors relating to the outer rectangle of the façade in the precise balance of a Mondrian painting. Surrounding it are a barn and chickenhouse, outhouse, cellar for storage, and an old harness shop scattered with buckles and fittings. But there is no sign of a vegetable garden or of flowers that might once have been planted and from which a few errant stalks somehow survived. The dusty, scrubby yard fades away to sagebrush desert.

Gannett, geographer for the Hayden Survey of 1879, noted that the area between the Green and Big Sandy confluence could not be profitably irrigated and must remain forever desert; this is even more true farther downstream, where the land is further complicated by broken terrain. A few grasses grow in the shade of the house and outbuildings. Before fencing this area was prime wintering ground for elk. Since sheep have grazed here almost no natural grasses now grow between the sage, and without them, the wind worries the soil, prodding it into the air in streaming funnels.

By the end of the nineteenth century it had become obvious that the Homestead Act was impractical, if not totally impossible, in the dry West. The Carey Act, passed in 1894, made desert lands available to the states; each of the states containing these lands was given large grants on the condition that the state would reclaim and irrigate them. Reclamation proceeded with such notable lack of enthusiasm that the time period was extended another ten years. The Kinkaid Act of 1904 quadrupled the amount of land given a homesteader, just enough to provide minimum subsistence at dry farming, where it was possible. But as the Congress giveth, it also taketh away—the Mondell Act of 1909 reduced acreage to 320 acres.

The Carey Act was amended in 1908 to grant additional lands to several states; the state was to file maps indicating irrigation plans and the source of the water supply, and upon approval by the Department of Interior these lands would be segregated and reserved from homestead entry. These terms were accepted by Colorado, Utah, and

Wyoming, with eventually hundreds of thousands of acres applied for by the three states. But by 1920 less than 3 percent of the segregated lands in Wyoming were irrigated; either the expense was too great or the expertise was lacking. By 1965 no more than 5 percent of the state was under cultivation. In the Green River Basin agriculture lacks not only favorable climate but good transportation facilities, and crops that can be raised are not the high-priced ones that justify expensive irrigation systems.

Altitude and climate make this region best adapted to stock raising if enough land is available to run large herds. The Stock-Raising Homestead Act of 1916 granted only 640 acres even after 1,280 had been judged necessary. One head in upper Green River country needs a minimum of 30 to 40 acres of pasture; 5,000 acres is minimum for a herd, and it takes more like 10,000 acres for profitable ranching. Those few who were successful depended upon almost unlimited free use of government land with which to extend their own acreage, and again much of the land fell into the hands of large outfits. The defeat of the basic concept of homesteading in the West was acknowledged in the Taylor Grazing Act of 1934, which attempted to curtail the unregulated use of land that fostered overgrazing and brought erosion. Under it nearly all the unhomesteaded pasture land was removed from homestead entry and could only be used under government lease. The whole history of land-use regulation in the West is flawed with proposals that ignore the basic facts of the environment and attempt to impose unrealistic solutions.

Small homestead cabins along the river, much less ambitious than this house, are often tucked in a cottonwood grove, and they project a kind of sheltered comfort. This house is wide open to the wind. A few sagebrush and willow were planted across the front fence line as a windbreak, but the wind ignores them and sweeps through anyway, rattling the rusted beer cans left by itinerant sheepherders, worrying the shreds of wallpaper. The wind lifts a piece of ragged wallboard and thuds it relentlessly against the floor. The kitchen linoleum curls at the edges, the trellis-and-cabbage-rose pattern awash with mouse and rat droppings. The stove is rusted out, pushed back on its hind legs and twisted askew. Through the window sagebrush desert stretches far and away, no trees, no mesas, no mountains.

I wonder what it was like to have lived here. It was lonely, of course, brutal in the winter, the house below freezing if the stove went out at night. I could have managed that, but not this wind.

Did whoever lived in this house take her pots and pans and pack them with reluctance and weary disappointment at leaving years of living here, poorer than when she came, or did she pack them with delighted haste, moving to a new house, with real plumbing, way back from the windy river? Or did she simply, one day, draw the outline of a cabbage rose in the fine incessant silt, get up from the table, leave the coffeepot half filled, the cups dirty, and walk out this lonesome door at which I stand, and go as far away from the wind as she could go?

As WE APPROACH Telephone Island, huge carp move out to deeper water, creating blossoming clouds of silt. The river is clotted with skeins and hanks of floating algae and pondweed. The warmer water and increasing turbidity favor carp over trout and whitefish; these carp must be at least eighteen inches long, big solid fish. If the proposed Lower Green River dam is built, the reservoir will back up nearly to this point and inundate twenty-one miles of river and further favor nongame fish over trout.

Late-afternoon sun glares off a row of Pacific Power and Light high-tension towers, strung across the landscape just above Big Island Bridge. The canoe spanks through riffles generated by the bridge piers. Severe and rectilinear, the bridge's stiff lines seem an anachronism in the flowing landscape. The new high-tension towers, mechanical mantises, connect to the Northwest Power Pool; electricity generated from coal mined near Rock Springs is sold to seven states west of Wyoming.

Ahead, the Union Pacific pipeline bridges the river. In the early 1850s Jefferson Davis, as Secretary of War, proposed the Pacific Railroad Surveys to find a practical route west, surveys not accomplished until the 1860s. When Congress enacted aid to encourage construction of railway lines from the Missouri River to the Pacific Ocean, in July, 1862, the inducement was ten sections or ten square miles of land for every mile of track laid. When not enough investors were forthcoming, the grant was sweetened to twenty miles on each side of the rightaway, all mineral rights included, engendering the famous race between the Union Pacific and Central Pacific. As the major holder of these rights, the Union Pacific conducted the first mineral explorations in this area.

Big Island splits the river. Smoke from the Big Island Mine and Refinery streams out to the east. The plant mines trona—sodium carbonate or natural soda ash. In the hand trona is slightly translucent milky white. It is converted into pure soda ash, essential in the manufacture of glass, and used in many chemical and sodium-based industries. It was discovered in 1938 in exploratory drilling for gas and oil, and is intimately associated with the oil and clay shales of the Green River Formation, laid down when the lake had no outlet. During dry periods when the lake evaporated, salts precipitated, and trona, being the least soluble, was deposited first. The lake reached this stage of evaporation at least twenty times, precipitating an estimated 300 million tons of trona in beds from one-half inch to thirty-eight feet thick. Another trona mine, about twenty miles west of the river, removes one million gallons of water a day from the Green to holding tanks that serve as a reservoir for its company power plant.

We have been twelve and a half hours on the river, of which ten or more have been solid paddling, sometimes easy but more often shoulder-socket wearying, against the wind. The day ends with a short stretch of happy water, black-green in the shadows; the canoe lifts its bow and perks through and beaches with a gentle hiss on a sandy island. A killdeer nest is nearby, and the parents complain in Morse code, a high, nervous, irritable calling fitting their specific name *vociferus*. They ply back and forth across the island, sharp black and white breast bands clear in the evening light. One lands and struts the shore, the patches on its rump the color of cinnamon. The swath where dam and dry sand meet is alive with half-inch bugs darting in a Brownian movement, and the killdeer scurries and stabs.

We are eleven miles north of Green River, Wyoming. Upriver there is complete wilderness, beautiful quiet, grassed banks, a munificence of wildlife. Here there are an irritable killdeer, a bale of mosquitoes, and a mucky river bottom draped with algae. In spite of unbeautiful things done to it, and a marked lessening of wildlife, the river retains its quintessential spirit in the spates of bright water that give the river its sense of lilt, of freedom, of riverness.

THE SIGNS of humanity have increased, not the least of which is the shift whistle at midnight and eight in the morning from the trona plant. The first one, at midnight, brings me right out of sleep, sure that an old side-wheeler is bearing down on the tent. At six o'clock I look out the tent flap to see three fishermen walking the beach; fortunately their fishing is unproductive and they leave.

When I strike the tent I dispossess hundreds of small flying and crawling insects from beneath it; at exposure to light they scatter. Even before I finish rolling the tent, big storm clouds, low and ominous, roll in from the west southwest. Virga curtain down in the distance. The breeze freshens. I get my rain suit out. It is right and proper that it should rain on last mornings.

A few drops pockmark the water as we shove off. A milk carton laps against the shore. The rain comes, bringing with it the brownish smoke and smell and drone of the trona plant. A huge horned owl sails out of a bush and lands midway up in a cottonwood tree, observing us, I sense, somewhat irritably. A red-tailed hawk skims off the shale cliffs on the right, from a distance its cry sounding like a richocheting bullet. The canoe skirts the cliff where the hawk nests, and it screams deprecations. Its agitated flying loosens a feather. The feather oscillates downward and a cliff swallow picks it up on the wing.

Having time before our deadline at Green River, we loaf downstream, for Perry is fascinated by the old abandoned buildings along the way. At a ranch, a Rube Goldberg irrigation setup lies disassembled and quiet, the big pump rusted out. The pipes are made of thirty- and fifty-gallon oil cans held together with inner tubes, and assorted hot-water tanks welded together. A Union Pacific switchman's bar leans against the fence; a baggage wagon stands half stacked with oil drums. Just the next field down the new rig is in place, with shiny gas and diesel pumps, pipes waiting in the river. Here on the Green, riverbanks are several feet above the river even at high water, and water must be pumped up to the bench level of the fields. Pumping is usually not begun until water level begins to lower after peak runoff, when predetermined amounts of water are allotted to individual ranches.

Farther downriver, a disintegrating wooden waterwheel leans crazily between steel beams and cement posts in the river. On shore, a rusting Lycoming engine hangs mounted backward in a tractor frame, in order to give extra traction. "DON'T SHOOT—HORSES INSIDE" is whitewashed in big letters on the walls of a listing shed. Hand-hewn ties lie stacked near the river. The smoother hand-hewn and planed ties were preferred to those cut at the sawmill, which retained a water-absorbent burr on the faces.

The river slides quietly through the landscape. We might be seeing it as Horace Greeley saw it in 1859, "a stream here perhaps as large as the Mohawk at Schenectady or the Hudson at Waterford. It winds with a rapid, muddy current through a deep, narrow valley, much of it sandy and barren." The rain stops. It is heavily still. In between the gray sky and the gray river a sonic boom lets loose, massive, ear-painful: the bombast of civilization is magnified by the quiet of the wilderness.

The last of a series of goose nests placed by the Wyoming Game & Fish Department stands forlornly. Constructed with a four-foot-square platform supported by metal posts, it is beginning to lean lopsided. From the Big Bend down, none we have seen have contained any sign of geese. All were labeled as to their purpose with a request that they not be disturbed, a request taken literally by the geese. A huge golden eagle soars from a far cliff. It loops across the sky, cer-tainly reason enough to discourage any sensible goose. Another bird comes sweeping down the river, this one white with yellow stripes and an engine on each wing. Herman, coming in to meet me at Expedition Island, dips his wings in recognition, and I nearly fall out of the canoe waving my paddle.

There are more and more changes in the landscape. At first they are subtle, roads that come over the ridgetop and turn and disappear. Then bigger roads. Then paved roads. Roofs. The sound of an irriga-tion pump throbbing. A man out fixing a pump, whanging at it with a wrench. We pass under the first highway bridge and I realize that my ears are hypersensitive: the high whine of tires on the pavement, the pounding of weight across the bridge, the exaggerated metallic grind of big trucks shifting gears. My ears are attuned to the whisper of water dripping off the paddle. The only birds now are magpies, cantankerously questioning the trees, the river, the sky, and each other. It is so easy to slip into the stillness of the river, to time days by the sun's going, to sense all the small silken silences, to adjust sight to the flick of a beaver tail or the flash of mink. But the opposite is not easy. It becomes more and more difficult to leave the river, to desensitize back to the level that makes the noise and smell and feel of mechanization livable, that puts jet scream and sonic boom into the background.

An abandoned segment of Union Pacific tracks lies high against a cliff ahead, designated as "Fish Cut" since many complete and ex-quisite fish fossils, discovered when the Union Pacific excavated, have been taken out of the Green River Formation here. The palisades that surround the town of Green River are ribbon-layered in shades of grayed salmon, jade, tan, pearl, oyster white, the cliff almost onyx-like, each bed marking a subtle change in current or materials deposited. The capping sandstones are a warm toast color, often undercut and cantilevered, a rough, formidable horizon.

The settlement of the town of Green River beneath these palisades did not begin until 1868, when a group of developers, seeing profit in the advent of the railroad, plotted the area for a town. But, when the Union Pacific arrived, it went right on through, bridging the river and bypassing a settlement of some two thousand people. However lack of water to the west caused railroad crews to backpaddle; population picked up by 1872 and the town has been in existence ever since. Since it is a railroad town, a large proportion of the town's population are employees who work nights. The "Green River Ordinance" was passed in 1931 to prevent solicitors and peddlers from ringing doorbells in the daytime, and has been adopted by many cities and towns.

We reach the main railroad bridge just as a multi-engined diesel goes across. The engineer waves. It is all I can do not to hold my ears with both hands. The high sun comes out and washes color out of rock and tree and river alike, just as the alien sounds of civilization wash the soughs of the river out of my ears.

We beach the canoe at Expedition Island, a teardrop spot of green in an otherwise sere landscape, greeted by family and an assortment of wading, splashing youngsters. Here, on the east end of a small park, a marker notes that Major John Wesley Powell, with ten men and four boats, pushed off on his incredible journey down the Green and Colorado rivers.

One hundred four years and one month later, we take out where Major Powell put in.

8

[Brown's Hole] is situated in or about latitude 42° north; one hundred miles south of Wind River mountains, on the Sheetskadee (Prairie Cock) River. Its elevation is something more than eight thousand feet above the level of the sea. It appeared to be about six miles in diameter; shut in, in all directions, by dark frowning mountains, rising one thousand five hundred feet above the plain. The Sheetskadee, or Green River, runs through it, sweeping in a beautiful curve from the northwest to the south-west part of it, where it breaks its way through the encircling mountains, between cliffs, one thousand feet in height, broken and hanging as if poised on the air. The area of the plain is thickly set with the rich mountain grasses, and dotted with little copses of cotton wood and willow trees. The soil is alluvial, and capable of producing abundantly all kinds of small grains, vegetables, &c., that are raised in the northern States. Its climate is very remarkable. Although in all the country, within a hundred miles of it, the winter months bring snows, and the severe cold that we should expect in such a latitude, and at such an elevation above the level of the sea, yet in this little nook, the grass grows all the winter; so that, while the storm rages on the mountains in sight, and the drifting snows mingle in the blasts of December, the old hunters here heed it not. Their horses are cropping the green grass on the banks of the Sheetskadee, while they themselves are roasting the fat loins of the mountain sheep, and laughing at the merry tale and song.

THOMAS JEFFERSON FARNHAM, 1839, *Travels in the Great Western Prairies, The Anahuac and Rocky Mountains, and in the Oregon Territory*

Cottonwood pods

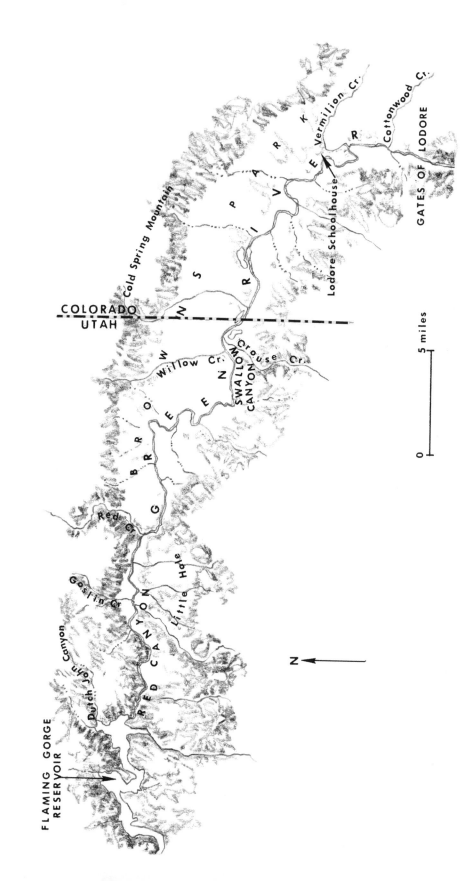

FLAMING GORGE DAM
TO THE GATES OF LODORE

JUST BELOW Cordwood Bottom, in the pale, dry narrows a few miles south of Green River, Wyoming, Flaming Gorge Reservoir begins. From here until midway through Red Canyon, the river is gone. Flaming Gorge Dam was closed in 1963, and the reservoir was filled to its capacity of 3,749,000 acre-feet for the first time in August, 1974. The first rendezvous site of 1825, where Henrys Fork comes into the Green, is inundated. Water obscures the lovely lower canyon series named by Major Powell: Flaming Gorge, Kingfisher, Horseshoe, and Hidden canyons. Here the *Comet,* a steamboat built in Green River in 1908, plied briefly between that town and Linwood, Utah. The reservoir hides Ashley Falls, where the general left his name in 1825, and covers the rocks that waylaid the 1849 bullwhackers trying to run Red Canyon. It floods the small farm once worked by hermit Amos Hill. And it backs the river up ninety-one miles.

Two days ago, the first of October, Perry Binning called and said he would meet me at Dutch John, about a mile east of the dam, to float Browns Park. Herman flies me to Dutch John, named for "Dutch John" Hanselena, a miner and horse trader from Prussia who prospected Red Canyon in the early 1860s. I look down on the gleaming bank of the river, released from the geometric curve of the dam. The river meanders gracefully, reflecting trees, a clear cobalt blue seen from ten thousand feet, patterned with marshes and sloughs and bronze-green bottomlands. Herman circles the airstrip and details appear: banks speckled with trees, little dry canyons snatching back from the river, crinkling white lines of rapids. Perry has said he is bringing a raft, but when I see the rapids, I wish it were the canoe. As we come in low to land, I can see Perry and Connie waiting. And they *have* brought the canoe!

Down at the boat ramp in Red Canyon, in shadow, it is sharply cold. The dam rises high and severe and also ominous, when I think of the massive volume of water impounded behind its thin shell. A notice reads: "Increased water flow through the generators may cause the river to rise several feet in a matter of minutes. Please be careful." The release of water from the dam depends upon hydroelectric power demands that change during the day, and fluctuations in the river can be rapid, varying from 400 cfs to 3,500 cfs. (The reservoir itself fluctuates twenty-five feet yearly.) A high release moves quickly downstream and can be dangerous for small boats or fishermen out on low, confining ledges; although flow is less variable the farther away one is from the dam, it noticeably affects the river as far downstream as Split Mountain.

Perry and I load the canoe, make last arrangements with Connie for take-out at the Gates of Lodore, and shove off at nine-thirty between high red canyon walls. We skim a clear, deep-green river shot with lines of crystalline sparks, absolutely enchanted canoeing. As we head into the early morning sun, swarms of midges catch the light like spinning gold dust. The river bottom is full of dark green moss; like the upper river, fresh out of the glaciers, the water is so cold and so swift here that water mosses thrive, almost covering the bottom from bank to bank in some reaches.

Dinner-plate-sized patches of pure gravel have been swept clear by brown trout that are now spawning, a useless gesture as all trout here must be stocked. Discharge is from the lowest level of the reservoir, and the water is preternaturally cold, preventing reproduction. Not only that, but supercooled winter tailwater temperatures down to 28° F. have occurred of late due to a combination of very cold water released from the dam and the cold air.

We bounce through a good chop that sprays copious amounts of water in over the bow. In the deep, cool canyon a draft of warm air and a shaft of sun are welcome: my jeans are totally soaked, my feet wet, my hands cold even with gloves on, yet I am so completely happy to be back on the river that it matters little. Cottonwoods and box elder along the shore are yellowing, transmitting the rising sun through topaz leaves. According to the moss and algae line on the

Tailwaves, back-waves, or standing waves, remain in place and break upstream

CURRENT FLOW IN RAPIDS

shore rocks, the water level here must fluctuate four feet or more; dried plants plaster the rocks, stranded by the river's present low level. Power demands are at a minimum from midnight until five A.M. and it is still too early in the day for much water to be released for peak afternoon loads.

Most of the white water in Red Canyon is produced by debris brought in by tributary creeks, blocking the river's flow with fans of boulders and gravel, debris brought in only during floods. In addition, the river is dropping a fairly swift eight to twelve feet per mile. The rapids are straightforward, not rock-garden obstacle courses that, in retrospect, seem much more difficult to run because they require such constant maneuvering, although probably safer as the water in these is generally shallow—and not nearly so numbing. A twelve-foot boulder lies exposed in midstream, fallen off the canyon wall. The water flows into a narrowing V, forced by the rock into a clear, smooth tongue of water, rising up and rolling, breaking into tail waves that dissipate the water's energy downstream. Generally when this gateway is passed there are no rocks under the tail waves, the exceptions providing some of the more exciting surprises. The variations of Red Canyon's rapids depend on the stage of the water, and the size and placement of the rocks. At this low water, there are probably even more than are marked on the map, riffles appearing over bars flooded out at deeper water. Rapids appear frequently now, light and larking, tongue well defined, and we run most of them right on.

NOW THAT FLAMING GORGE is covered, Red Canyon is the first red rock canyon on the Green River. The walls are a soft rose red in the morning light, eight hundred feet high, rising back to two thousand on the mountainside to the south. Powell, who ran it in May, named the canyon for these red walls of ancient Uinta Mountain Group quartzites that form the spine of the Uinta Mountains.

The Uinta Mountains, some 150 to 160 miles long and 30 to 50 wide, run east and west, keen, snow-slashed peaks steeping in the sunlight, unique in their trend among the Rockies. ("Uintah" is said to mean "land high up where the timber grows", and is spelled with an "h" if a political division, without if a natural land form.) After the Civil War much attention was given to this range, and all three of the great territorial surveys, led by F. V. Hayden, Clarence King, and John Wesley Powell, did classical geological research in the area, aided by the completion of the railroad at Green River that facilitated transport of supplies. Unlike most mountain ranges, most of the Uinta peaks are named after American geologists.

The Uinta Mountains rose during the same period as the Wind River and other Rocky Mountains, urged upward by movements that began in the California-Nevada area and pulsated eastward sixty to seventy million years ago. The mountains are formed out of sediments laid into an ancient east-west trending trough. These sediments accumulated to a depth of nearly two miles, brought in by rivers and streams running down from the Ancestral Rockies to the northeast,

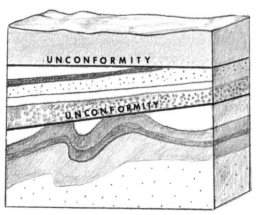

UNCONFORMITIES

A long period of erosion or nondeposition is an unconformity.

Sedimentary strata tilted and eroded; more sediments laid on top.

Older strata folded and eroded; sedimentary strata laid on top.

large ranges no longer in existence. The oldest rocks underlying the range are Red Creek quartzites, which may be two to three billion years old and perhaps 20,000 feet thick. A period of erosion intervened before the Uinta Mountain Group sediments were laid, creating what is known as a geological unconformity. The deposition of the Uinta Mountain Group was terminated by renewed uplift. Sediments that now lie some 30,000 feet below the surface in the adjacent basins were raised to 12,000 and 13,000 feet above sea level, and once covered the mountain crests.

Renewed uplift caused the range to rise again. Regional uplift caused severe bending along the flanks, stresses that led to large-scale faulting: the 120-mile-long Uinta Mountain Fault on the north side thrust the mountain core some 20,000 feet upward. The final determination of much of this terrain depended upon glaciation; although there were no glaciers here in the eastern end of the range, those that covered at least a thousand square miles in the west directly affected the surface drainage by the outward pouring of water during warming periods. These periods undoubtedly coincided with those of the Wind Rivers, and left moraines extending forty miles into the Green River Basin, as well as a complex series of terraces within Browns Park.

The red walls flanking the river are composed of hard quartzites and shales and conglomerates, colored by the precipitation of iron oxides from underground water. Most are so slightly metamorphosed that, even though a billion years old, the original character of the sediments is still apparent. Some of the rocks scattered along the river look almost like bricks in size, texture, and color. A loose boulder on shore contains gravels and large pebbles from the old Red Creek Quartzite, held in a matrix of rust-red sandstone. It is so strongly cemented that it has characteristically broken through the pebbles rather than around them, and lies like an oversized chunk of *Blutwurst* in the sand.

We continue to run riffles, one after another. A heavier sound than that of the light rapids we've been running carries up from downstream. I make a quick check of the map. It is too soon for Red Creek rapids and absolutely nothing is marked. The noise gradually intensifies. Around two more bends and still nothing. We begin to paddle very slowly and carefully. A stream coming in at this dry end of the year could not make such a solid sound. And then in front of the canoe —suddenly the river disappears. There is no place or time to land. Fortunately we are lined up right with the tongue. As the canoe shoots through I take a deep breath, sure I am going out and under. The bow points straight down. Water pours in. The canoe stabilizes in the calm water just beyond. Awash and amazed, we look back to a solid white step, four or five feet high, tongue pushed far to the right, a foaming plunge into frothing icy water. It looks like a rim of bedrock, probably not even showing when the water is high. We pull over as soon as possible to bail. But I begin to feel uneasy: if something as thumping as this fall is unmarked, then Red Creek rapids, reported to be the swiftest in this canyon, must be truly formidable.

After this fall we enter the quiet of Little Hole, where the steep red rock walls flare out to form a protected opening. The river has, in the slowed gradient and before it was dammed, built a gentle flood plain. "Hole" is the designation for valleys rimmed by hills or mountains where trappers "holed up" for the winter; there are several along the river in the next hundred miles, Brown's Hole and Pat's Hole being the best known. On the high terraces to the south there are some small gardens and hay meadows, irrigated from Davenport Creek. Still farther above, the high, rolling hillsides of the Uintas are gold-plated with aspen. Since aspen here reproduce by underground suckers, they form solid groves that gleam like some Mycenaean treasure just opened to the sun.

RED CREEK is not only a stiff stretch of white water for a canoe, but bears some of the more rugged history of the river. Jesse Ewing lived at Red Creek for a short time; previous to coming here he had been a station keeper on the isolated South Pass post of the Overland Stage route. A bear had clawed his face so severely that he was described as the ugliest man in South Pass, an epithet which also applied to his disposition.

He came south to prospect Brown's Hole in 1867. In order to secure enough money to conduct operations, he took on a series of partners, the length of the association depending on how long the partner's money held out. A young man named Robinson was one of the less fortunate. Accounts vary; one says Ewing bullied him into cutting railroad ties to sell in town and then attempted to keep the money and chase him away; another says he was simply ill fated enough to be prospecting too close for Ewing's pleasure and refused to move on. Ewing achieved a permanent separation by slashing Robinson's body to ribbons and leaving it on the ice for the river to dispose of in the spring, staining the ice with blood. Ewing reportedly announced to a group of miners: "If you guys want to see a handsome corpse, go up yonder on the ice and take a look."

Being lonely, an almost *a priori* assumption for a man of such temperament, he applied for a "coupon woman." She turned out to be one Madame Forrestall, who had formerly bootlegged liquor to the Indians, a woman whose outlook on life reportedly matched Ewing's. However, the advent of a stranger fleeing from the law created a *ménage à trois* on Red Creek. The handsome outlaw, who had been helping Ewing mine, pleaded indisposition one day and Ewing went off to work his claim alone. When Ewing returned from work, he was greeted with a warm blast from his own Winchester, solving all his problems on the instant.

With this lurid history in the back of my mind I wait to hear the sounds of Red Creek Rapid, those nuances that say how far, how soon, provoking a tenseness that is the not-unpleasant price of preknowledge. The sound floats upstream far ahead, and by the time we reach the rapids the roaring consumes the wind. Red Creek carries a large amount of dissolved salts that prevent good soil-holding vegetation along its banks; in addition, it has a large drainage basin. It is therefore subject to infrequent but intense floods, dumping much coarse rock debris into the river. The river is not competent to carry it away, so rocks stud the whole channel, forming an obstruction over which the water pitches as it drops steeply downstream, the average gradient twelve feet per mile in this reach. Woolley's river survey party of 1922 aptly described it as a "veritable dam of boulders" for their wooden boats.

As we approach, the right side of the river looks like good passage; the water piles and splashes into a tongue that pours into the rocks and disappears. We get out to look the rapid over. Huge rocks off the right cliff are now visible, forcing the water into a narrow channel and then piling it up against the cliff in a dangerous chute that could take the canoe like a hazelnut in a nutcracker. The near side of the river looks possible but big slabs lie just under the surface, and the gradient is steep enough and the river low enough so that the water lathers over them in small falls. A flat tongue enters on the high side of this rock-bound slot and we try to estimate if there is enough water over the rocks to let us through. The farther down we walk the worse it looks. The total shooting turbulence of the river, all those lethal rocks —I must look pale green. I certainly feel pale green. Perry says, "We can run or line the canoe through. It's up to you." From somewhere a voice, *surely* not mine, answers, a little quavery but *very* positive, "I wouldn't miss it for the world."

We walk the canoe as far back upstream as possible and climb in. We align the canoe to the tongue with care, with much care. As we enter the tongue a stiff breeze catches me full face. I am surprised that we go so fast. In position, a minor adjustment, centering on the tongue, steady, the current propels, slick, quick, quickening. The roll increases, the bow holds straight, paddle at the ready, no need to put in the water, watching for the big rock on the left, a light pry, and a quick gentle hand lifts the canoe and passes it through and not even a rock ticks the hull. Water piles gunwale high as the canoe rears into the tail waves, out of that sleek tongue, hardly taking a drop of water. The rapids tail out into a rock garden, and now the bow ticks rock after rock in the shallows, and it seems a long time of intense concentration and hard work. And then it is over and done with and time for elation and lunch—except I would prefer to nose the canoe back upstream and run Red Creek Rapid again. My confidence is at such a high that it is well we are not in Lodore: I would have no hesitation at trying Triplet Falls at this moment.

Over lunch we agree that canoeing is one of the best ways to learn the river, for one must mark what makes the river run and mark it well. As far as I am concerned, a canoe is one of the most pleasant modes of transportation invented; it fits the human body, and the rhythm of paddling suits human musculature and leverage. Perhaps a kayak is a more intimate way to go with the river, but a canoe is more comfortable for long miles. It is silent; it requires no fuel other than a good breakfast, lunch, and dinner for the boaters. In quiet water there is time to absorb the countryside; in fast water there are challenge and excitement. Its quiet going does not disturb wildlife on the river. It can be at once companionable and solitary. But, most of all, it is your decision both to run and how to run that streaming rapid that turns water iridescent in the sunlight. Although I have gained an even greater respect than I already had for the boatmen who run the really big rapids, being a raft passenger will never be quite the same again.

BROWNS PARK proper opens after Red Creek, to cradle the river all the way to the Gates of Lodore. Browns Park is a layered landscape: steep dark red slopes, heavily evergreened, form a high near-even horizon, nested with the pale, rolling, and notched hillsides and mesas of the Browns Park Formation (named by Powell), giving way to terraces along the river. The valley of the park lies roughly parallel to the axis of the Uintas, carved out wide and flat-bottomed by an ancient stream system. Into this hammock the pale sediments of the Browns Park Formation were deposited.

Tradition has it that the area was named for a French Canadian trapper, one Baptiste Brown, an employee of the Hudson's Bay Company. A volatile sort, he and his squaw picked up and moved here sometime around 1827 after he disagreed with the company; there is record of his being snowed in by the winter of 1835–36, and the valley was spoken of as Brown's Hole by 1839. It was a favorite wintering area. Since it was protected from winter winds by surrounding mountains and enjoyed a slightly higher temperature and less snow, cattle and horses could be wintered here. Sealed off at both ends by deep canyons, it was a natural corral. Powell reported large herds of cattle both in 1869 and 1871, as did the Hayden Survey in 1870. Tradition also has it that Powell took out the apostrophe and changed "Hole" to "Park."

Although it is a propitious wintering place, there was little permanent settlement until the 1870s, and the families—Bassett, Hoy, and Crouse—provide as much lively history as the outlaws, with whom they coexisted on practical and pragmatic terms. Roughly between 1875 and 1905, Browns Park was both a way station of a cattle-rustling route that led from Hole-in-the-Wall, Wyoming, to Robbers Roost on the San Rafael Swell in Utah, and a more or less permanent hideout for many who found total honesty a personal encumbrance.

The arrival of the railroad through Rock Springs and Green River, Wyoming, brought with it an era of cattle barons. Untold thousands of cattle were shipped and driven to Wyoming, Montana, Utah, and Nevada, requiring large numbers of cowboys. Only men with large capital could operate on such a grand scale, and they were generally unsympathetic, to put it gently, to the aspirations of small upstart operators. Cowboys who had ambitions to become ranchers were thwarted by monopolistic companies, and many turned to rustling, with ingenious and malevolent energy. It was the custom of the range that mavericks could be branded by whoever found them, and from this it was only a short step to culling out and rebranding those that undeniably belonged to someone else. There were many ways to change a brand, and an artistically altered brand could not be positively detected unless the animal was killed and the original scar examined from the inside. The outlaws' Wagon Wheel brand could cover almost any other mark and soon became recognized as a universal rustler's brand, and any animal decorated with it could reasonably have been expected to have been stolen.

The isolated fastness of Browns Park provided ideal storage for illegal cattle. As it lay at the junction of three states, a herd could be driven over the state line easily and quickly, and the law was notably reluctant to enter. (Neither did any of the three states, Wyoming, Utah, or Colorado, ever collect any taxes or spend any money for schools, roads, or bridges in the park.) All the assorted refugees from the law had intimate knowledge of dim trails and widely spaced water holes, and since they had as little compunction about shooting a sheriff from the back as the front, sheriffs became dedicatedly apathetic when it came to Browns Park. Members of the "Wild Bunch" flourished in these years, led by the redoubtable George Parker, better known as Butch Cassidy. The group became known as "that wild bunch from Brown's Hole" because of their overenthusiastic gunplay at whatever town they chose to celebrate Saturday night, usually Vernal or Rock Springs. But it is said that they always generously repaid whatever damage they caused, and if not friendly with the towns' elders, yet they were seldom betrayed. In Rock Springs or the work camps of the Union Pacific, everyone seemed aware that cattle brought into town were rustled, but it seemed a waste of time just to kill a steer in order to read the brand wrong side out, and beef on the table was beef and never mind its provenance.

THE AFTERNOON river is golden and olive and clear, the surface netted with debris from rising water. Ripples pattern the sandy bottom, sinking into shadowed pools. Three feet beneath, crisp dark fronds weave in all the various filamentous, intertwining subsurface currents. Often a single plant grows, forming a mound on the bottom, where it catches sand that builds up around its roots. As the current flows over, it tends to form a vortex that eats away sand on the downstream side, eventually loosening the plant and tumbling it away. Since underwater plants spread largely by vegetative means, the tufts and handfuls floating in the currents beneath help to colonize downstream.

On the left bank, the stone building beneath the cottonwoods was the old Jarvie store, modernized with an irrigation pump and a new trailer. John Jarvie, who established the first post office in the park and ran the store here, was murdered by a half-breed and his partner in 1909, the body set adrift in a skiff, a grisly flotsam found months later in Lodore Canyon. One of the few ferry crossings in Browns Park lay between Jesse Ewing Creek and the Jarvie Ranch, where the river banks are open and low. A mile below is the site of abandoned Bridgeport Post Office, Browns Park's connection with the outside world between 1881 and 1887. After it was closed the lack of mail delivery isolated the park's inhabitants; mail could be brought in monthly from Vernal, at $50 a run, but the road was so hazardous in winter that the postman refused to deliver. Another short-lived post office was established in 1889 on the Bassett ranch, and after that the mail came only weekly from Maybell, Colorado, until modern rural free delivery.

Whiskey Creek slips in through a terrace that it has notched deeply. In recent years many of the streams of Browns Park have renewed downcutting. The result is a lowering of the water table and a change from the grasslands, so characteristic of the park in trapper days, to the greasewood deserts we find when we get off river.

Thinking that the rapids are over, I am pleasantly surprised to hear the river's burbling float upstream and to enter a narrow rock-studded reach. Although the current switches through the rocks, the river steers us and we bob and swivel through. The rock-garden rapids precede the windless respite of Swallow Canyon. Now that the birds are gone for the year, it seems ghostly quiet. It is a small, charming canyon cut through a spur of the Uinta Mountains that projects northward. This whole area was once covered by the softer layers of the Browns Park Formation, on which an ancient river system initially established its course. When the river cut completely through, it reached the harder quartzites of the Uinta Mountain Group beneath. Confined in a channel determined originally in the softer strata, it continued cutting in the same channel, into this spur, a geologic process defined by Powell as superposition.

On a low ledge toward the mouth of the canyon, a beaver works on his lodge, stuffing sticks under a triangular overhang, the only one we see in Browns Park. Crouse Creek enters the river just below the mouth of Swallow Canyon, a lovely shaded slot of a canyon with green thickets. Butch Cassidy allegedly had a cabin high on a sandstone ledge up the canyon where Mrs. Crouse delivered jam and goodies. Perhaps, in a time of more open hospitality, Cassidy was a personable addition to a lonely, isolated household. Or perhaps the fact that he often left his hostess a five- or ten-dollar gold piece under his plate assured him of a devoted welcome wherever he hitched his horse.

One of the triumvirate of early Browns Park families, Charley

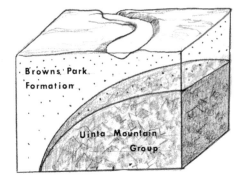

SWALLOW CANYON: SUPERPOSITION

1. The Green River established its course on the easily eroded Browns Park Formation.

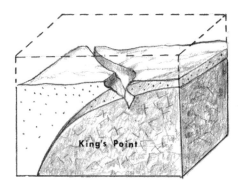

2. As it cut through the softer formation, it reached the hard quartzites of a northward extending spur of the Uinta Mountains (called King's Point, after geologist Clarence King, leader of the Fortieth Parallel Survey). Its course was then superposed on the harder formation.

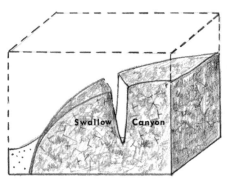

3. The river, with heavy post-glacial flows of water, and rejuvenated by uplift in the Uinta Mountains, cut a narrow canyon through the hard rock spur to form Swallow Canyon.

Crouse, bought this bottomland and canyon in 1880 and raised horses here. He was a salty character, as handy with a knife as others were with firearms, and possessed of a quick and mean temper. One of the ferries in Browns Park was run by a Negro named Albert Welhouse, known as "Speck" for his blotched complexion. Filled with a little too much liquid enthusiasm, Welhouse and Crouse engaged in a wrestling match that turned nasty when the Negro threw Crouse. Crouse retaliated by slashing him in the groin and abdomen. Browns Park first aid was simple and effective: Minnie Crouse dumped her supply of flour on the massive wounds and wrapped him in a blanket. Charley Crouse reportedly nursed him back to health, not out of altruism, but because the going rate for posting bond for murder cost more than the medication.

At the Colorado border we enter Browns Park National Wildlife Refuge. As a migratory wildfowl area it is dependent upon yearly flooding. When Flaming Gorge Dam was built, the yearly inundations stopped and wildfowl populations declined sharply. Now nesting sites are periodically reflooded and many flocks again nest here.

We pass beneath the only car crossing in the park, a narrow suspension bridge built in the 1950s that bears a sign at each end: "200 sheep or 30 cattle or 3½ gross tons." The river gradient is slowed to less than two feet per mile and I feel as if in a painted canoe upon a painted river. Silt carried in from side canyons builds aprons out into the bottom; although the water is clear, they have a way of slipping up beneath the boat, and once the canoe knifes into the sand and anchors stubbornly, it needs much poling and pushing to get it free. All along the river the squawbush is a glorious tangerine; rose bushes are stained a deeper bronze-red. Vines of clematis overlie many shrubs, blurring outlines with their soft white seedheads. Grasses glow golden red, almost henna: scarlet and orange and salmon, a resonant land-scape doubled in the water.

At low water it is impossible to see much of the countryside so we disembark and climb a forty-foot terrace above the river. Many large anthills are made of fine gravel, sprinkled on top with bits and pieces of rabbitbrush that looks freshly harvested and left outside to dry. Downriver, J. S. Hoy Bottom is accented with black-trunked cottonwoods turning molten gold, the grasses beneath, brass. Dozens of big snags and whole trees recline in the water, branches stretched out in supplication. Across the river, Warren Bottom is stalked with sedges that shine copper in the ruffling breeze. But up here the terrain is windswept and dry, with only rabbitbrush, buffalo grass, silver sage, and small gray-green plants curling into themselves for winter.

J. S. Hoy brought a Texas rancher's cattle into the park to winter, and, recognizing the park's unique possibilities, he encouraged his brothers, Valentine and Harry, to settle here. The Hoys had covetous dreams of making Browns Park their own preserve, never accomplished because of the unwelcome tenacity of the Crouse and Bassett families.

Western clematis or virgins bower
(*Clematis ligusticifolia*)

Valentine Hoy was the first of the "law and order" men, deter-mined, since the law appeared disinterested, to stamp out rustling and to disperse the outlaws in the park. Ironically, his death did just that. He was shot while leading a posse in 1898, and this activated the latent citizenship of every resident, and for the first time, a sheriff from Colorado entered the park. At what must have been one of the most jaw-clenching trials in history, J. S. Hoy presided as justice of the peace for the Precinct of Lodore at the trial of Harry Tracy, the man who killed his brother. Tracy's companion was lynched and hanged from the Bassetts' corral gatepost, since there were no big hanging trees that far back from the river, and left there for a week.

The decisive exodus occurred in 1900. A man named Tom Horn was hired to eliminate certain undesirables for $200 a head. He shot Matt Rash while Rash ate lunch. (Rash was engaged to Ann Bassett at the time, and she believed that Horn had been hired by the Hoys.) Next, Horn killed Isom Dart while Dart was answering a call of na-ture, surely the epitome of efficient untactfulness. Since no one fancied being next, there was a unanimous exit of outlaws. Although rustling was not entirely abandoned, large-scale rustling was, and the more dedicated proponents moved on. Besides, rustling itself was losing its economic impetus with changing times and the influx of sheep, which no cattle rustler considered worth stealing.

To the north lies Cold Spring Mountain, where Herbert Bassett brought his Virginia-born wife after the Civil War, moving in with his uncle, Sam Bassett, a retired scout on the Overland Trail. Herbert Bassett was an asthmatic and appeared content to let his spirited wife, Elizabeth, enjoy the plotting and scheming that attended survival in the park. A strong-minded woman, adored by those who chose her company, intensely disliked by those who did not, she was, among other things, a prototype feminist, a Machiavellian conniver, local surgeon after Browns Park's only doctor died. And perhaps even a cattle rustler. Called "Magpie" by the Indians for her loquaciousness, she was an intelligent, generous, resourceful, ingenious, assertive, and vivacious woman. She had two daughters, Josie and Ann; the latter described her mother, mounted on her thoroughbred saddle horse, Chalky, dressed in a handsome dark blue habit, as "a picture to remember."

One of the few times the Guelph and Ghibelline relationship of the Bassetts and Hoys was abrogated occurred when the Middlesex Cattle Company, a Texas outfit whose massive herds would have starved out local cattle, attempted to run their stock in Browns Park. Elizabeth Bassett's fine hand undoubtedly was behind the schemes to prevent this invasion. She was accused, with others of her coterie, of rustling five hundred head of Middlesex cattle, and to avoid being caught with the evidence, of driving them over the cliffs at Lodore.

The first white child born in Browns Park was Ann Bassett, a willful and elusive spirit. Schooled in the wilds of Browns Park and a superb horsewoman, her lately-widowed father sent her East to be "finished" at Miss Porter's. Possessed of a flinty vocabulary that could make the toughest ranch hand blush and a flagrant disregard for the legal restrictions of ordinary mortals, the boarding-school experience was short-lived. She went back home and tried to run Browns Park her way, and if she was not always successful, at least life around her was never dull. Josie, too, was a lively woman, who recalled and recounted the history made on her doorstep.

Women in history along the Green are few: the nameless Indian squaws; the first woman in the park, "Snapping Annie" Parsons; the elusive Madame Forrestall; George Bagg's wandering-eyed wife; the resourceful Minnie Crouse; and Elizabeth, Josie, and Ann Bassett. The fortitude, spirit, and intelligence of the last three embellish the history of the whole river.

WEATHER IS BLOWING in from the west, thickening clouds tarnishing the silvered river. The vertical knife-edge bays of the Gates of Lodore now loom on the horizon, raw and treeless, brighter than the olive-green mountains. To the north a single building stands on a low river terrace: Lodore Schoolhouse.

A rough road leads through a leggy cottonwood grove to the school and the graveyard beside it. A large marble headstone marks the grave of Harry Hoy. And others. The graves are heaped with big river stones, grown over with cheat grass and evening-primrose, some graves fenced, some not. Several are identified with simple metal markers from the mortuary in Craig, Colorado, a metal frame with a stamped metal plaque fitted in, or a cracked glass over a slip of paper. Wind worries the grass. A once-vivid-fuchsia plastic rose, now faded nearly white, pitches across the ground, revolving to show its original color. There is a constant restless whispering, a snatching sound in the wind. The soil is pale and rocky and hard, laid under a wide sky and an unquiet wind.

Squawbush (*Rhus trilobata*)

The building is not the original schoolhouse where Speck Welhouse presided over the bar at dances and Herbert Bassett collected guns at the door. Browns Park children now go to a newer school on Vermilion Creek, although this building is still used for hoedowns and meetings. Today it stands empty. Inside, a forlorn still-life of pot-bellied stove, metal card tables, and plastic spoons; outside, a white plastic cup overends across the ground with a scrabbling sound.

The hitching rack stands in front, weathered gray, where reluctant children no doubt left their transportation. I stand on the porch facing out to the southwest. The river shimmers below. The cottonwoods rustle. The Gates of Lodore stand sharp and forbidding but enticing. The river dominates the landscape—fluid, evocative, animated. How any child could repeat multiplication tables with this Pied Piper view is beyond me.

We push off into a probing wind and changing weather, a drying aspiration in the air, geese restive, a turning of the day, a veering of the season. Groves with hundreds of cottonwoods line both sides of the river, some green, some gold. Geese, standing on the sand bars, are beginning to flock up for winter. They beat the river to a white froth as they spring into the air.

The topographical map shows a homestead cabin downstream; actually there are several buildings. I stand in the center of the smallest cabin, still partially roofed with willow withes, and I can almost touch all four walls. It has a small fireplace and a window, just my height, for leaning out of. It has, in short, charm, and I envy the wife who set up housekeeping here. The other house has a sod roof, its grasses quivering in the wind. One wall is fallen out; papers tacked up, year after year, for insulation, now peel off in reverse sequence: Denver *Post*, 1934; *Woman's Home Companion*, 1933; *Saturday Evening Post*, 1930. Outside an upright piano lies on its back in the grass, keys gone, the sounding board still strung, creating an abstract pattern of pegs and strings, thin shadows and rust. I run a fingernail across the wires; the sound is faintly tinny, lightly harplike, evanescent, no aftertones, weaving dry in the cottonwood air.

Just downstream, an old cable stretches across the river. A wooden car swings lightly in the middle. Usually the cars, if they remain, are anchored to one of the suspension pillars at the side. This one sways forlornly in the wind, going nowhere from noplace, and as we go beneath it, it seems symbolic of this landscape, this time of day, this time of year.

VERMILION CREEK cuts through the pale soil of a terrace to enter the river. Tamarisk turn orange along the shore, brazen against a blurred watercolor sky. Twenty geese take off from a sand bar downstream in a glorious ruffle and flourish of wings; thirty-six more follow, honking. The river begins to cloud with silt, and from the Gates of Lodore down there are no more glimpses of rippled sand, cobbled beds, or streaming algae and moss.

Fort Davy Crockett lay on a curve of bottomland where Vermilion Creek enters the Green, probably built about 1836 (the year of the Alamo), near the site of Baptiste Brown's cabin, by three traders named Thompson, Craig, and Sinclair. It never was, in truth, a fort, just a rude post, and opinions of it depended upon how glad the traveler was to see even minimal comfort. Thomas Farnham, after a very difficult journey in late summer of 1839, blessed it:

> Such kindness can be appreciated fully by those only who have enjoyed it in such places; who have seen it manifested in its own way; by those only, who have starved and thirsted in these deserts and been welcomed, and made thrice welcome, after months of weary wandering, to "Fort David Crockett." . . . It was a bright ethereal night. The Fort stood in the shade of the wild and dark cliffs, while the light of the moon shone on the western peaks, and cast a deeper darkness into the inaccessible gorges

on the face of the mountains. The Sheetskadee flowed silently among the alders—

Dr. Adolphus Wislizenus, who arrived but a few days after Farnham, was less enamored:

> The fort itself is the worst thing of the kind that we have seen on our journey. It is a low one-story building, constructed of wood and clay, with three connecting wings, and no enclosure. Instead of cows the fort had only some goats. In short, the whole establishment appeared somewhat poverty-stricken, for which reason it is also known to the trappers by the name of Fort Misery (*Fort de Misere*) . . . our store of meat was exhausted, and we had hoped to supply ourselves here with new provisions. But the people at the fort seemed to be worse off than we were. The day before they had bought a lean dog from the Indians for five dollars, and considered its meat a delicacy. I, too, tried some of it, and found its taste not so bad.

Trade was carried on amicably with both Indians and whites, although relationships were strained when Thompson stole some horses from the Snake Indians in the fall of 1839, and a party including Joe Meek, Joe Walker, Kit Carson, William Craig, and Robert Newell had to go downriver on the ice to retrieve them and restore them to the Snakes, and get back to Brown's Hole in time for Christmas. The post was in operation through that winter, but was abandoned in February, 1840, because of Indian hostility, and was in ruins by 1844 when General Frémont's party crossed the river from the west and camped here.

The river bends south, to a confrontation with the Gates of Lodore. On the left bank, patches of dark rock of the Uinta Mountain Group appear beneath the Browns Park Formation—a contact between the oldest and youngest rock formations in Browns Park, one laid over two billion years ago, eroded, now capped by a formation laid less than sixty-three million years ago. The dark rock builds toward the south, to a foreboding of mountains into which the river disappears. As Sam Bassett wrote in his journal, November, 1852, when he entered Brown's Hole: "To the South, a range of uncontested beauty of contour, its great stone mouth drinking a river."

9

FRIDAY, THE 8TH: *we proceeded down the river about two miles, where it again enters between two mountains and affording a channel even more contracted than before. As we passed along between these massy walls, which in a great degree excluded from us the rays of heaven and presented a surface as impassable as their body was impregnable, I was forcibly struck with the gloom which spread over the countenances of my men; they seemed to anticipate (and not far distant, too) a dreadful termination of our voyage, and I must confess that I partook in some degree of what I supposed to be their feelings, for things around us had truly an awful appearance. We soon came to a dangerous rapid which we passed over with a slight injury to our boats. A mile lower down, the channel became so obstructed by the intervention of large rocks over and between which the water dashed with such violence as to render our passage in safety impracticable. The cargoes of our boats were therefore a second time taken out and carried about two hundred yards, to which place, after much labor, our boats were descended by means of cords.*

GENERAL WILLIAM ASHLEY, 1825, *Journal*

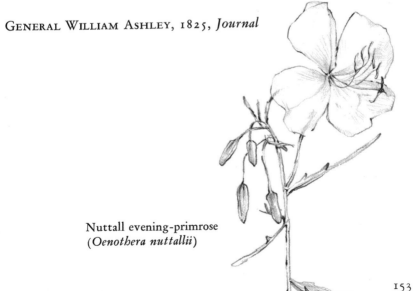

Nuttall evening-primrose
(*Oenothera nuttallii*)

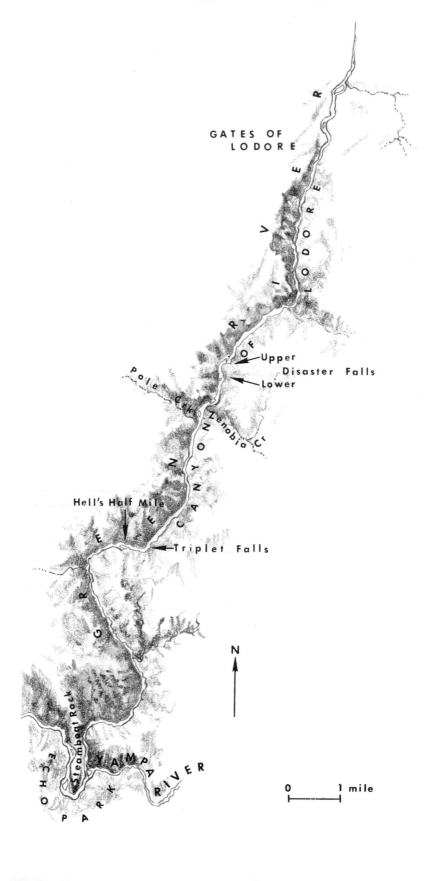

GATES OF
LODORE

Upper
Disaster Falls
Lower

Pole Ck.

Zenobia Cr

Hell's Half Mile

Triplet Falls

N

Steamboat Rock

YAMPA RIVER

ECHO

PARK

0   1 mile

THE GATES OF LODORE
TO ECHO PARK

LODORE: a word full of dolorous long O sounds, a heavily romantic name that matches a sonorous canyon. One of Powell's crew on the 1869 expedition, Andy Hall, recalled a poem from schooldays, "The Cataract of Lodore," written by Robert Southey, the nineteenth-century English poet. It is a verbose poem, a compendium of rhymes, but it has a vibrant language that somehow seems appropriate to this canyon the more one knows of it. Despite objections from a chauvinistic member of the crew who felt that it was wrong to apply a foreign-inspired title to an American canyon, it became Lodore and it could be nothing else.

Each canyon of the Green has its own distinctive presence but none is as dramatic as Lodore. The cliffs rise two thousand feet, immediate, all the more striking because of the pale landscape from which they spring, almost without transition. The Gates of Lodore hinge inward, cruelly joined, hard rock, ominous, and when mists skulk low between the cliffs, they become an engraving by Gustave Doré for one of Dante's lower levels of hell.

I see the Gates of Lodore next on a forbiddingly chill October afternoon, with the sound of leaves rattling dry over the ground, the sky as overcast and brooding as one in a Brontë novel. I am one of a small group, a few passengers but mostly boatmen, running with Ken Sleight on his last trip of the season: Dan Lehman, Clair and Bob Quist, with all of whom I've run before, and a couple more. People are milling about, getting rafts rigged, checking and loading gear, distributing life jackets.

It is a time of transition on the river, some green still evident, not all yellow yet, some rabbitbrush still in bloom, some in seed, some wind-cleaned, some not. The wind issues straight out of Lodore, flowing the big sagebrush bushes into feathers. Shredded gray bark pulls away from beneath an old sagebrush trunk as thick as my arm. Cottonwood leaves scuttle across the sand like yellow crabs. Shreds and snippets—ivory twigs, copper oak leaves, bits of bark—slip, hang, flutter, snag, snatch free and catch again, beat frantically with the wind, held against going, a season on the wane but not allowed to leave. The few leaves on a scrub oak are just tacked to the branch tips; the wind worries off more and sends them spinning. The willows are already shorn of yellow, and as the reds and yellows go, warmth seeps out of the landscape, bleaching to November gray, a draining of the golden time.

The river answers back to each gust of wind in a thicker rippling, more audible, coming up into the bank and its tiny gullies in determined waves. At the water's edge is a flat area where the waves lick against and under a narrow scalloped shelf. On a thin sand spit beneath the water, thin ripples are laid, an inch apart, parallel to the shore. The water eddying in and out runs the sand in tiny clouds, leaving a hesitant line of black debris at high-water mark. Sun sweeps honey across the river and it is at once warmer, and then immediately the shadows sweep upstream and it is chill again. Even when the wind stops for a minute where I am there is always a restless simmering somewhere else, and then it is back to whistle in my ears, water my eyes, blow sand in my teeth. The wind is bothersome, but it belongs, a part of the river and its perimeters.

When low-lying clouds break away from the cliffs, a bank of snow-frosted trees materializes out of the fog, a precise line of white beginning far up the slope, the visualization of the separation between freezing and nonfreezing, fall and winter. Wind blows ripples upstream, against the current, *à rebours*. Times of transition seem as difficult for nature as for people.

LODORE CANYON, where the river breaches the end of a mountain range, is such a striking dichotomy that it could not help but intrigue the geologists who pondered the reason behind this puzzling passage. The relationship of the Uinta Mountains and the Green River led Powell and his colleagues to develop a theory of drainage that des-

Golden rabbitbrush
(*Chrysothamnus nauseous*)

POSSIBLE SEQUENCE OF GREEN RIVER DRAINAGE THROUGH LODORE CANYON

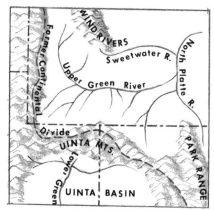 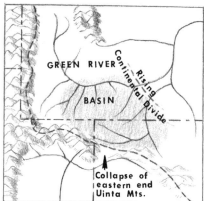

1. Some 25 million years ago, the Continental Divide lay west and south of the present Divide in this area, along the crest of the Uinta Mountains. The upper Green River drained eastward into the North Platte River; the lower Green River drained south from the Uintas through the Uinta Basin, much as it does today.

2. Browns Formation (shaded) began to fill the valley north of the Uinta Mountains. Some 12–15 million years ago, the eastern end of the Uinta Mountains collapsed. At approximately the same time, the present Continental Divide began to rise to the northeast.

ignates streams as antecedent (the river here before the mountains, cutting down at the same rate as the mountains rose beneath), or superposed (the river letting down through soft rock into underlying hard rock and then confined in that channel, as at Swallow Canyon). Powell was the first to speculate about Lodore, and proposed it as an example of antecedence; another geologist, S. F. Emmons, immediately countered, citing it as an example of superposition.

Current geological thinking accepts superposition, plus stream capture and a complex series of events to the north that caused a change in drainage. A relatively long period of crustal stability followed the first uplift of the Uinta Mountains, during which much erosion took place. Renewed faulting and warping caused drainage to begin to run eastward, cutting the valley now known as Browns Park. Into this newly excavated valley the Browns Park Formation was deposited, probably filling the whole valley. Toward the end of the deposition of this formation, but mostly afterward, the eastward end

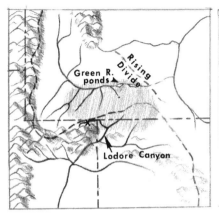 

3. Between 2–12 million years ago, streams draining off the Uinta Mountains flowed not only to the north and south but eastward as well, and such an east-flowing stream (*) began to turn south, initiating cutting in what would become Lodore Canyon. The upper Green River, blocked by the rising Continental Divide, began to pond on the Browns Park Formation.

(Adapted from Hansen, *The Geologic Story of the Uinta Mountains*, 1969, U.S.G.S. Bulletin 1291, pp. 62–65)

4. With rejuvenation of the entire drainage system with renewed uplift, and a warming post-glacial climate that released massive amounts of water, the Green River began major canyon cutting, such as Swallow Canyon. The upper Green River was captured by an east-west stream running on the north side of the Uinta Mountains, and diverted into Lodore Canyon and the lower Green River drainage. The ancestral Green, to the north, disappeared, although evidence of its course remains in the adjusted drainage patterns of present-day streams and lacustrine deposits.

of the Uinta Mountain arch collapsed. The compressional stresses that had domed up the mountains relaxed, allowing the eastern end to drop some 4,500 feet as a graben, a large trough bounded by faults. The crest of the Uinta Mountains had formed the Continental Divide, but the collapse of the eastern end altered the Divide's direction, and the present Divide across central Wyoming began to rise, blocking the ancestral Green so that it could no longer flow east into the Platte River–Gulf of Mexico drainage system. The river ponded into a chain of lakes.

As surface movements became more active from time to time, the river was impelled to cut deeper; most of the canyon cutting was preglacial. Rejuvenation of the entire drainage system instituted major canyon cutting. The Green River bore down through the soft Browns Park Formation, letting down in some places into the hard rock of the Uinta Mountain Group as it has at Swallow Canyon and Lodore. In the latter, given impetus by the thousand-foot difference in elevation between the Green River Basin and the Uinta Basin, the Green River shot nearly a straight channel, a deep narrow gorge, in what Powell was to call Lodore.

And, once the river drained south through Lodore, it entered a different drainage system, that of the Colorado River, and flowed, as it does now, into the Gulf of California.

THE FIRST EVENING out I climb up the bank to find the pipe laid by John Grounds in 1934. Wade and Curtis, for whom this campground was named, were only caretakers for Mr. Grounds, who operated a tourist camp here, boating passengers down from what is now the ranger station (he built the small log cabin still standing by the river there). According to Mr. Grounds, "We also put in more than a quarter of a mile of two inch pipe from a spring down to the lower cabin. Here, we had a strawberry bed and a number of fruit trees. Another thing to be remembered is, that when we did these things, it was right in the darkest days of the Depression. In 1935, we were operating four boats between the two camps." When Grounds left at the beginning of World War II, his squatter's rights were lost and the land returned to the government.

I claw my way up to a prow of rock, one of a series of fiercely jointed battlements. The somber aspect of the inner canyon comes from the combination of dark purple-red rock, dark green trees, and dark shadows, combining in certain lights to a lurid Victorian red. Even from the air, on a summer morning, this canyon is a brooding, dark-shadowed slot.

Above and across the river is a wider terrace, from which huge buttresses spring, ballasting the base of another steep, vertical rise. The river cut some fifteen hundred feet into the canyon and then slowed, widening rather than cutting down. Probably uplift in this area rejuvenated the river, giving it impetus to erode to its present base some seven hundred feet lower, forming this two-tiered canyon. The river cuts most effectively at periods of high runoff, the carrying power of the river increasing geometrically with increasing velocity. The erosive energy of a large volume of fast water is extremely effective. Then, instead of carrying the sands and silts it usually does, it carries larger particles, its higher waters plucking rocks off banks and using them as pestles in a mortar. When Julius Stone entered the canyon in 1909, it was being cored for a dam, and the depth measurements provide a clue to what lies beneath the opaque waters:

> At times of low water the river is only a few feet deep, but at flood time the sand, gravel, and boulders of the channel are stirred to great depths. Borings near the mouth of the canyon at the side of a proposed dam which would control the flood waters of the Green River for purposes of irrigation, indicate that a channel has been scoured out to a depth of one hundred and three feet below low water level, but six miles below the proposed dam the drill penetrated to a depth of one hundred and sixty feet without encountering bed rock. This means either that the river scours to a depth of more than one hundred and sixty feet, or that the canyon was once deeper than it is now and has been partly refilled with sand and boulders.

The river through Lodore has an average drop of twenty feet per mile, still an actively eroding river.

Below me, thin rapids like pulled silk bound a sand bar, a gentle hissing sometimes slipping up the cliffside. The boatmen work on shortening some oars, sawing off and whittling down the handles. It could be an illustration out of Major Powell's diary. The reflections in the river begin to clear; the wind is dying and the river is slowing. Looking down into the canyon, I am suddenly depressed. I have a strong sense that canyons are not for people, they're for rivers. Canyons are for going through and coming out of, not for staying in, and now in the chill drizzle of the October evening I feel the coldness of rock and running water as an ice edge that goes through to the marrow. Perhaps it is the somberness of the canyon, perhaps it is the knowledge of dangerous rapids: I feel an unease in Lodore I feel nowhere else on the river—as Powell felt it, "a black portal to a region of doom."

I rationalize that I am cold and hungry and therefore my spirits are low. But there is something beyond low blood sugar. It is the oppression of the bloody rock walls of Lodore itself.

ONCE WE ARE on the river the noise of rapids comes upstream all day, vibrating off the rock walls. Cascades of thick water pour over rocks. At a turning, the cliff is masses of light and shadow and the big river is marbled and swirled with silt. A trio of Rocky Mountain sheep—ram, ewe, and small lamb—walk a short way from the river, turn, and watch the rafts go by. Reedgrasses screen the shore, drying into pale yellow plumes.

The river jogs right and begins its fast drop of twenty-two feet per mile for the next ten miles. Ahead a huge rock anchors a line of splashing water, a sharp turn, and nothing beyond: Disaster Falls, a series of rapids consuming almost a mile of river, and in its time, many boats, a frothing series of standing waves and sheets of sound. Standing on the bank, I listen to the boatmen evaluate the rapid. These big rapids are relatively stable features, since the huge rocks that cause them are moved only during rare flood periods, periods which now are minimized by the dam upstream. What does change in these rapids is the water level, at different times both of the year and of the day. The water shoots by, foam webbing the surface, a roiling rich milky tan, piles of water, a polemical confrontation of river and rock.

Ashley entered Disaster Falls in 1825 and capsized. In 1849 the second recorded descent of the Green was led by a young bullwhacker named William Manly. The leader of Manly's wagon train announced that they would go only as far as Salt Lake City and winter there. Impatient to reach the gold fields, uneasy about job possibilities in the winter, Manly and seven others announced that they were striking off on their own, and did so when the wagon train reached Green River near Fontenelle Creek, advised by both the surgeon and captain on the train that this "stream came out on the Pacific Coast, and that we had no obstacles except cataracts, which they had heard were pretty bad."

When Manly stumbled on a sunken barge that had once been used as a ferry, he took it as a good omen. They patched it up, loaded their gear, and when the wagon trail pulled out for Salt Lake City, Manly and crew pointed down the Green. Near Ashley Falls the barge wedged hopelessly on the rocks, so they hewed two fifteen-foot canoes out of pine boles, lashed them into a rude catamaran, and when this didn't hold all their gear, built a third. Manly's group made it through Lodore, Whirlpool Canyon, Split Mountain, and Desolation Canyon, but south of Gray Canyon were deterred from continuing by a wise Indian. They packed out overland to California, where Manly published his account of this journey forty-five years later.

Here, at Disaster Falls, Powell in 1869 momentarily lost one of his wooden boats, the *No-Name*, and all his barometers. Not until lighter, flat-bottomed boats were designed and built, and a different technique employed for running rapids, was the fast water in Lodore handled with any aplomb. Both were the product of the ingenuity of Nathaniel Galloway, a trapper from Vernal. Powell had had his boats built on the assumption that, if they were sturdy enough, they could withstand the buffeting of water and rock; they were oak-planked and double-ribbed, with decked compartments fore and aft, heavy boats that had to be manned by two oarsmen. The oarsmen rowed backward into the kicking water, rowing as hard as possible to go faster than the current and to provide control for a third man at the rudder. The rudderman faced forward, tried to steer, and shouted orders to the oarsmen over the pound of the water.

The "Galloway method" of running rapids was to face down-stream—that is, rowing backward. It is a technique still used on the river. The advantages are that the boatman not only can see what is ahead but maintain better control, able to go slower or faster than the current; although usually the former, a strong stroke or two gives considerable acceleration and control. The disadvantage in rowing backward is that the boatman does not have the leverage of a normal stroke; most boatmen counter this by quartering into the tongue, assuming a position from which they can turn either way.

Galloway's best-known trip is described in *Canyon Country*, written by Julius Stone, a trip that began September 12, 1909, and followed a free river from Green River, Wyoming, to the Gulf of California. Stone was an Ohio industrialist who had boats built to Galloway's design, an outdoorsman who grumbled when Galloway wouldn't let him run all the rapids in Lodore. No mean boatman himself, Stone characterized Galloway as so dextrous that "one would not be surprised to see him run a boat on a heavy dew if it were necessary." Two years later, Ellsworth and Emery Kolb, also starting from Green River, and also using Galloway-type boats, ran every rapid all the way to the Gulf, a journey entertainingly chronicled in *Through the Grand Canyon from Wyoming to Mexico*.

Lodore was successfully run by three French kayakers in the late 1930s; one of the three was Geneviève de Comont, who went all the way down to Lees Ferry in her sixteen-foot folding kayak. The principal load on the trip was beer, causing river historian O. Dock Marston to remark that they seemed "to fear bad drinking water more than bad running water." Since Lodore is now part of Dinosaur National Monument, only specified raft sizes are allowed for safety.

Currently acceptable boats are large neoprene rafts that have been described by Mr. Marston (a wooden-boat devotee) as "nearly foolproof, for large parties, especially those containing women, children, the lame, the halt, and the blind."

After we run Disaster, I look back upstream to see the drop that didn't seem like much until we went over it, cushioned by a great sheet of water through which rocks are darkly visible. But I am finding it difficult to be spectator. The boatman intervenes between passenger and river; it is his skill and judgment, not yours, that reads the water; it is his hand, not yours, that guides the boat. It is he, in short, who has the fun and thee, the passenger, who gets wet.

WALKING DOWN the portage trail beside Triplet Falls, I scuff a soil almost as red as the rocks; even lichens on the stone seem to partake of the same dark color. I recall that Powell portaged two and lined the third of the three rapids, and when I come level with the top one, I understand. Powell estimated a fall of "15 feet in 10 yards" with the last short and abrupt run of Triplet "tumbling down 20 feet over a group of rocks that thrust their dark heads through the foam."

When the flow of the river changes from ordinary streaming flow to shooting flow, characteristic of rapids, the velocity increases greatly and there is a lowering of water surface—hence that sensation of declination when the raft sweeps into the rapid. When the opposite occurs, the surface water rises, causing stationary waves and backwater effects. I stand, twenty feet above the river, immobilized with fascination. The entrance to the first rapid rolls right into a turbulent tail wave with an irregular configuration that implies rocks beneath, then swings short against the opposite cliff. The main current is into the cliff, and a boat pushed into this wall with this much force flips in a second. The main push of the current bounces off the wall and shoots between it and a rock, forming a gateway that is just wide enough to wedge a boat but not let it through.

A huge boulder studs the water below, the first of a line that stretches to push the tongue of the rapid far to the right. The water is roiling, flailing, falling back on itself, and without sunlight it looks cold and mean. I pick up a stick and throw it as far as I can out into the river. It lands in the main current, sweeps into a trough, immediately up-ends, flies out of the water and flips back into a tremendous ivory spume of a wave and then disappears for good, dragged underwater by the current to appear who knows how far downstream. The back waves curl and fume, three to five feet high, ten to twenty feet wide. Their constant roaring is punctuated by pulsations that build higher and slap resoundingly on the large boulder right beneath me, hypnotically beautiful, hypnotically dreadful.

Walking back through the woods I can still hear the rapids boom, sound trespassing into this gentle, subdued land world: pale gray-blue berries on the junipers, a stalk of snake grass with one pure coral segment as if strung with an Indian bead. The path is spongy with pine needles and huge mats of haircap moss, luxuriantly green from all the moisture. But always, sifting through the filtering green, I hear the heavy beat of the rapids.

I ride with Bob Quist. Had he not chosen to become a boatman (and a very fine one) he was probably born eighty years too late—he should have done music-hall recitations: his vocabulary is Rabelaisian, his timing, dramatic. He takes Southey's poem and opulently embellishes it with gestures (no small matter when you have two oars to cope with). Ahead the rapids ruffle the top of the water. Bob gets a firm grip on the oars and bellows over the pound of the river, "Hang on!" The raft bounds into slick and opalescent troughs, into water spun and syruped into thick loops—magnificent water, charged with energy, revealing little of what enrages it. Each wave is a watery lion's paw, playfully smacking a gray mouse of a raft with strength to spare. It is pure river on the river's terms.

RAPIDS AT NIGHT are something else again. One night in Lodore I spread my ground cloth on a flat bar near the water where the sound of fast-moving water is insistent. Near the bank an eight-foot log is entrapped in a cluster of boulders. It floats free and wedges, floats and wedges, seeming to need just an inch more clearance to break through and go downriver. It is shiny brown, bobbing gently, just broaching the surface. The water swashes around it, curling and nudging, sheeting over, as if anxious to be rid of it. The log rocks as softly as if in a cradle. It has an air of patience, one stubby, craggy branch outstretched, some old sea monster brought to shore to die, an animal whose time is spent but not yet gone, bearing the brunt of the river, beyond pain.

The river at night loses the light that makes spray fanciful and rolls slick and darkening, sound ominously magnified, hundreds of cubic feet per second, a rushing that is the sound of power unhampered by tide, answering only to gravity, the cold heat of tons of silt abrading rocks to simpler size. The sound is unrelenting; there is no pause, no respite.

I sleep in stop-motion, awakening to think I've not been asleep but to see the constellations revolved. I lie on my back, sleeping bag gathered up to my nose, and watch for Orion to rise. I fall asleep and wake again, and there it is, a big dynamic constellation with the spirit and configuration of its name—a force stretched out from center, the vitality of diagonals striding out obliquely across the sky, the eternal hunter. The sound of the river, warmth, and Orion are the three points that determine my plane of empyreal existence.

HELL'S HALF MILE was not exactly Powell's preference for a rapid's name, since he tended more to the romantic, but he acquiesced to his men, who, after all, ran it—all the rapids in Lodore bear such straightforward names. The portage trail for Hell's Half Mile has almost as many boulders in it as the river. It is a bare dirt path, obviously well used. There is something about looking rapids over beforehand that adds another dimension to running—a different point of view, an apprehension that is akin to anticipation, a heightening of sensibility and awareness. It is a necessity in a canoe, and even with a raft on the bigger rapids; changing water level may alter the way in which a rapid is run, especially at lower water as in October.

Great red boulders have blasted downslope, forming a phalanx to the right. The only passage is pulled far to the left of the river, a broad tongue pouring and dropping through the passageway, straight into two large rocks with formidable holes on their downstream side, boat-sized holes with no room for maneuvering between. Position must be perfect or in missing the first rock the raft dumps into the second. After the initial drop, the water separates into channels of rock gardens and chutes, stretched and divided into shallows that would be infinitely easier to run at higher water. It is a rapid that demands a nicety of adjustment, measured in quarter oar strokes, finesse, skill, and confidence. Ken Sleight recommends that all passengers walk since the river is low enough to make the rapid dangerously difficult. Those who want to ride may do so. Most choose to walk, leaving but one passenger per boat. It never occurs to me not to go —once one accepts the river, one accepts it under all conditions. Dan

Lehman hands me two straps to tie onto the D-rings mounted on the pontoons so that when I sit centered on the cross tube, I will have something to hang on to, a necessity when the raft is wet and slippery and tilted at any angle except horizontal. I notice that the boatmen take time to secure duffel and gear more snugly, to check lines, oars, to bail out any remaining water.

We swing first out into the channel. The rapid begins suddenly. The straps go taut, the only reality in a suspended weightless spray-filled horizonless implosion. The bow springs high, the raft tilts steep, light comes through a carved screen of spray, a ten-foot wall perforated with sound. The boat swings and pivots. I hold my breath. I feel as if the top three layers of skin are gone in a total exhilaration of water streaming down my face, down my neck, totally soaked in spite of a rain suit, disembodied yet physically involved, aware of every rapid I've ever run, aware of superb boatmanship and a superb river.

Safely through the rapids, we pull ashore for lunch. I nearly trip coming off the raft, just making it to shore without falling in, muttering something about my luck not yet running out. To be helpful, I catch the bowline of the last boat coming in; it bounces off another raft and swings away. Instead of letting the rope play out, I simply hold on, knowing what is imminent but powerless to act. On the steep, muddy bank, I feel myself slide slowly and irrevocably down into the water until I am sitting waist deep, laughing so hard I can't get up.

THE RIVER cuts back in time. The Lodore Formation, named by Powell, appears on the crest of the ridge above Triplet Falls, and reaches the river at Alcove Creek, a somewhat sandier, smoother red, but still massive rock. Limestones, laid down 340 million years ago, form a gray cliff above it, rising like some bared reef a thousand feet above my head. At the end of the canyon, the river follows and then crosses the Mitten Park Fault, a dramatic fault erupting into a notched skyline. The Yampa River joins the Green at Echo Park, and the aggrandized Green slides along Steamboat Rock. Supposedly echoes come back sixfold or more off this rib of Weber Sandstone, hence Powell's name of Echo Park, called locally Pat's Hole.

The park is lovely, hazed with lavender rockcress in spring, gilded with cottonwoods in fall. There were ranchers and squatters in this

Globemallow
(*Sphaeralcea coccinea* var. *dissecta*)

inaccessible country as far back as the 1870s, and Pat Lynch probably came along about that time and lived here until his death in 1917. He was a Civil War veteran who claimed to have taken part in the battle of the *Monitor* and the *Merrimac*. He came west, thinking he had killed a man. Also having served a stint in the army, he drew pensions from both army and navy and was considered well-off by other settlers.

He lived several places along the Yampa and Green, added his personal petroglyph to a cliff of Indian designs, and left his own artifacts in an archeological site on the Yampa: suspender buttons and cartridge cases. I never go into Echo Park without half expecting to see him stalk out from the grove of cottonwoods, or at the very least to see his boot prints on the beach sand. He left, for whoever might come after, these often-quoted lines in one of the caves in which he slept, an inscription that transcends artifact and artifice:

> If in these caverns you shelter take
> Plais do to them no harm
> Lave everything you find around hanging up or on the ground.

His grave, long unknown, was found several years ago by Ernest and Billie Untermann, a husband and wife geological team who have done definitive work in this area. They located a fine white marble headstone, wreathed with cocklebur and globemallow. It read: "Pat Lynch, U.S.N." A large feisty rattlsnake lay coiled beside it.

10

Friday, September 24, 1909.

Off once more at 1:10 for Jones Creek, where we arrive at 3:15 and go into camp in a delightful bower of box-elders. No tents are needed. Indeed, there is no room for even the small ones we have. At 5:30 Galloway comes in with thirty-one trout, which I fry for supper. We eat all but three. The sky is clear, there is no wind, the weather is perfect; and everyone is as happy and full of good spirits—and trout —as he can be.

Saturday, September 25, 1909.

Last night, beginning at 8:25 and continuing until three this morning I saw a beautiful sight. The contour of the top of the cliff on the south side of the river coincided almost exactly with the position of Mars as seen from the spot where I lay, and as the radiant planet seemingly advanced westward in the sky, it was alternately hidden and unmasked by the serrations of the cliff. There were seventy-five or eighty of these obscurations and apparitions before it passed wholly from sight.

JULIUS STONE, 1932, *Canyon Country*

Boxelder *(Acer negundo)*

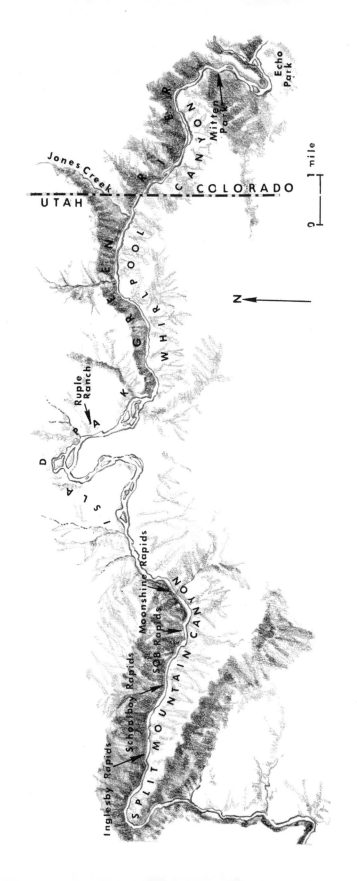

Jones Creek

UTAH · COLORADO

Echo Park

Mitten Park

WHIRLPOOL CANYON

GREEN RIVER

Ruple Ranch

PARK ISLAND

Moonshine Rapids

SOB Rapids

Schoolboy Rapids

Inglesby Rapids

SPLIT MOUNTAIN CANYON

N

1 mile

0

ECHO PARK
THROUGH SPLIT MOUNTAIN

HERE LIE a Green River raft, a pump, ten paddles and life jackets, assorted duffel, food bags all over the ground. It is May and of course it's raining and since this is an Outward Bound trip, the seven of us are expected to get it all together and on the river. Our instructor is Mark Leachman, slender, quiet, bearded, hidden beneath a high-crowned, broad-brimmed hat. He is a very, very good boatman and an excellent teacher. When he says, "Listen up!" we *listen*. There are twenty-eight of us in all on this trip, among them my daughter Sara.

We have been issued rain suits, heavy slickers almost totally water-proof except for the shocker that goes down the front of your neck when you're leaning back to backpaddle in a rapid. Since it's raining, we have them on, sweating through trying to get the raft inflated. Uninflated, it looks like a mistake: an amorphous wrinkled flotsam, no front, no back, all middle. When the first pontoon is full, it sits there like a lopsided doughnut. As we pump air into the other side, the raft rises out of some primordial vulcanized sleep to become something resembling a boat. At command, the seven of us carry, drag, lug, and stumble it onto the bank edge and push it over. It plops in with a large smack, tugging with the current.

Next come the big Coast Guard–approved bright orange life jackets. The extra bolstering in front makes everyone look like orange pouter pigeons. They are constantly in the way: you can't get things out of your pocket, you can't get things into your pocket, you can't lean over far enough to pick up something dropped in the bottom of the raft. Amazingly, after a few days, one does acclimate well enough to be almost efficient, in an elephantine sense. But not yet. Still, we somehow all manage to get into the raft without getting into the river first.

It is my first experience with paddling a raft. It handles like— well, nothing in my experience. I am reminded of the description by Andy Hall, the young bullwhacker who served as boatman and cook on Powell's first expedition. In Hall's idiom, his boat would "neither gee nor haw nor whoa worth a damn"—as if it "wasn't *broke* at all!" This raft does not crease the water as a sailboat does, or arrow it as a canoe; it seems more to pivot, and were it not so heavy, to skitter. We practice the six simple commands: forward, right, left, back, rest, and hold. It seems impossible to believe that at the end of this trip Mark will have us running rapids with style and respect for the river, and with the elation that comes with accomplishing something new and difficult with éclat.

AT ECHO PARK, the river, out of Lodore, makes a hairpin turn around the prow of Steamboat Rock before it enters Whirlpool Canyon. Steamboat Rock comes down to the water in an elegant line, almost the same color as the flat swirling river, but more variegated: the weathered beige of the Weber Sandstone is bannered with gray, tinged with yellow, scrubbed with black, strung with desert-varnish pennants. Manganese and iron oxides, with other trace elements, are dissolved and carried in rain water. When rain and surface water drain over rock surfaces, they redeposit these minerals on the rocks in dark, often shiny, streaks. When it rains, many areas of the cliff face may remain dry, but rivulets gloss the streaks of desert varnish, following patterns that have carried rain water for centuries. The deposition of desert varnish is slow, measured in hundreds of years, especially in this arid country where rainfall is so sparse.

Steamboat Rock is massive and monumental, rooted in the Mitten Park Fault, a spectacular example of drag faulting. The rock forma- tions in the fault are compressed upward, so twisted and gnarled that the rock almost loses its quality of rockness, as Baroque architecture passes into sculpture. The drag is pronounced, particularly on the upthrown side on the left, rock strata bent in the direction of the thrust. Several hundred feet of the Uinta Mountain Group, which disappeared just upriver in Lodore, are pulled up into view again.

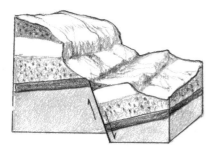 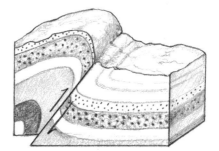

Normal fault   Reverse fault, showing drag

NORMAL AND DRAG FAULTING
(Adapted from Hansen, 1969, p. 116)

Weber Sandstone twists upward like the bare ribs of some Norse boat; the gray limestones stand vertical, on edge. The contrast between cold gray and sandy red, between vertical and horizontal, clearly revealed because there is no obscuring vegetation, illustrates the process of drag faulting as clearly as a textbook diagram.

The fault's name? Pat Lynch named this small park after his mule, Mitten.

Whirlpool Canyon is bounded by the Mitten Park Fault on the east and the Island Park Fault on the west. The afternoon wind coming around the corner of Steamboat Rock is sufficient for sailing. We rig our rain jackets with paddles in the sleeves, use two more paddles as centerboards, and sail down the river. But, as we turn into Whirlpool Canyon, the head-on wind is so strong that, even with eight people paddling, the raft seems to plow back upstream. Alongside, short sticks entrapped in the vortices of the eddies whirl around as if stirring a witch's brew. Having picked up the Yampa River, the Green charges into Whirlpool with vitality and verve.

Whirlpool Canyon is the antithesis of the sunny, sandy openness of Echo Park, where the water is flat, the rocks golden sandstone. The Uinta Mountain Group rocks are somber, sheer to the water. The waves are high and fast and lurch upstream. The wind makes it difficult to maneuver, exhausting to paddle, and cold in the shadows. I put on my wool mittens and they rub my hands raw where they're sunburned, an occupational hazard of boating. Spray spatters my sunglasses. No one talks, except usually quiet Allie, who is captain and keeps yelling tersely, "Keep paddling!" The raft bucks through big, malicious waves. The boat hangs between wind and water, poised, seemingly going nowhere. Only the cliffs seem to move, ever so slowly, upstream. The ancient brooding rocks come right down to the water, striped like a Dobos torte or slabbed with ripple-marked sandstones stacked like cards against the canyon wall.

About three miles downstream the river widens enough so that sand beaches intervene between river and wall. Two Canada geese nest on one of these. They stalk with necks extended, wary, facing away from the raft, suspicious but unwilling to fly. Finally, complaining in anserine irritation, they take off in a great sweeping arc. With eggs in the nest they do not remain away long, and even before we are out of sight they are back down.

We pass "Stateline Rock," where boatmen assure passengers that they are leaving Colorado and entering Utah. And then, Jones Hole ahead. It has been a long day of paddling for me, perched in an awkward position, and I am sure I will be sore, stiff, and a walking wounded. Instead, as I half-jump, half-fall off the raft, some peculiar elation hits: I have survived another day on the river's terms, and weary as I am, my only regret is that I have to put the paddle down. The river pours by and I want to go with it.

Nuttall violet
(*Viola nuttallii*)

Jones Hole Creek empties into the river, having cut a narrow canyon into the sandy-red Lodore Formation, whose cliffs now flank the river. Like Lodore, the lower part of Whirlpool Canyon is steeper, flaring at the top to a mile and a half across. In autumn, big groves of cottonwoods let the sun shaft through to leaves on the ground, an underfoot goldness. In spring, violets make a Botticelli carpet under trees just leafed out into pale yellow-green, and one spring the cicadas sang green rondeaux. In spite of the fact that as a campground it is woefully overused, it is still a Midas place.

I walk to a ledge at the far upstream end of Jones Hole. It is just big enough for a sleeping bag, about six feet above the water, floored with abrasive gray limestone embedded with shells. When I slept there last October, a boxelder smoldered as red as the cliffs across the river, and in a crevice, a small rosette of distilled-lavender asters bloomed. It was a solitary spot in a vast canyon, right above the river that purled quietly beneath, facing a cliff outlined with stars. That night a misting rain fell, then cleared, and the stars came thinly through, small raindrops breathing down even as the sky blackened. I awoke to a loud clanging: one of the boatmen was out on the basketball-sized cobbles that pave the river bed, trying to get wash water. The river had dropped a foot or more during the night, baring almost thirty feet of shoreline. The sun rose behind a cloud, turning it blinding white, an incandescent river morning.

But this year a surge of high water has dumped a pile of logs and brush that leave room only for chipmunks and ground squirrels.

POWELL NAMED the creek here Bishop Creek, after his chief topographer on the 1871 expedition, and Jones Hole after Stephen Vandiver Jones, the assistant topographer. But it seems not to have been called Jones Hole by local residents until after an episode involving one Charley Jones in 1883. In an attempt to reclaim his wife and children, who had left him, Charley Jones knifed a hired man. Thinking he had killed him, Jones holed up for the winter in this remote canyon that now bears his name, going out the next spring when he discovered the man had not died.

Jones Hole Creek runs muddy today, a colder brown than the river; it cuts into the Green like a scimitar, curving downstream, maintaining its separate identity as far as I can see. The Island Park Fault that terminates Whirlpool Canyon downstream swings northward, and it is in this zone of weakness that this creek runs. The creek used to be prime fishing; one of Powell's men caught 20 trout here, and Galloway, in 1909, reportedly snagged a total of 129. Fishing has declined with the increasing popularity of the campground and large boating parties that enjoy wading and splashing in the creek. Trout are almost never caught in the main stream of the Green in this reach, for it is too silty; rainbows and browns in Jones Hole Creek have not been introduced and are thought to have come in from the Yampa or the upper Green River before Flaming Gorge Dam closure. And Jones Hole Creek was certainly fished by prehistoric Fremont Indians who frequented the area.

A short walk upstream still leads to a wall of Fremont drawings —a walk through thickets of waist-high rustling horsetails, through garlands of butterflies, yellow violets and wallflowers, gold parsleys and twinpod, starflowers and opulent drifts of pale blue chiming bells, along a stream brightened with yellow monkey flowers and clumps of watercress. On a sandstone wall, high above the creek bottom, are the drawings, both pictographs and petroglyphs. The latter are chiseled into the stone surface, while the pictographs are painted with hematite pigment, applied with a twig or branch, fingers, or a yucca-fiber brush. The wall is long, and there are many figures arrayed over the surface, placed with no interrelationships, no perspective, among them a square-shouldered human figure with a horned headdress about fourteen inches high, stiffly drawn, a typical Fremont representation. The animals are more naturally limned: cleft feet of deer, long curling horns of mountain sheep, added to a simple rectangular body. Circles and a careful pattern of triangles arranged in rows, a grid of holes pecked out of the rock, some spatter marks, a series of circles—enigmatic, evocative. A rough rectangle is divided into squares; to its right, which is upstream, is a zigzag, a common abstraction for water. The two forms together, and their orientation, imply a net set for catching fish. Although there is no historical evidence whatsoever for interpretation, it is hard to ignore the implications of such widespread symbols oriented to the landscape in which they occur.

The Fremont Indians who produced these wall paintings lived in this area between A.D. 300 and 800 or 900, the northernmost extent of a culture found first along the Fremont River (now called the Dirty Devil, the name originally given it by Powell) in south-central Utah. Long considered a "peripheral" and offshoot culture, it is

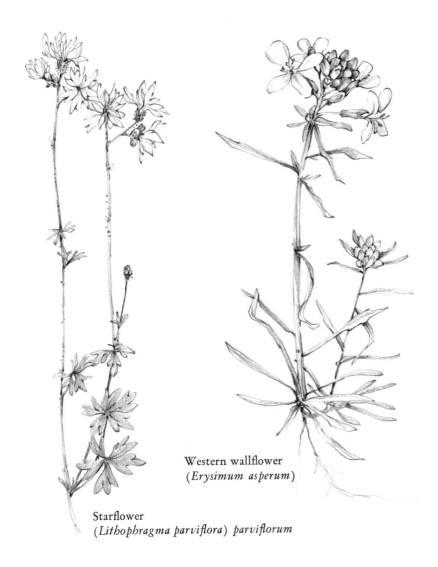

Western wallflower
(*Erysimum asperum*)

Starflower
(*Lithophragma parviflora*) *parviflorum*

now recognized as having had a fully-achieved cultural pattern that spread over most of Utah, with recognizable regional variations, two of which occurred along the Green River drainage. The Fremont lived a seminomadic existence with few material goods, and probably began the practice of agriculture when corn, squash, and beans were introduced into this region. Storage cists of corn are tucked away in protected caves and overhangs, or in pits in the ground provided with covers. The Indians also gathered many wild seeds, bulbs, and nuts,

Fremont pottery shards

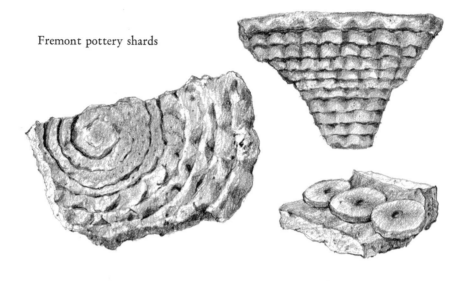

among them rice grass, prince's plume, yucca, beeplant, wild onion, prickly pear, squawbush, and mariposa lily.

Small points and snares are the tools of the hunter, and as in other prehistoric cultures, the Fremont wasted little. They wove strips of fur into a net of fiber cords to make light, warm robes. From bone they made awls and punches that hold, even today, firm and heavy in the hand, useful, sturdy objects. Also from bone they fashioned counters for games, smooth on one side, sometimes decorated on the other. Some have holes drilled in them and were undoubtedly worn as ornaments, and no wonder—they are small, light objects in the hand, clicking together pleasantly, scattering with a winsome clatter like thin dominoes.

Pottery is the mark of a civilization that needs vessels for cooking, storage, and carrying. The Fremont made a utilitarian plain gray ware out of alluvial clay and tempered it with whatever was at hand, and shaped it into ollas and pitchers. So seldom are they decorated that a small pitcher I saw, sitting on the shelf in the University of Utah anthropology laboratory, attracted my attention because of the pleasure and care an Indian hand took—molding small clay disks, perforating each with a small hole, and applying them in a neat overlapping row. The Fremont Indians made fine baskets; a bundle of fibers, often yucca, wound around a split willow rod core and sewn together to form a closely-woven container. Both baskets and pottery

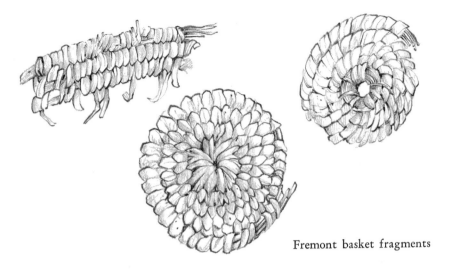

Fremont basket fragments

were sometimes lined with gilsonite, a tarlike substance found in the Uinta Basin that made them waterproof.

Unique to the Fremont culture are small clay figurines, probably made for religious purposes, and an ingenious moccasin design. The figurines, like the pottery, are gray; they are unfired, decorated with a fingernail imprint for an eye, a pinched-out nose. The lower part is unfinished, serving as a handle perhaps, and one fits into my hand as if planned, a miniature face staring upward with an inscrutable expression.

Moccasins were made of mountain-sheep hide, designed so that the dew claw forms a kind of hobnail. Never mind that this made the seams come on the foot at all the points of wear and that a great amount of industry was probably expended in keeping them patched; what intrigues me is that glimpse of patterned perception that saw, on the fleet foot of a mountain sheep, a glimpse of human utility.

ON A BRIGHT May afternoon the raft cavorts through the remainder of Whirlpool Canyon with great good humor, bucking the roller-coaster waves head on. Strictly speaking, these are not rapids in the sense of rocks and falls that require precise maneuvering. Although the waves are big, there are no hidden rocks or surprises, just an increased drop in a narrowing channel that pushes the water into foam-

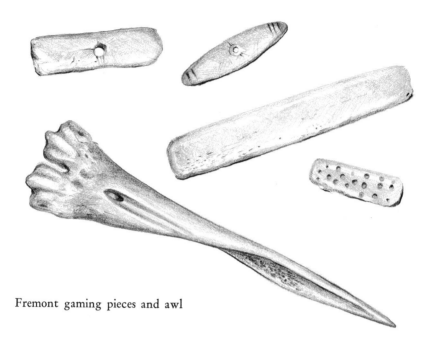

Fremont gaming pieces and awl

ing haystacks. None of the rapids in Whirlpool are named except for one unofficially called "Greasy Pliers," obviously a boatman-named rapid commemorating the loss of that indispensable tool. Our raft wallows over the waves like some huge inchworm, and at any one moment the crewman in front of me may be three feet above or three feet below, paddle out of the water or submerged nearly to the top.

The rock formations disappear in order as we travel downstream, first the Lodore Formation, then the intervening limestones, and finally Weber Sandstone coming down to the water's edge, forming cliffs full of crusader castles and old fortifications from ancient deserts—and who knows what intrigues and machinations go on inside, or what veiled eyes watch through slotted windows. Reddish at the base, gray-white to tan toward the top, the cliffs rise, divided into bays; trees grow within the hollows but not on the edges, emphasizing the knife sharpness of the ballasts between. The lightness of the water and the fantasies of the rock give as light-hearted a character to the lower part of Whirlpool Canyon as the dark rocks give somber aspect to its entrance.

The Island Park Fault marks the end of Whirlpool Canyon. Island Park itself separates Whirlpool Canyon and Split Mountain, and the river meanders and braids across it, as if it had all the time in the world, looping a length of seven miles across three air miles, a peaceful cul-de-sac between two racing gorges, named by Major Powell for the numerous islands around which the river flows. Some are sand-bar islands, flat, like a piece of tan paper pasted on the water; others are bigger, carrying cottonwoods and brush, or sprigged with a row of this year's tamarisk, that make a thin green haze, last year's row farther back and a little taller, studded with cocklebur and annual grasses.

Henry C. Ruple, who originally homesteaded Island Park, came here about the same time as Pat Lynch. The latter used to tie a few logs together and float and walk down Whirlpool Canyon to visit the Ruple Ranch. At the conclusion of the visit, he borrowed a horse from Mr. Ruple and rode back up to his current lodgings on the Yampa or Green. There he let the horse go, and it would find its way back to the Ruple Ranch.

Before Flaming Gorge Dam was built upstream, the river froze over in the winter, thick enough to drive a team of horses across, temperatures down to 40° F. below for six weeks at a time. G. E. Untermann and his wife lived here for several years, Mrs. Untermann having been a Ruple before her marriage. Mr. Untermann tells of the winter of 1936–37, when he chopped holes in the ice so cattle could drink; the last ax blow would release a fountain of water that froze on boots and trousers on contact, and had to be whacked with the flat of the ax to make movement possible. Three to four inches of new ice froze in the holes every night. Sometimes the ice would cut off cottonwoods along the river as neatly as a buzz saw.

In the springtime, newly green cottonwoods edge an island stretching flat with sagebrush. The water is peaceful, reflecting the sky in a lavender blue. Vortices ease out from the bank, a flat swirling that is soporific to watch; there are intimations of the lower Green in this quiet, wide river. And then Island Park ends as it begins, with a fault. The rock strata rise and curve above a loose talus slope to crenelated cliffs, rock faces broken, ledges and sharp slopes sprinkled with trees, and in the far, far distance, a ridge with a thin dotted line of spring snow.

IF LODORE is an anomaly, Split Mountain is incredible. From the air one can see how the river hooks into the mountain at one end, runs for some five miles right down the middle, then angles out at the

Cocklebur
(*Xanthium strumarium*)

other end, as it entered. Calling it Craggy Canyon in 1869, Powell
took a second look and changed it to Split Mountain two years later,
and it is precisely that, a mountain cut by a tensile copper wire of a
river.

Split Mountain is small as mountains go, about ten miles long and
five wide. As an entity it was probably contemporaneous with the
main Uinta Mountain uplift. As at Swallow Canyon, the river is
superposed. Split Mountain simply did not exist as a positive topographical entity when the river first flowed above it millennia ago.
Probably the whole Rocky Mountain region at that time had only
mild surface relief, more rolling than mountainous. The river flowed
across and then through softer rock layers left now only in the
adjacent valleys. When it reached the underlying Weber Sandstone,
it continued to cut downward in the same channel. The river has cut
through all the sedimentary formations that record a rising and
falling of the land, some sediments laid down underwater and some
not, some on the oscillating shore, some continental, some marine.
The way in which these sediments eroded provides the panorama of
Split Mountain.

Split Mountain is a morning canyon; of all the Green's canyons, it
is the most upbeat, a pure delight of sun and water and rock. (I have
felt this way even while running it on a dark, freezing, foot-soaked,
hand-numbed October evening, shivering and stiff.) At its entrance
the Island Park Fault soars upward in massive ribs, a rising line that
is infectious. Split Mountain is one glorious chute, rapid after rapid,
with just enough time to get your breath in between before the line
of foam and the din downstream announce another. The river drops
140 feet in seven miles, a drop that ensures fast rapids, and the river
profile shows four sharper inclinations, all named: Moonshine, SOB,
Schoolboy, and Inglesby. Like the rapids of Lodore, these were boatman-named some forty years ago by Bus Hatch, one of the best boatmen on the river when only wooden boats were used. Moonshine is
named for Moonshine Draw on the left, obviously commemorating
some illicit activities on the mountainside. SOB was, in a wooden
craft, that kind of rapid to run; Schoolboy, because after much
fretting Hatch considered it that easy. And Inglesby commemorates
a dentist who went overboard here. They can be run in succession,
bright rapids, spanking rapids, sunshine rapids, and best of all morning rapids.

Of the times I have relished Split Mountain's rapids, perhaps it is
on the Outward Bound trip that I enjoy them most. We have worked

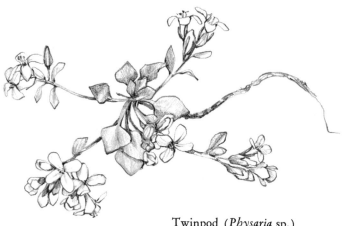

Twinpod (*Physaria* sp.)

together for five days, have learned the raft's temper and the river's power, and now begin to concentrate on the refinements of running. Mark draws diagrams in the sand and we talk over how best to run, what position the raft should be in on entrance, what landmarks there are to orient by, the danger spots. About two hundred yards beyond the entrance to Split Mountain lies Moonshine Rock, an immense boulder fallen off a high slope or tumbled in by Moonshine Draw. From the river, at high water, the rock shows only as a large, ominously slick surface. On its downstream side is a stationary wave with a hole of sobering dimensions. A short chute of slick swift water follows, and then the tongue of the rapid itself; in midstream are the rocks that must be slipped around, and then the river jogs straight into the cliff and piles up against the wall in an entrapment to be devoutly avoided. The raft's attitude going into the tongue should be about forty-five degrees, a strong pull out of the current to avoid the wall, and then into haystack tail waves that pile up in sleek, opaque café-au-lait pyramids.

We adjust life jackets to breathless; during rapids, the bottom and midships fastenings are cinched in tight to prevent the jacket from popping over your head in case of being thrown out. (In that case, proper procedure is not to swim but to face downstream, knees slightly bent to act as shock absorbers against the rocks.) We pile into the raft, backpaddle to get to midriver upstream, edging into position, already sweeping so swiftly downstream that we immediately enter the pouring tongue. We swivel to confront the rollers. The raft bucks; a sheet of water comes point-blank over the bow. Everyone paddles even though the paddle may be biting thin air because stopping means a loss of control. Water pours over the side, cascades of spray and splash inundate everyone, no time for anything but putting the paddle in the water, bracing, watching the paddle in front of you, keeping the beat, pushing back tons of water, switching to one back stroke to turn, pulling away from the cliff and out of the current and suddenly—it's over, in seconds, too swift for exhilaration. That comes with looking back over what you've come through and the sight of another rapid in a thin rim of unfurling white on the river horizon ahead. Moonshine is a rapid I got to captain, although not to my satisfaction—I have not yet learned to allow for the time lag in the raft's response. At this moment I want only to go back and do it over and do it better while it is fresh in my mind, with more style, more precision.

I look back through hexagons of water on eyelashes, flaring with sunlight, to see caramel waves breaking upstream. I feel surfeited with sun and spray and dazzle and May. In the brief quiets between rapids, when there is time to wipe sunglasses and look about, I savor the heightened awareness that rapids bring, that make one more responsive to this total world of rock and sunshine and river. Split Mountain ends with sedimentary beds canted downward at a steep angle, a definitive satisfying end. At the boat landing we unlash gear, tip the rafts up on their sides and slosh them clean, open the valves and let the air out. We fold them and carry them to the truck, six river days encapsulated in a neoprene packet.

The rest of the group goes home, but my husband, Herman, and boatman Clair Quist meet me at Split Mountain and we shove off in Clair's ten-man raft within the hour, my continuity of river unbroken. The elation of Split Mountain persists almost as long as the view of it lasts downriver, but my knowledge of having cleft through that mass of rock on a beautiful May morning, suspended on a crystalline lather of spray, remains with me still.

11

The river enters this meadow between two high cliffs which, after forming a sort of corral, come so close together that one can scarcely see the opening through which the river comes. According to our guide, one can not cross from one side to the other except by the only ford which there is in this vicinity. This is toward the west of the northern crest and very close to a chain of hills of loose earth, some of them lead colored and others yellow. The ford is stony and in it the water does not reach to the shoulder blades of the horses, whereas in every other place we saw they can not cross without swimming. We halted on its south bank about a mile from the ford, naming the camp La Vega de Santa Cruz. We observed the latitude by the north star and found ourselves in 41° 19' latitude.

VÉLEZ DE ESCALANTE, *Diary, September 13, 1776*

Easter daisy
(*Townsendia exscapa*)

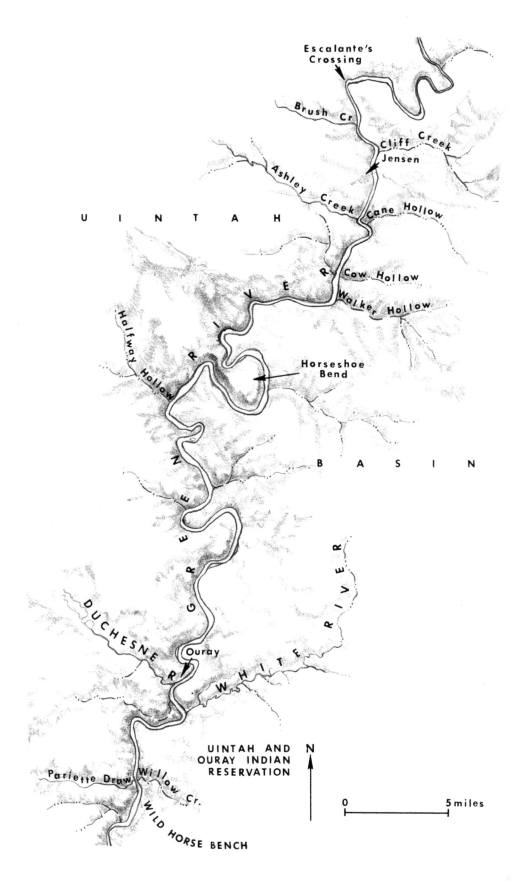

Escalante's
Crossing

Brush Cr

Cliff Creek

Jensen

Ashley Creek

Cane Hollow

U   I   N   T   A   H

R

V

E

R

Cow Hollow

Walker Hollow

Halfway Hollow

Horseshoe
Bend

G

R

E

E

N

B   A   S   I   N

R

WHITE RIVER

DUCHESNE R.

Ouray

UINTAH AND
OURAY INDIAN
RESERVATION

N

Pariette Draw

Willow Cr.

WILD HORSE BENCH

0   5 miles

SPLIT MOUNTAIN
TO WILD HORSE BENCH

SPLIT MOUNTAIN is an end: the river cuts through no more mountains. The change from mountain to basin is sudden and complete. The river enters the Uinta Basin, the topmost province of the 150,000-square-mile Colorado Plateau, through which it continues until its confluence with the Colorado River.

In the gentleness of a spring afternoon there are still reminders that the plateau is a land of extremes: of oven-hot summers and arctic-blizzard winters, of arid deserts and a big cool river, of open flood plains and stark, narrow canyons. It is an area still largely wilderness. In thousands of square miles there are only a few towns. It is 182 river miles from Jensen, Utah, to Green River, and Ouray is the only settlement on the river between them, and it has a population of around fifty.

The main mass of the Colorado Plateau lies in eastern Utah and northeastern Arizona, bounded on the north by the Uinta Mountains, on the east by the Colorado Rockies; on the west and southwest it stands above the Great Basin, slipping off into the southeast below Grand Canyon. The plateau accumulated and preserved sediments for some 250 million years, and the color of these, combined with their cliff or slope-forming characteristics, gives visual impact to the whole plateau, especially where the river has cut through them. At the time of the general uplift of the Rocky Mountains, uplift in the plateau was also considerable; it hung together intact as a strong and rigid block, elevated to between four and six thousand feet above sea level. This elevation instituted the period of deep canyon cutting that is such a marked feature of the landscape. Erosion still continues to be more active than deposition, and soil development proceeds very slowly; consequently there are vast vistas of bare rock magnificently exposed.

The once romping river becomes, until Desolation Canyon, a somnolent river, flowing through softer rock formations that allow it to spread widely and run quietly, and it is somehow as if the river rests. There is placid floating for the three of us, a time of peace and greening trees and early flowers and such quiet, of a big river heavy with springtime runoff, when the river imprints a new sense of suspended, extended time. For the next week, time on the river is no more hurried than the slow cooing of a mourning dove; every morning begins with a meadow lark and every evening ends with a waxing moon that finally hangs full over the ghostly cliffs of Desolation. If there were to be but one springtime in the world, this is how I would wish it to be.

THE GREEN RIVER, as it enters the Uinta Basin, scribes a rounded W, looping from east to west, through low crinkled cliffs of Mancos Shale and Morrison Formation. The shales are pale buff, soft, rounded divides and velvety smooth shadows, rutted with quirky drainage lines, looking like a piece of old leather. Just below Split Mountain the river cuts through the Mancos Shales that rise higher as the river cuts deeper, and then become completely eroded away, not to be seen again until the foot of Gray Canyon, where they floor the Gunnison Valley.

The distinctive Morrison Formation appears in candy-striped slopes: pale olive, lavender-green, pink, gray, marbled with a little scrub but supporting no trees. It is one of the few consistently and easily identifiable formations, pastel stripes and rounded slopes persistent even though individual beds are discontinuous. Most of the formation consists of fine muds and silts, laid by rivers; there are some sandstones and freshwater limestones that accumulated in small standing ponds. The surface upon which these rivers moved was flat and poorly drained. Occasionally animal carcasses and old logs washed down one of these ancient streams, caught on a bar, became covered with silt and layers of sand. The bones and fibers of this flotsam were preserved by an infilling of silica into the porous structure of the bone or wood, resulting in a nearly unbreakable stonelike fossil. The Morrison Formation here has yielded varied and distinctive dinosaur fossils, many species not found elsewhere. They are unique in being so superbly preserved and so numerous.

Although Powell listed fossils in his reports, he did so mainly to establish chronology and did no extensive digging. Some forty years later a canny scientist named Earl Douglass, already well known as a geologist, paleontologist, and botanist, suspected that the giant bones local sheepherders talked about meant a real find. Hired by Andrew Carnegie, he came west to look, stayed at a local ranch but found nothing. When he was ready to give up, the ranchers, who knew a good boarder when they saw one, encouraged him to stay, and two days later, August 17, 1909, he stumbled across a row of Brontosaurus vertebrae weathered out in relief, just below the mouth of Split Mountain: "At last in the top of the ledge where the softer underlying beds form a divide—a kind of saddle—I saw eight of the tail bones of a Brontosaurus in exact position. It was a beautiful sight."

Douglass worked the quarry under the most primitive of conditions, chiseling and scraping out tons of bones. He made homemade plaster of Paris out of gypsum in the Morrison ledges, and re-entombed 700,000 pounds of the bones, packed them to a railroad that even today is a long way off, and shipped them back east, most of them to the Carnegie Museum, which financed his work. He tried to stake a mineral claim in order to protect the many fossils that were coming to light but discovered that mineral claims do not include dinosaur bones. In 1915 he was successful in having 80 acres set aside as Dinosaur National Monument; in 1938 the site was enlarged to slightly more than 200,000 acres.

When Carnegie wished him to spend his winters at the museum, Douglass demurred and became a consulting geologist for the University of Utah. He never completed his stone cabin at "Lizard Farm" and it is to be regretted that the Park Service tore it down. The dry farm must have been the perfect place to live, near his work, here where the Green shimmers downstream and the pale rim of Split Mountain is notched like the back of a Stegosaurus.

MAP SPREAD OUT on my knees, I watch for the ford ahead. The Mancos Shale along the river bank presents a solemn aspect—the explorer Escalante rightly described it as "lead-colored." Where these

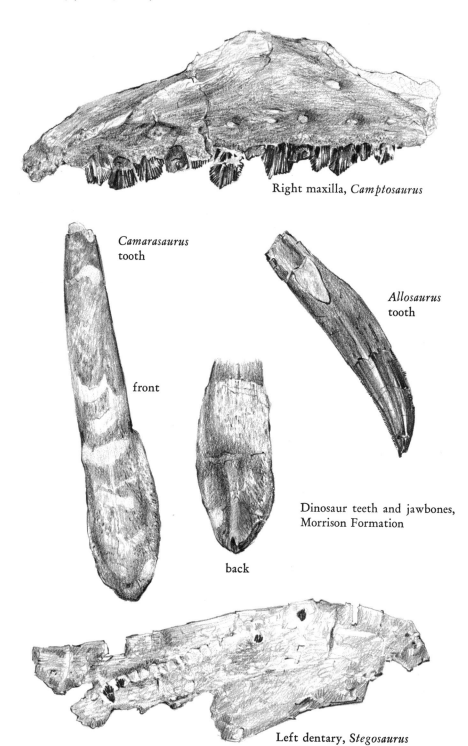

Right maxilla, *Camptosaurus*

Camarasaurus
tooth

Allosaurus
tooth

front

Dinosaur teeth and jawbones,
Morrison Formation

back

Left dentary, *Stegosaurus*

rolling cliffs reach the river's edge, the river turns south almost at a right angle. Then the cliffs break back, and in the right bank a dugway is cut. Here Fathers Francisco Antanasio Domínguez and Vélez de Escalante, with their cartographer, Don Bernardo Miera y Pacheco, and ten others, made the first documented crossing of the Green River, on September 16, 1776.

The ford was long known in this area and an Indian guide apprised the expedition of its utility; it was used for over a century longer, known as the "Uinta and White River Trail" according to township survey plots of 1878–79. The gravel bottom made a serviceable road for wagons before a ferry was established downriver at Jensen. It is difficult in the high water of May to envision this as a good crossing; it is not until October, when the river slides over the rock bottom at low water, that its virtues are apparent. (I saw it then at midmorning, near the time of day the expedition crossed, and it was easy to imagine the creak of wood, the hollow splashes of horses' hooves in the water hitting stone, the remote sound of voices urging, directing, and then the lonely procession rising out of the river on a heading south.) Domínguez and Escalante set out from Santa Fe in July, with instructions to find a new route to the California missions, specifically to Monterey, founded in 1769. They returned to Santa Fe in January, 1777, without having been able to establish such a route, but Escalante's diary provides the first recorded descriptions of the country, and Miera's maps influenced cartographers on both sides of the ocean.

The expedition camped September 13–16 a mile downstream from their proposed crossing, arriving the day the British entered New York. Now, nearly two hundred years later, at this same site, the cottonwoods are just leafing out, and yellow-flowered bushes form the undergrowth. I am determined to camp here too, but it is not to be: mosquitoes, with which Escalante may not have had to contend in the fall, swarm out in multitudes and Herman balks.

Escalante was a remarkable journal keeper. It is hard to write while on the trail, and equally difficult to remember everything when the day is over. I suspect that Escalante wrote everything down at the end of the day, since he more than likely kept his journal packed away in waterproof coverings, and because his entries are almost stream of consciousness: he notes in the same paragraph their use of the quadrant (a primitive sextant), the black-trunked cottonwoods along the river and what an expedition member carved on them, the shooting of a buffalo, and a horse race in which the horse broke his neck. He wrote in an even hand that varied little during the trip; there are few errors, and these are neatly struck out. Margins are even, pages well ordered. Escalante had an observant eye that recorded anything of note, a perceptive eye that scrutinized people as well as places, a proper eye that noted latitude readings, and a devout heart that made obeisance to God.

The Spaniards came to this trip little knowing what they might find. Certainly trappers and traders had brought back descriptions of terrain, and Indian guides told of fords and possible routes. Spaniards had seen parts of the upper Colorado, but there is no written record that they had crossed into the Green River drainage. Canyons blocked exploration much more effectively than mountains, and "Tierra incognita" and "Partie inconnue" are written more across canyons than across mountains on maps of the time.

Once the expedition crossed the Colorado River (above present-day Grand Junction, Colorado), they were in country altogether new to white men. Having no knowledge of the terrain to the southwest, they concluded that the Green River, the largest one they had seen since leaving Santa Fe, was a separate drainage system from the river they had already forded. They named it Río San Buenaventura, after the thirteenth-century theologian and biographer of St. Francis, a melodious name that flows like the river.

When Miera plotted the river he made a conjecture, and one that so coincided with what later traders and colonists and explorers wanted to believe that it took seventy years and a major expedition to destroy it. From Miera's map it is patent that he assumed that they were on the western slope of a divide from which rivers could flow, uninterrupted, to the Pacific. Later map makers copied this river of illusion, often adding fancies of their own. Most of the maps were made in Europe, and in 1804 Humboldt, whose influence as a geographer and essayist was considerable, printed a map in conjunction with his political essay on New Spain that accepted Miera's conjectures. Above my work desk is a map copied from Humboldt, printed by A. Brué in Paris, 1825. Both the headwaters of the Río San Buenaventura, shown rising in a ridge of mountains, and the final reach, extending inland from the Pacific coast, are drawn in a firm line. In between there is a hiatus across which is lettered "Partie inconnue." Running beneath this lettering, a light dotted line connects the two ends of the San Buenaventura. This intermittent line is tentative, yet very precise. It is of such lines that dreams are made.

Until 1844 maps showed the San Buenaventura. More accurate maps, sketched by traders and trappers, did not carry the authority to dispel a myth; for instance, Jedediah Smith, at Ashley's bequest, went up the California coast in 1826 and concluded that the river did not exist. Unfortunately, Smith's sketched maps did not survive. Practical manifestations of the belief in an inland waterway were manifold: the Bidwell party, 1841, took along materials to build boats so that they could float from the Great Salt Lake to California; a party from Browns Park, under the leadership of Joe Walker (who had served with Bonneville), planned to trap their way to California. As late as 1849, bullwhacker Manly set out down the Green with the conviction that he would beach his craft at the Pacific.

Frémont's expedition was the last to search for the inland water route, as entries in his journal between December 12, 1843, and April 14, 1844, document. Finally he gave up:

> It has been constantly represented, as I have already stated, that the bay of San Francisco opened far into the interior, by some river coming down from the base of the Rocky mountains, and upon which supposed stream the name of Rio Buenaventura had been bestowed. Our observations of the Sierra Nevada . . . show that this neither is nor can be the case. No river from the interior does, or can, cross the Sierra Nevada—itself more lofty than the Rocky mountains; and as to the Buenaventura, the mouth of which seen on the coast gave the idea and the name of the reputed great river, it is, in fact, a small stream of no consequence . . .

Although the hoped-for inland water route was nonexistent, an efficient transcontinental route did materialize, but it took twenty-five years and millions of dollars. In 1869 a spike driven at Promontory, Utah, forged the link between East and West.

That same year, John Wesley Powell left Expedition Island and filled in the vertical blank spots between Green River, Wyoming, and Green River, Utah.

THE WIDTH and gentleness of the river below Split Mountain is indeed an enticement to make one believe that it is navigable for untold miles. The river moves evenly, falling an average of less than two feet per mile, recipe for a quiet river. After we set up camp, Herman gets out his octant (a refinement of the sextant) to check Escalante's reading. Clair, the bearded one, stands in his characteristic pose, weight on one leg, hand on hip, the other foot pointed out, and observes closely. He takes the octant and makes an accurate reading the first time he has it in his hands. Escalante recorded 41° 19'; Clair reads off a more accurate 40° 25'.

The morning sun lights an impoverished land: greasewood wide-spaced, dirt and sand between, a little grass, a low, prickly, gray-green matted cover only at the river's edge—woefully overgrazed land, pitted with cattle tracks, hardened to a cementlike surface. Chalky patches of alkali indicate a soil in which no sage can grow; prickly pears sprawl in the sand, broken and wrinkled for lack of water. Almost every twenty feet is a large anthill, seething with big brown ants.

The climate here is arid to semiarid; rainfall varies from five inches and less annually, in the deserts, to twenty or so on the mountains and high ridges. Since rainfall is spasmodic in most areas, rapid runoff and sheet erosion result, producing a tormented badlands landscape shattered with cliffs. Scant rainfall results in scant vegetation; only the higher plateaus and ridges are dark with evergreens. Below 6,500 feet, rainfall and snow are so light that evergreens disappear; only sagebrush persists, and still lower sage cannot endure, leaving the dry land to shadscale and greasewood and cactus. This landscape is an illustration of what Powell foresaw for arid western lands. In order to run enough cattle for subsistence, a 160-acre homestead would be overgrazed and unable to recover from year to year, terminating in a near desert of undernourished plants. Somehow a true desert is less bleak than this vista; a desert seems at equilibrium within itself, while this is but the tattered remnant of something better.

WE STOP at Jensen for butter, irritating the red-winged blackbirds in the willow thicket to wheezing. The town was named for Lars Jensen, who ran a ferry here around 1885. A cock pheasant flies across the river just in front of the raft, squawking like an old phonograph record. The raft drifts downstream, rotating slowly in the current. Honey reflections slide on the putty-colored water. Silver-dollar-sized pods of foam catch the light across the water surface, spinning downstream at different rates of speed, those in the swifter channel near the outer bank outpacing those close by.

Sometimes a wide upwelling ends in a swirling vortex, like the seething of some giant cauldron, the visible manifestation of turbulence beneath the smooth surface. Formed by underwater currents, the

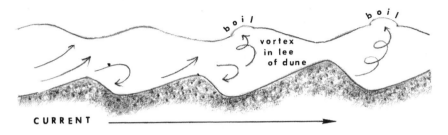

UPWELLINGS AND BOILS
(Adapted from Morisawa, 1968, pp. 56 and 69, Figs. 4.6 and 5.1)

vortices are sometimes a foot in diameter, sometimes several feet. Sometimes they are silent, sometimes they hiss and bubble as the water effloresces and curls in upon itself, blossoming silt. The greatest velocity of the river is somewhere below the surface, causing eddies to spin up from unseen underwater obstructions. The upwellings form in the lee of sand dunes on the bottom of the river, at the sides of channels, or at every sunken log and boulder, appearing downstream from whatever obstacle instigated them.

Thin coins of spume merge, stretch, separate, round, elongate into crescents, are destroyed by a vortex, then reunite and loop into Art Nouveau curves in hypnotic succession. Sometimes they are spaced so evenly that the river resembles nothing more than a giant chessboard on which bubbles are pawns, cliffs are castles, but there are no knights, no bishops, no kings, no queens. There are no gambits and no pieces are lost. In the heat of morning, when the birds become silent, the upwellings are the only sound in the beautiful quiet, almost birdsong-like in themselves, silken sounds, intimate incurlings, rustling softly. It is this stillness that I remember when I am off river.

THE BANKS are divided by the river but sewn together by invisible lines of bird and butterfly flights. A cottonwood stands almost submerged in the high water; as we pass I pull a catkin to draw off one of the top branches. The new leaves, rolled inward, are as shiny as if varnished.

The burring of an irrigation pump grows louder. A log house and a couple of sheds nestle under a big cottonwood; the field around is freshly plowed, one of the few we see actually under cultivation. The brief growing season here limits even irrigated farming to such short-season crops as alfalfa or clover seed, etc. And the remoteness: the nearest railroad is still a hundred miles away, an impractical distance for shipping produce.

The river crosses the axis of the Uinta Basin and the rock strata begin a gentle dip in the opposite direction. The river runs nearly through the middle of the 9,750-square-mile basin, cutting through

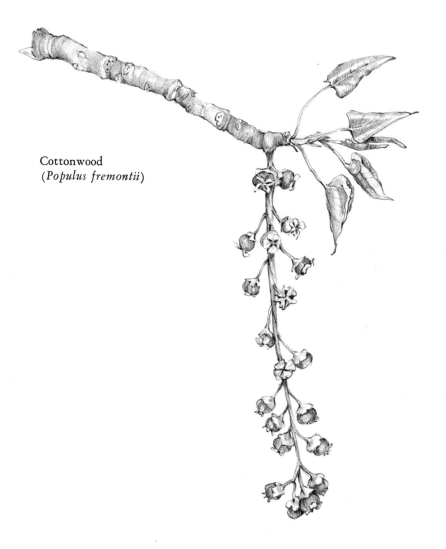

Cottonwood
(*Populus fremontii*)

some 9,000 feet of strata. Like the Green River Basin, the Uinta Basin contained a vast lake, some 5,000 square miles at its largest. Like its counterpart to the north, its sediments grade from predominantly lake in the center to fluvial deposits at the edges, where streams fed into the lake. It lay in the basin approximately thirty-three million years, at its greatest extent connecting with the lake of the Green River Basin around the eastern end of the Uinta Mountains. The second period of elevation in the Rocky Mountains severed their connection.

Someone is hammering, slowly, deliberately. A bent-over figure at the top of a bank resolves to that of a boy pounding an old fence apart. He holds the hammer with both hands, the body motion of each blow preceding the sound, this non-correlation giving a sense of unreality. We draw closer. A nail screams as he pulls it out and the board comes loose with a hollow thwack. He never looks in the direction of the raft. Usually people wave. Perhaps we no longer exist.

Split Mountain is diminished, beginning to lose its interior color and modeling, now simplified like a scenic wallpaper, back wall darker, front wall paler. It is a measure of how far we have come. It disappears behind the cliffs flanking the left bank, just before we enter Horseshoe Bend, where the river makes a huge bulbous loop. Should the river ever again have cutting power sufficient to break through the neck, it will leave the horseshoe empty and run half a mile straight instead of nine miles around. At its present rate of flow it seems impossible, but then the river has millions of years and a grain at a time moves mountains.

Cliff swallows swarm like gnats, in and out of the light, visiting a cluster of nests hung on the cliff. Sometimes it is difficult to differentiate between swallow and shadow. The overhang is crowded with nests, and a score or more birds hang on the cliff face in the process of construction, against a constant background rattle of wings and an incessant high twittering. They exchange places in a continual grand right and left, small creatures, with sharp wings and square tails, hurtling through the air like paper airplanes. They have recently arrived from farther south and will summer here, raising a brood, leaving in September.

The search begins for a campground without mosquitoes. The sun is still hot at six-thirty and we've been on river since nine o'clock, eating lunch on board, floating and rowing, taking only necessary rest stops. The first good sandy spot is infested. We drift on, alongside cliffs tiered like a wedding cake, layers askew, icing melting and dripping. The next potential campsite is infested. I think it injudicious, knowing Herman's fanatic aversion to mosquitoes, to quote George Bradley's opinion, written during Powell's first trip, on the mosquitoes of the Uinta Basin:

> The mosquitoes are perfectly frightful. As I went through the rank grass and wild sunflower sometimes higher than my head they would fairly *scream* around me. I think I never saw them thicker even in Florida than at this place. . . . One of the men says that while out on the shore of the lake a mosquito asked him for his pipe, knife and tobacco and told him to hunt his old clothes for a match while he loaded the pipe—but I didn't hear the mosquito ask him though there are some very large ones here.

An area of low cliffs coming down to the water has little vegetation and turns out to be acceptable to Herman. By this time it is dusk, and a wind has picked up to the point where it begins to bother me. I pitch the tent, usually a three-minute task, and it seems to take hours. I feel as if I work in slow motion. The wind picks up the ground cloth in spite of the rocks with which I weight it. In the quieter layer of air near the ground the mosquitoes speckle my hands when I try to pound in a tent stake. Letting go to swat means starting all over again and recapturing the elusive tent loop; bedrock lies so close to the surface that the stakes will not hold by themselves and the tent corner plucks them out of the ground. I hold my breath, wedge a stake in as far as possible, hold it with one hand and stack a cairn around it, and only then take time to dispose of mosquitoes. By this time even they are finding it difficult to find fresh skin between the welts. My hands, still raw from woolen mittens and sunburn, feel like two uncooked hams. It is dark by the time I get the tent secured, and the wind still blows and the mosquitoes still whine and I seriously question what I am doing here, and there is murder in my heart when Herman, freshly fortified with repellent and a generous drink, asks if the tent is ready for his sleeping bag.

Worse yet, this terrace gives no compensation of a beautiful view. A telephone pole stands dead in front of the tent. In the wind, its wires whine and hum. Beneath it are some barrels, toppled over, and, rusting in a wooden frame, a washing machine in advanced state of rigor mortis that died with its legs in the air. I am reminded of another entry in Bradley's journal about his sleeping space one night in Lodore: "If I had a dog that would lie where my bed is made tonight I would kill him and burn his collar and swear I never owned him."

Cymopterus
(*Cymopterus bulbosa*)

THE TERRACE rises forty feet above the river, paved with river rocks since the river once ran this high. Most are wholly or partly encrusted with shells of alkali. Between them the soil is desert dry. Nevertheless, there are many flowers, sprinkled like confetti across the ground, festive in the morning light: orange globemallow and white tufted evening-primroses, pink phlox, scarlet Indian paintbrush, yellow Rocky Mountain beeplants, white onions exploding into bloom like miniature sky rockets, a lavender cymopterus, deep purple in bud, lavender in flower, already rustling clusters of papery pods. A funnel-lily sends up lead-colored leaves and stems, topped with a spray of blue-striped white-petaled flowers.

Funnellily
(*Androstephium breviflorum*)

The morning is calm, bright, and clear, going to hot and dry. We pass signs of settlement: oil drums, a big steel dory on shore, a small aluminum rowboat with a motor moored to the bank, a floating pump, a rubber tire hanging from a big cottonwood, unswung. The river runs so smoothly that I spend most of the morning seated on the pontoon drawing the plants from Horseshoe Bend—another early cymopterus, this one with green-striped creamy petals and intricate leaves and seed pods, a stalk of peppergrass, the funnellily. Clair leans over to look at one drawing. "Not too shabby," he says, and I could not be more pleased had I been granted eternal absolution.

Beavers slide out of the thickets at the edge of every bottom. Here the river is too wide and too deep to build lodges, so they burrow in the bank. At Hammacker Bottom one swims out, inspects the raft, snaps his tail and dives, surfaces, repeats, over and over, until we suspect that he is doing it just to hear himself. Three beavers farther downstream munch willow shoots; they scoot into the water but none of them have loquacious tails. One of the members of Powell's 1871 expedition remarked on the beaver holes in the banks here and described the beavers as "chattering like a group of children."

Large fields are plowed at Hammacker Bottom, irrigation pipes in place on the ground, but the pumps are silent and there are no signs of activity. I suddenly realize that it is Sunday, but, as far as I am concerned, after two solid weeks on the river, days of the week have lost their meaning. The river veers gently left, entering Brennan Basin. Several oil wells are visible from the river. The porous reservoir rock for many of the wells in the Uinta Basin is Weber Sandstone, the rock of Steamboat Rock and the walls of Whirlpool Canyon, now lying far under the surface. The wells, drilled in the 1950s, produce a black intermediate oil, most of it trucked to Salt Lake City. The pumps make a faint intermittent, syncopated sound; a working well on top of the ridge rocks back and forth, Sunday or not.

Three grebes work the shallows on the far side of the river, cobra-like necks making them easily distinguished from ducks. When they dive, we watch and wait, trying to anticipate where they will emerge. They seem to stay underwater forever, finally rising far away. Grebes, like all diving birds, expel much of the air from their lungs, making it easier to dive; since their blood is richer in hemoglobin and so retains more oxygen than that of other birds, there is sufficient oxygen available to their systems to enable them to remain submerged for good periods of time, and their general metabolism slows when under water. The length of time they seem to be submerged is further enhanced by the fact that they often do not come up again in midriver, but behind the rushes and sedges at the bank, so they are probably credited with longer dives than they really make.

Although the river makes repeated meanders, there are also many small islands around which it flows. At this high water, most are flooded. One contains a thicket of young cottonwoods, another is nearly all tamarisk. Stabilized by herb and tree roots, the islands survive from season to season. Each is teardrop-shaped, broad end facing upriver. Chunks of sod that fall off river banks, if carried to an island, can root almost immediately. Wind-blown seeds, such as willow seeds, snag in the damp surface and find prime colonizing areas with fertile silt and ample water. Vegetation screens out more silt during periods of high water, and the cobbled island eventually becomes a mud flat at high water, an island at low.

A high-voltage line strings across the river, hung with orange balls to keep crop dusters from hitting the wires. As we come around a curve, there is the first view of the Tavaputs Plateau, level and remote, pale blue with snow lines; to the north Split Mountain is still just visible. The river is suspended between two rocky masses that are almost too far apart to see, in a flat flood-plain hammock hung by ropes of white rapids at either end.

OURAY NATIONAL WILDLIFE REFUGE begins just below Brennan Bottom. The river becomes almost lakelike, bordered on both sides with unleafed tamarisk brush, backed with cottonwoods that have river reflections gleaming in their leaves. Red-winged blackbirds by the dozen perch in the tops of the willows, meadowlarks make enraptured announcements. Three neat gray sheds housing throbbing diesel engines drown out the birdsong and mark the northern edge of the Ouray and Uinta Indian Reservation. Federal trust responsibilities on the reservation ended in 1961 and the Utes now govern themselves. This one is the second-largest reservation in Utah and borders the Green River on the east almost as far south as the Gunnison Valley.

We pull off river at Ouray to go to the trading post. It sells pickled eggs, fresh eggs, hooks and eyes, white gloves, pop, beer, hem tape, baking powder, sausage, sewing-machine threaders, earrings, buttons, brooms, knives, but no paper clips, which are what I need. A phone booth stands outside, lined with embossed metal patterned with a geometric flower design beginning to disappear under many coats of paint and many scribbled telephone numbers. I check in with our daughter Jane, who says that Skylab took off this morning. On the river we are averaging three miles an hour. Here there is point-to-point

Wild onion (*Allium textile*)

time and we traverse this country now as a hundred years ago, or perhaps even more slowly: in 1897 Butch Cassidy rode from Ouray to Browns Park in two days. Via the river, it has taken about a week.

The underside of the highway bridge is lined with cliff-swallow nests, made of the small gravel taken from the river bank, more granular than the usual clay ones. A blue truck pounds overhead; the vibration bothers the swallows not at all. Downstream, the Duchesne River enters on the right. A great deal of water is taken out upstream for irrigation, and at high flow the Green River backs up into it. In the top of a tall cottonwood half a mile further, a pair of huge gray-and-white birds nest. The female sits while the male flies out and circles back, screaming. When wings are outstretched, the dark band at the "wrist" on the white underwing is sharp, and that plus their large size mark them as fish-eating osprey, rather rare along the river. Their nest is a platform of sticks. A great deal of poking and pushing is going on, and the female's reluctance to leave the nest suggests that there are young. The male sits on a bare branch and vocally shakes his fist at us until we leave their territory.

The White River enters on the left, the last access from the east until the foot of Desolation Canyon some 125 miles downstream. Here Etienne Provost spent the winter before meeting Ashley in 1825, in a grove of cottonwoods upon which his horses could feed. Indians often wintered here, and a Spanish trail crossed here before 1830. Antoine Roubidoux's old trading post once stood at this confluence. Powell wintered near here before his first expedition, and on that trip

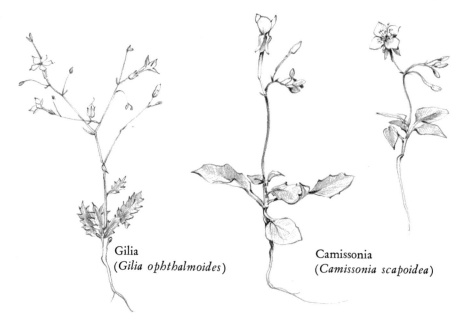

Gilia
(*Gilia ophthalmoides*)

Camissonia
(*Camissonia scapoidea*)

went out from here for supplies and mail. And plans have been announced for a billion-dollar oil-from-shale refinery here, using a process "which uses no fuel or water to extract oil from rock."

A ragged ledgy cliff rises two hundred feet above the river. Three men stand on top of it, taking potshots at the river. Since we are within range when we pass beneath, I feel as if it were 1863 and we were running the Yazoo River above Vicksburg. As we slip out of range, they wave at us with big, friendly sweeping motions. We wave back, much relieved that they have not been tempted to use the raft for target practice.

The river swings hard left. Because Clair knows of Fremont Indian drawings on the row of cliffs here, we go ashore. Some are unmistakably modern. But others are old: eight circles, one inside the other, chipped into the lighter, unweathered rock, and horned figures, and notations so weathered with time as to be indistinct. At the foot of the cliff, minute desert annuals—stickleaf, gilia, camissonia—all of which grow larger in more favorable sites, here are all a hand width apart and only an inch or so high. They bloom early, dropping their seeds into mud cracks, germinating only when spring dampness triggers them. A tiny lizard is so close to the soil color that I see it only by its shadow when it scuttles away. I take along a branch of sagebrush to draw because it carries a big, woolly gall on its stem.

The river loafs through the flat open country. Cottonwoods rimming the bank contain half a dozen huge nests, each with a crook-neck watcher: a heron rookery. None leave the nest. It is brooding

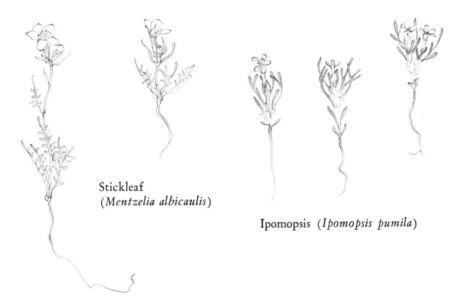

Stickleaf
(*Mentzelia albicaulis*)

Ipomopsis (*Ipomopsis pumila*)

time and the big birds sit with shoulders hunched, bills tucked in,
all looking like misanthropic dowagers. On either side, total wilderness
flanks the river: there are no towns, no houses, no ranches, no oil or
gas wells. The quadrangle to the west bears the confusion of section
and township lines that must drive modern cartographers to distrac-
tion. Early surveying was piecemeal, especially in the back country
where there was no immediate need to lay out fences and boundaries.
Often transitory landmarks were used—an old tree, a mound of dirt.
West of the Colorado state line and east of the Green River Valley,
no land survey corners were found when searched for in 1910 during
an official survey. East of the Green River, land lines were projected
from corners found in valley lands. West of the river, more settlement
and farming lands, laid out by subdivision and often fenced, afforded
a more complete starting point. The old Indian Treaty Boundary cuts
diagonally across the Uteland Butte and Ouray quadrangles, and
down the whole canyon to Green River, Utah, the maps are a confusion of offsets and setbacks. This remains wilderness, on the maps
as well as on the ground.

Sagebrush with galls
(*Artemisia tridentata*)

WITHIN THE DAY tamarisk have changed from bud to hazing green. Against the late-afternoon deep blue sky, river and butterflies are the only moving objects in the landscape. The afternoon sun incandesces in the sharp green of fresh-leafed cottonwoods on an island, making them look lighted from within, glowing with a green fire. On shore, an old homestead cabin stands near the river, and three big cottonwoods, broken off midway, stand like columns of an antebellum mansion. In the monumental stillness not a leaf moves.

Ten years ago this was represented on the topographical maps as an island; the narrow river channel has now filled in, but the river's former flowing is clear: once it ran over this whole nose of land, and back from the river one undulating rise after another marks former point bars and channels, now paved with maroon soil and river stones, broken with ragged ledges of bedrock. The whole countryside is ablaze with spring desert flowers, as if one of everything had been planted long ago—small furry daisies, milkvetch, mustards, strawberry cactus, phlox. We climb to the top of Wild Horse Bench, and there to the north, just visible, faint but unmistakable, is our last view of Split Mountain. Tomorrow we will be in the canyons and swifter water (and, Clair claims, no mosquitoes), but I have loved this dry, empty country, not much used for anything, impoverished perhaps, but beautiful in rock and sand and far vistas.

At the river's edge two tiny wrens sing high up in the cottonwoods under which we put our sleeping bags. Leaves on the ground are all shades of russet and bone, tan and brown, and they pile up around the big silvery logs. There is no wind. Smoke from the dying fire floats like a canopy over the river. The only sound is that of water steaming in the kettle. The moon hangs globelike from a cottonwood branch.

The quiet going of the river permeates the beginning, tentative night sounds; when fading light limits vision, small sounds become magnified, ears become more sensitive. During the day I do not hear the river as much because I am absorbed in the visual—the slotted reflections, the spinning vortices, light on the cliffs, the cast of new leaves and the hues of early flowers. Now, in the dusk, the river muses, as if to itself. The fire dies down and out. The wrens sleep. I fall asleep listening to moonlight and the old cottonwoods leafing out.

12

These peaks were gradually dropping down in height; and at one open section, with alfalfa and hay fields on gently sloping hillsides, we found a small ranch, the buildings being set back from the river. We concluded to call and found three men, the rancher and two young cowboys, at work in a blacksmith shop. Emery had forgotten to remove his life-preserver, and the men looked at him with some astonishment, as he was still soaking wet from the splashing waves of the last rapid. When I joined him he was explaining that no one had been drowned, and that we were merely making an excursion down the river. . . . These men, while absolutely fearless in the saddle, over these rough mountain trails, had "no use for the river" they told us; in fact, we found this was the usual attitude of the cattle men wherever we met them. McPherson's respect for the river was not without reason, as his father, with two others, had been drowned while making a crossing in a light boat near this point, some years before. Some accident occurred, possibly the breaking of a rowlock, and they were carried into a rapid. McPherson's men found it necessary to cross their cattle back and forth, but always took the wise precaution to have on some life-preservers.

ELLSWORTH KOLB, 1914, *Through the Grand Canyon from Wyoming to Mexico*

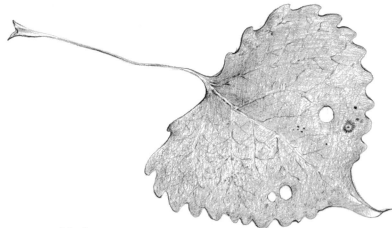

Cottonwood leaf
(*Populus fremontii*)

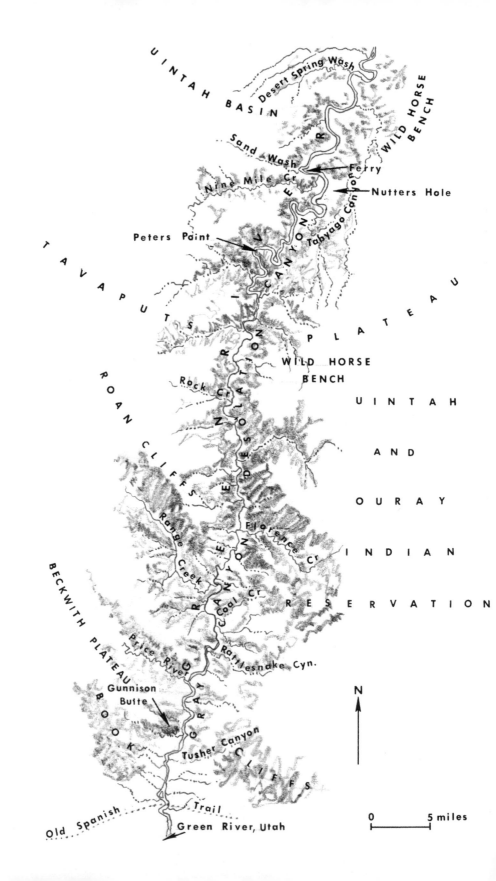

UINTAH BASIN

Desert Spring Wash

WILD HORSE BENCH

Sand Wash

Nine Mile Cr

Ferry

Nutters Hole

Tabyago Canyon

Peters Point

DESOLATION CANYON

GREEN RIVER

TAVAPUTS PLATEAU

WILD HORSE BENCH

ROAN CLIFFS

Rock Creek

UINTAH

AND

OURAY

INDIAN

RESERVATION

Range Creek

Florence Cr

GRAY CANYON

Coal Cr

BECKWITH PLATEAU

Price River

Rattlesnake Cyn.

Gunnison Butte

BOOK CLIFFS

Tusher Canyon

N

Old Spanish   Trail

Green River, Utah

0   5 miles

WILD HORSE BENCH
TO GREEN RIVER, UTAH

AT WILD HORSE BENCH the scale of the maps changes. The large quadrangle maps are at a scale of 1:2,400; the maps south to the town of Green River are 1:62,500, and the illusion is that we go more slowly, remaining on each map longer. Actually the current has picked up although not enough to cause any great acceleration, and although each of us has other places to be, we go with the river and worry not about arrival. A meadowlark with a gold-nugget breast perches beside the river and sings into a yellow morning breeze.

The cliffs begin the day two hundred feet high; by midafternoon they reach to six hundred feet, now massive, dark, dull purple-brown shales with lighter lenses of sandstone. There is an infinite combination of layers, gray sandwiched with tan, tan layered between buff, stripes of beige and ochre and sepia, the record of an ancient shifting shoreline. The Green River Formation appears again, walls sometimes flat and striped, reminding me of the cream and gray-green marble façades of San Miniato or the Cathedral in Florence. At other times that cliff is eroded into stepped-back ledges alternating with rounded slopes, like old temples fallen in upon themselves and recognizable only by a detail of carving or a shattered column. At first there are bottomlands bearing the name of the homesteader who worked them, but they become increasingly narrow as the cliffs sweep in toward the river and the map becomes cloisonnéed with elevation lines.

A row of cumulus clouds masses over the Tavaputs Plateau. The

mature cell of a thunderhead cauliflowers up ahead, already dissipating
and wisping out on top, but still capable of dumping rain. It is deep
Wedgwood blue beneath, on top sharp white. Other clouds drift
across the sun, bringing the cliffs into alternate light and shade, spot-
lighting prominences, a backdrop for *Der Fliegende Holländer*. In
the distance virga scarf down toward the ground. A great blue heron,
the same dusky blue as the virga, beats by, trailing long legs. A flock
of sandpipers flash white on their underwings as they wheel away.
Thunder gutters in the distance.

Vermiculate lightning covers the whole quadrant of the storm area.
Now there is only this one vast cloud, consuming all the moisture
pulled up from the ground or residual from previous rains. Gradually
it sulks to the east and filters upward. When one is living outdoors,
weather patterns become of paramount interest. Perhaps the modern-
day convention of discussing the weather is only a remnant of times
when, without roof or raincoat, people were truly affected by sun
and rain. All afternoon we watch the clouds develop and move, and
we calculate, speculate, feel the changing air pressure, react not only
to the different states of outer change but to the inner reactions that
affect the whole psyche.

THAT EVENING, Herman and I walk back half a mile from the river,
across the trough-and-channel terrain of abandoned meanders, to an
oil-shale cliff against which the river once pushed. Rows of willows
mark the old strand lines. Much of the ground is encrusted with alkali,
coating my boots with a fine chalk. The maps show, all along, the bottomlands on either side where the river once ran; present meanders
are consistently smaller than those abandoned, constantly reiterating
that this river once ran heavier and wider.

The cliff is made up of oil shale, weathering to an ashy white. I
pull a piece out of a shattered ledge. On one side are small angular
impressions that are the negative casts of crystals formed when the
lake in which these sediments lay evaporated. Split open, the rock is a
rich chocolate brown that indicates good-quality oil shale. Under the
hand lens, the fresh-broken edge shows fine lines, an alternation of
darker and lighter laminae, forming a series of varves. "Varve" is a
Swedish word meaning a periodic repetition; a dark and a light lamina
together form a single varve. The sediments drifted so quietly into the

lake that seasons can be counted: the lighter layer is wider and coarser, formed by sediments carried into the lake by streams in the summer; the darker layer formed in the fall and winter, rich in organic matter from summer plankton blooms.

Oil-bearing strata of the Green River Formation underlie some 16,500 square miles of adjacent lands in northwest Colorado, southeast Wyoming, and northeast Utah. Indians used "the rock that burns" for campfires; there is a story about one Mike Callahan, who built his fireplace out of an interesting dark brown rock and got a nasty surprise when he lit the first evening fire. Kerogen, which comes from a Greek word meaning "wax forming," is the compound that distinguishes oil shale from regular shale (and oil shale is not a true shale, but a marlstone). Oil shales formed in the basin lakes during periods of withdrawal, when the lakes were less than one hundred feet deep. Reduced depth and increased temperature resulted in increased plankton production, and the organic ooze congealed to a gelatinous putrid mass of matter, layer after layer over 6,500,000 years, compacting into a rock that underwent complex chemical and physical changes to become oil shale.

There is no free oil, or very little, and that oil trapped in the rock cannot be removed by ordinary petroleum solvents, and herein lies the problem. In the only presently workable method, shale must be mined, crushed, fed into a retort and heated to 900°F. in order to convert the kerogen into oil vapors and gasses. Since the tailings from this process take up from 10 to 50 percent more space than the original rock, are sterile, have the consistency of fine powder, and compact to a near impervious hardness, the residue from retorting is a large white elephant that will fill up canyons and upon which little will root. Runoff from it will carry salts into the upper Colorado River drainage system, where excess salts are already a problem. Vast amounts of water are necessary for processing, up to six million gallons a day (or 20,000 acre-feet annually for a production of 100,000 barrels a day), plus the demands for domestic use that accompany rapid settlement, amounts of water that are not available in oil-shale areas without impinging upon present domestic and agricultural uses.

The *in situ* process (which takes less water), in which fracturing is done by underground explosion, looks promising but is not yet practical. The Paraho retort process, which uses no water, is now under testing. Underground nuclear explosions are also being researched, but the specter of leakage into underground water may make this process unacceptable. Some environmentalists question whether the amount of recoverable oil is even sufficient to make expensive operations in remote country feasible. It is, as one environmental writer put it, a Pandora's box.

I start up the scarp, which turns out to be steeper than it looks, paved with very small chips of shale. It isn't so bad going up, but the way down gives me pause. There is nothing but space to hang on to. There are no irregularities for good footing, no way to wedge a foot into the side of the slope, and the fine debris is as slippery at this angle of repose as if it had been greased. I cannot imagine how Major Powell, one-armed and barometer laden, took readings on these slopes, making them every half hour in conjunction with those taken at base camp. Herman patiently talks me down.

Clusters of white mustards, wild four o'clock, skeleton plant and purple scorpionweed are a startling green against the pallid ground. A fat rose and tan and cream sphinx moth rests under an overhang, waiting for the four o'clocks to open. I stay behind to draw and it is dusk when I start back to camp. The evening fire glimmers faintly. Powell and his companion too, out late on a high shelf in Desolation, gingerly working down the loose slopes in the dark, were guided by "the gleaming camp fire," thankful to be back. I feel the same, walking toward the protective palisade of cottonwoods, where Clair has cooked pork, sauerkraut, potatoes, and applesauce for dinner, Herman's favorite.

The cottonwood leaves whisper rain, as they always do. Part of being on the river is coming to an understanding with these old trees that ring years of sun and wind and rain in their gnarled trunks. Across the prairies a row of cottonwoods means shade, water, rest. Along the river they mean the same. Their bark is shades of gray, tan in the thumb-deep cracks, rutted vertically, cracked horizontally. Sometimes the big branches lift straight up but mostly they lean out, wide and sheltering. They dangle catkins in the spring, ripen cottony seeds that candlewick the water and tuft the air and hang on every bush and shrub within miles. The leaves are a satisfying triangle, round-notched, strongly veined, a unifying green neither warm nor cool but perfect with blue sky and putty river. Before they fall they glaze waxy yellow, fading finally to the white of bleached bones. They layer the ground, interwoven with their knobby twigs, in a cushioned footing. The old trees die with dignity, falling in ranks, bark coming off in plates inches thick, silver wood furrowed with intricate beetle paths, crumbling back into the earth. An old cotton-

Wild four o'clock
(*Mirabilis multiflora*)

wood is protector of anthills, shelter for wren, shade for small plants, platform for osprey, perch for heron, shovel for Fremont Indian, all things to all creatures. Stonewall Jackson's reported last words were, "Let us cross over the river, and rest under the shade of the trees." Surely he meant cottonwoods.

To the east a full moon rises, etched with the black lines of an unleafed willow bush. The river runs mauve, reflecting the pink and gray and lavender of the cliffs in amorphous swirls of color. Tree branches darken to silhouette. The inside leaves of the cottonwoods hang still; only the very outer ones quaver in the evening drafts. Colors seep out of the river, the cliff, the sky, leaving only lambent river, webbed with chryselephantine fretwork, holding the sky light after that light fades.

Frog calls deepen and amplify. The male frogs are well tuned up; a deeper-voiced bullfrog leads the chorus beginning in iambic, switching to troche. Others join in, each species orchestrating its particular song. It is a warm night and frogs up and down the river answer. The moon brightens, a thick Albert Pinkham Ryder moon that draws an upside down exclamation point on the river. The river, in this nacreous night, holds the light like the underside of a mirror and slips toward morning.

THE FROGS are still going strong at daybreak. Water glints in the marsh; the river is up. A wren rejoices but Clair blasphemes—the lid of his favorite cast-iron Dutch oven slipped out of his hand and into the river and disappeared forever, for in this silt-laden water visibility ends at one inch.

At Sand Wash Ferry a delta sloping out into the river is now stabilized with shrubbery and cottonwoods and the river no longer breaks into rapids around it. Up from the river, a four-room cabin is dug into the ground, with framed windows and a sod roof. An old iron ferry boat rusts in the brush, decking so near the color of the rusty, ungreen thicket that it is nearly invisible, a willow growing right up through it, the iron scabbing off. On the opposite shore a twenty-foot opening, thickly brushed on either side, extends out into a landing platform. The ferry ran until the 1930s, carrying sheep and equipment, held by a cable at the crossing connecting to a road to the east.

Nine Mile Creek bounces in with a good rush, the first creek with any push to it; yesterday's thunderhead must have dumped water upstream. The oil-shale slopes flanking its entrance are purpled with

Scurf pea (*Psoralea* sp.)

scurf pea and scorpionweed. Nine Mile was originally known as Minnie Maud Creek, named after rancher Alfred Lund's two daughters. Numerous Indian ruins have been found there: storage cists, artifacts, pictographs, adhering to the highly conventionalized Fremont tradition, and small, nearly inaccessible constructions built high on isolated promontories. No artifacts are associated with these, and for lack of concrete evidence they have been called lookouts. Roof timbers indicate a severe drought in this area between 1270 and 1295, probably sufficient to cause the Fremont to abandon agriculture and to return to a primarily gathering and hunting economy. When life

Boxelder
(*Acer negundo*)

exists on an ecological margin, a very slight shift in climate can make a major change in culture.

According to Powell, Nine Mile is the beginning of Desolation Canyon. In the paleness of Desolation lies its charm. The long slopes of oyster-white shale flanking the river are interrupted only by the shadows of stringing ledges or small green shrubs that follow a seepage, or the hard edge of cap rock. The strata dip northward so imperceptibly that the reiterated beds look horizontal. Even the old cottonwoods have pale bark the same color as the cliffs, and weathered logs are paler still. The soil is pallid. Everything is muted to an ashen denominator in which cottonwood leaves gleam emerald. The more friable cliffs are triangled with fresh falls, cascading down the face like chocolate shavings. Sometimes seeps leak thin shiny banners down the slope. The cliffs are buff and pale putty; the river is dark putty with cream foam, reverse reflections of each other, a natural palindrome.

A beaver slips down the bank into the water. The ones we see now are always alone, probably those two-year-olds who have left the parental lodge and are out looking for *lebensraum* of their own. A recently discommoded young beaver is somewhat sad to watch; unlike its hyperreactive parents, it moseys along the river edge, stopping often at the shore, looking for a suitable place to settle.

The river is narrowing, flowing a little more swiftly. The cliffs become more terraced, less sheer, ballasted by sandstone ledges. Each ledge has a series of convex triangles of debris below it so that the slopes become a succession of spread fans, one on top of the other. As we come around Little Horse Bottom, the first waves gently rock the raft. The cliff makes a small tight horseshoe on the right. Of Green River Formation, it looks like an engraving, hand tinted in pale greenish-gray and sepia. The fine-lined horizontals, short, broken verticals, and the succession of fine repetitive lines literally resemble the contour lines on a topographical map. The cliffs rise a thousand feet above the river and could have materialized out of a geological illustration for a Powell report. The detail verges on the incredible, drawn with a hard precision. It is such a quiet running, without birdsong, that it seems as if the raft were drawn on the river and we are an illustration in a U.S.G.S. publication of 1879, a dot in time on the river, drawn in sepia ink with a crowquill pen.

A BREEZE coming upstream wrinkles the river, making the whole surface shimmer like lamé. The raft swings, itself a large piece of debris rotating in the current. Occasional upwellings surround it, the river's breathing and snorting.

In May boxelders bloom on the bank across from Peter's Point, a craggy reddish-brown marker, shadowed with apses and arches in chunky rough rock, thirteen hundred feet high, named for Indian Peter Post. While we are sitting on the grassed bank opposite, talking, there is a muted rumble. Near the top a block larger than a dining-room table cracks loose, drops out, hits a high ledge and kicks up a plume of dust, bounds to a lower ledge and settles. It is absolutely astounding to see a ton of rock, for no reason at all, simply let loose. It takes a minute for realization to coincide with sight. Only the settling dust marks that it even happened. I wish it had gone all the way to the river—it would have made such an eloquent splash.

The cliffs become craggier as we go downriver. Cottonwoods appear again along the river—boxelders dominate upstream, as if the two could not share the same bank. Rapids announce downstream, good bouncy water with no rocks showing. They begin to come every mile or so now, caused by washes of rock brought in at the foot of small canyons or draws. The pace increases, rapids coming at every turn, usually just a brisk cross chop, sometimes more.

Rock Creek bubbles in on the right. Rock Creek Ranch lies in a meadowed crescent beneath the cliffs, a gentle spot in the midst of rough canyons, level and protected, almost literally beyond nowhere —the topographical maps for the area are bereft of both township and section lines. Many old places along the river look derelict; Rock Creek Ranch does not. I sit beside the house on an old log, a house carefully built of blocks of warm rose sandstone masterfully cut, precisely laid. Even the chicken house is cut stone, carefully fitted, hung with a sturdy wooden door, and neatly plastered inside. The fields below were cleared, the rocks thrown into a breakwater, and once alfalfa and corn grew here, irrigation coming from the creek above, around the cliff, down to the meadow. In the orchard there are mulberry, apricot, pear, and peach trees that still make a froth of flowers in the spring. At the edge of the meadow a rim of cottonwoods glistens. At my feet shards of a blue bowl lie, convex sides up, pale sky blue.

On the raft again, I watch the ranch diminish. It is the quality of the green and the quality of the river, the sturdy endurance of what was built here that keep this place from being sad. It does not seem abandoned, only waiting, holding promise of new green. I would like to think that once again there will be a handful of fresh apricots picked off a laden tree and laid carefully in a pale blue bowl.

THAT EVENING, even though it has clouded over, the beach sand where we land remains warm. Drifts of small scurf peas, that look much like lupine, lavender the ground, many with leaves rolled over small

Rice grass
(*Oryzopsis hymenoides*)

dark larvae. One caterpillar, a late hatcher, probes about, still inside its green cylinder. Seated on a big cottonwood log, drawing it, I am visited by the largest, wooliest bumblebee I have ever seen, bright orange-yellow, very nearly the size of a postage stamp. Spiders constantly crisscross the sand at my feet, and the rice grass, just spreading into bloom, is full of ladybugs. A translucent sheath encases fat white buds striped with pale green, opening into a graceful fine-spun panicle. Indians often ground the seeds, which are high in food value, into flour for bread.

Sand-verbena
(*Abronia elliptica* [?])

The river runs just beneath the dune upon which we sleep. I listen to the small gossiping sound of the waves coming and going on the shore, beneath the steady pound of the rapid—persistent, a high, demanding continuum. I sight across the river and watch the waves, springing up and curling back on themselves, shooting up great globules of water like the stylized ocean waves on an old Chinese scroll. Each wave has its own moment, and the water passes in peaking or foaming, unfurling or flipping, in a unity of color and direction but an infinite variety of shape, river moving downstream, wave staying here.

The sand is so smooth and fine and warm that it is a sacrilege to mar it with footprints. I sleep fitfully, keyed to the sound of the rapids. In the morning, all around the dune, are the little investigative tracks of darkling beetles. Mice and lizard prints calligraph the sand, precise patterns laid in loose, open arcs. The lizard prints look as if a chain had been placed on the sand and gently pressed in, leaving neat imprints half an inch across. Beetle tracks are myriad, a double scallop an inch apart, a wavering streak down the middle from the dragging body. In contrast to the animal wanderings, the rice grass leaves scribe precise curves like a compass in the sand.

The three of us eat one of Clair's splendid breakfasts under a lusty old cottonwood. Nearly all the cottonwood leaves are perforated with eighth-inch holes, old and new. Many of the branches are only partly attached to the tree, yet are leafing out as if they had not split away. The new leaves are like malachite, carved and shaved to a thin translucence, hanging languid in the morning light, two shades of green: brilliant lime where only one leaf thickness is lighted, deeper green where they overlap, constantly shifting shadows. They luminesce, light contained within the leaves themselves, as phosphorescent rocks give off an unearthly glow. They are not the richness of yellow or the coolness of green, but a thinner, harder, more penetrating color that cuts like a laser into the spring river edge.

GRAY CANYON begins at McPherson's Ranch. At one time the ranch produced fruit, vegetables, and forage, irrigated by Florence Creek. McPherson settled here, not knowing that Florence Creek was a way station for the Wild Bunch, who had long used the pastures to rest horses and stock. He was on his way to get married when he met a posse and reluctantly had to join them, furnishing one of the more original explanations for not getting to the church on time. After the rustlers were cleared out, he settled here permanently with his family, and the hospitality of the ranch is mentioned in all accounts of river travel. Julius Stone, in 1909, wrote that "we stop at McPherson's ranch where we are treated to peaches, pears, and apples from the trees, also watermelons, cantaloupes, and tomatoes from the vines, all of the finest quality and flavor. The unfailing courtesy received from everyone we meet is in fine contrast to the scant consideration sometimes accorded wayfarers in the East." Most boatmen I know still get a wistful faraway look when they describe the quality of McPherson's orchard. In 1942 the ranch was bought for inclusion in the Uintah Ute Reservation and it is no longer farmed.

Powell originally called it Coal Canyon, and changed it to Gray Canyon on the second expedition. Brown sandstones and gray shales replace the ashen oil shales of Desolation Canyon. Coal beds are often present in the lower parts, and the dark streaks appear and disappear along the river. Land on either side of the river remains open only a mile below the ranch. Ten ducks flush out of a marsh and I realize that we have seen no geese for several days. Rapids are not conducive to water-fowl nesting and the rapids come solidly now, with names like Range Creek and Wire Fence, at the mouth of every draw.

Coal Creek was proposed as a dam site in an extensive preliminary survey of the Green River begun in 1910 under the Carey Act. This whole area was to be webbed with a canal system served by gravity canals and fifteen pumping stations. Later reconnaissance studies concluded that this grandiose scheme would be impractical, not only in the cost of the installations, but because three-quarters of the soil is unfit for agriculture, being too alkaline. The amount of excess alkali in the rocks and soil is obvious in every white patch and every white trail down the rocks, and every dark line of seepage bounded by a white one.

AT OUR LAST CAMPSITE, about ten miles upstream from Green River, Utah, a trail of ants threads from their hole in the sand to an old log half buried in the beach about four feet up from the water line, a distance of about sixteen feet all told. The ants emerge from a half-inch hole in a small hill within a foot of the rising water. The sand is damp and the waves are beginning to wash toward it. The log is higher, drier, and warmer, and so the ants, in a trail two to five ants wide, transfer the small wide dots of larvae to safety.

Milkvetch (*Astragalus ceramicus*)

A hellgrammite comes out of the water, a repugnant three-inch troglodyte, with eight pairs of legs and a flat head with murderous-looking scythelike jaws. Its large size is achieved during a two- or three-year period spent under a rock in the swiftest part of a rapid, after which it comes ashore to pupate under a log or stone, emerging as a dobson fly. The hellgrammite crosses the ant trail and the ants swarm on it. It coils and flips, a Gulliver beset by Lilliputians. Being now on the upshore side of the ants, it appears disoriented and turns to cross the column again to the safety of the water. Again the ants seethe over it. It twists and writhes, finally rolling back into the water, taking with it the few ants still clinging. The ant column, momentarily disarranged, reorganizes immediately.

I go back down to the river's edge after sunset to check the ants. There are only a few still following the path up the beach. In the morning, the beach is pitted in a granulated fretwork from last night's shower, the fragile rim of each alveolus formed by sand grains that flew out on the impact of a raindrop. The river sand is so fine that even a light breeze picks it up and the smooth sand surface is restored, grain by grain, even as I watch. The ants have totally disappeared. The river rose during the night and flooded out their anthill.

GUNNISON BUTTE rises on the right skyline, a reminder that Green River, Utah, was once called Gunnison's Crossing, after Captain John W. Gunnison. The original crossing was one of the few places for miles in either direction where there was a stable bottom and easy access to the river. Used as a ford by the Utes from times unknown, it became one of the major fords on the Old Spanish Trail, that began in Santa Fe and ran northwest to this crossing. At best never more than a trail, the Old Spanish Trail was practical and usable during the spring, summer, and fall. So much stolen livestock traversed it in the 1820s and 1830s that it earned the sobriquet of "Horsethief Trail." It was not until the winter of 1830–31, when William Wolfskill led twenty-one trappers west, that it was opened all the way from New Mexico to California.

The acquisition of Oregon in 1846, the termination of the war with Mexico in 1848, and the rush of gold seekers in 1849 pressured for better communication and transportation between the Mississippi River and the West Coast. At the close of the 31st Congress in 1852, an appropriation was made for a railroad survey, and in March of the following year exploration was authorized to follow a central route suggested by Senator Thomas Hart Benton. Although Benton would have preferred his son-in-law, Frémont, to be appointed, Captain Gunnison was made head of the small survey group that included a botanist, a geologist, a cartographer, and a military escort.

The expedition was directed to the Old Spanish Trail crossing of the Green River by an Indian guide. Here Gunnison was to split the expedition into two parties, one under his command, the other under Lieutenant Edwin Beckwith, who described the crossing:

> We crossed the river by an excellent ford, which we had observed the Indians crossing, from a few yards below our camp (on the Spanish trail) to an island opposite, and from its upper end to the shore. The river is 300 yards wide, with a pebbly bottom, as we forded it, but with quicksands on either side of our path. The water, rising just above the axletrees of our common wagons, flows with a strong current, and is colored by the red sandstone of the country through which it passes, having here the same red muddy character which the Colorado has far below, where it enters the Gulf of California.

Gunnison and his small party proceeded to the Sevier River. There all were ambushed by a group of revengeful Indians, Gunnison shot while he knelt and washed his face in the river. None survived. Beckwith took the remainder of the expedition to Salt Lake City, where they wintered. They returned east the next spring, going north to cross the Green River above the Uinta Mountains. They followed it nearly to its source, preceding the Hayden Survey by twenty-six years.

A PUMP transfers water from the river to a broad farm on the right bank. In the West, water rights must be applied for, and can change hands quite apart from the land on which the water is used, in sharp distinction to an eastern water owner's more permanent and absolute, or riparian, rights. In the East, rainfall normally exceeds evaporation, and the riparian doctrine gives the owner of the streamside property exclusive rights to its "natural use." Where water is plentiful, this system is practical. But west of the ninety-seventh meridian water is scarce, and the doctrine of prior appropriation holds: the state ordinarily possesses title to all water within its borders, and individuals appropriate it on a basis of "first in time, first in rights," and these rights may be forfeited by non-use. Irrigation rights carry a limitation of cubic feet, adjusted so that users up and down the river may remove specified amounts, which are both sufficient to needs and will not overtax the amount available.

In the Gunnison Valley agriculture can be successful only with irrigation since rainfall ranges between five and ten inches yearly. Although there are some excellent bottomlands, their extent is limited, and individual tracts are often small and irregular; in addition, those up canyon are isolated. Much of the remainder of the land is poorly drained and patched with alkali, the Mancos Shale flooring forming a variable soil that has a tendency when wet to imbibe roads, air strips, and miscellaneous farm machinery. Rustlers ingeniously took only small groups of cattle through at a time during the wet season, or made a circuitous trip to avoid leaving track molds that hardened into cemented evidence until the next gully washer. In fact,

Clam shells, Mancos Shale

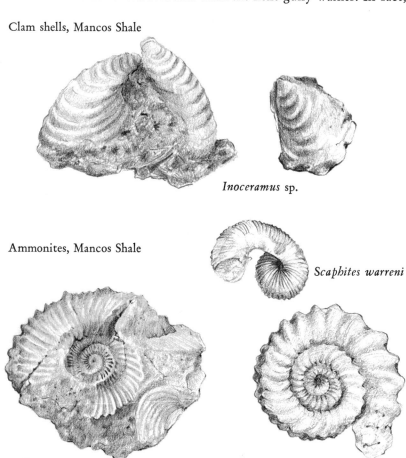

Inoceramus sp.

Ammonites, Mancos Shale

Scaphites warreni

Collingnoniceras sp.

C. woollgari

the landscape looks today just as it looked to Dr. James Schiel, geologist with the Gunnison expedition, in 1853:

> There could be no thought of any subsistence by the hunt, for one can travel for weeks without finding any game besides a pair of lonely jack-daws, or a few contented lizards, which seem to represent the animal life here. . . . The soil is so dry and bad that even the fields of artemisia and cacti, which in the Grand River territory are a nuisance for the traveler, disappear soon and only single specimens remind us of their existence.

A familiar sound comes upriver, that of a rapid, yet somehow steadier. Ahead a straight line of dancing water marks the top of a diversion dam. The raft slips down the spillway into the continuous smack of a three-foot backwave. On the left bank a big waterwheel stands silent. When the Kolbs came through in 1911, Ellsworth noted several waterwheels along the river here, some

> twenty feet or more in height,—with slender metal buckets each holding several gallons of water, fastened at intervals on either side,—were placed in a swift current, anchored on the shore to stout piles, or erected over mill-races cut in the banks. There they revolved, the buckets filling and emptying automatically, the water running off in troughs above the level of the river back to the fertile soil.

Around the farmhouse, iris and peonies are blooming. Years ago a housewife put her mark on the river and it blooms every spring.

As we approach town, gutted, wheelless cars lie like grotesque carnage on the river bank, piled there to keep the new shorter channel, cut when the highway bridge was built, from shifting. The roofs of Green River appear through the trees. Founded officially in 1878 as a mail relay station between Salina, Utah, and Ouray, Colorado, it is one of the few Utah towns without a Mormon background.

An apocryphal story avers that Gunnison Butte once bore a profile closely resembling that of Brigham Young. Since the town was a railroad community rather than a congregation of the faithful, the profile received less than proper respect. One dark night, after a lengthy session of hundred-proof debate, it is said that some of the more energetic of the town's notables made their unsteady way to the appropriate promontory, and with a little dynamite surgery irrevocably altered the Butte's configuration.

Wild larkspur
(*Delphinium nelsonii*)

13

In its descent from the east the railroad runs into a shallow valley, which conceals the view of the surrounding country, and finally comes out on the east bank of Green River at a little village called Elgin. The change from the barren slopes of shale to the beautiful green of the cottonwood trees and the brilliant fields of alfalfa is very grateful to the traveler, and he welcomes the sight of running water. It is true that Green River is generally muddy, but even if it is he looks upon it with pleasure and almost with reverence, because a stream of this size that can persist through so many miles of semiarid land excites curiosity and admiration. The river is spanned by a fine steel bridge, and a mile farther west is the station of Greenriver, an oasis in this inhospitable desert, at the lowest point on the Denver & Rio Grande Western Railroad.

MARIUS CAMPBELL, 1922, *Guidebook of the Western United States, Part E. The Denver & Rio Grande Western Route*

At the San Rafael a heavy rainstorm came up, and presently we detected a loud roaring we could not account for. At last, however, it was discovered to arise from the accumulated rain-water which was pouring over a near-by cliff in a muddy torrent. The whole country was extremely bare and barren, mostly rock, and the rain gathered as on the roof of a house. The river had narrowed up before we reached the San Rafael and had entered low, broken walls. The current was rather swift, but there were no rapids. As we went on, the sight of the rain cascades falling with varying volume and colour, some chocolate, some amber, was very beautiful. They continued for a time after the rain had ceased, and then, as if the flood-gates had been closed, they vanished, to reappear every time it began to rain afresh.

FREDERICK S. DELLENBAUGH, 1904, *The Romance of the Colorado River*

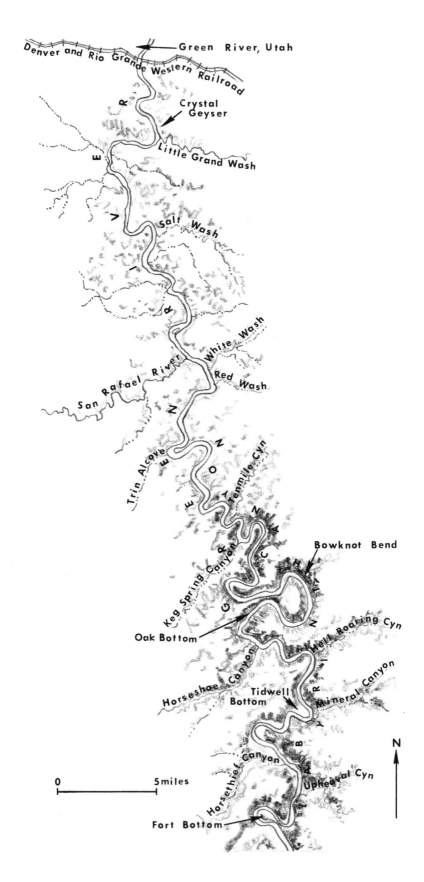

GREEN RIVER, UTAH,
TO FORT BOTTOM

HERMAN LEAVES ME at Green River and I continue on down to the confluence with a group. I have never departed Green River other than under a high overcast, and this time is no exception. Colors are muted, far cliffs hazed, even people's voices, waiting to be on river and under way, are quiet.

A more festive leavetaking was described by Frank B. Stanton in *Down the Colorado*. He was chief engineer for Frank Mason Brown of Denver, who organized the Denver, Colorado Cañon and Pacific Railroad. Coal was needed on the West Coast, and there was coal in Colorado, and Brown, a promoter and entrepreneur, believed that a railroad could more reasonably be constructed along the slight grade of the Colorado River than by putting tracks over mountain passes. On a preliminary reconnaissance trip, Brown's party left Green River (then also called Blake), May 25, 1889:

> The work of loading the boats and preparing the raft occupied the whole morning of May 25th, and, by that time everything being packed, we lunched on cold bread and river water, and ten minutes before one pulled out from shore. The whole population of Green River, both male and female, were on the river bank to bid us farewell. The postmaster took photographs of our fleet as we floated away, and everyone gave us several rousing cheers as we rowed down on the quiet water below the railroad bridge.

Only ten days previous, Frank C. Kendrick, on the preliminary survey, had pulled *up* the Green River. Engaged by Stanton in March,

Kendrick left Moab to survey the upper Grand River (now called the Colorado). Kendrick and his men spent seven weeks reaching its junction with the Green on May 4th, and were then "ready to take a 75 mile pull up to Blake." They rowed, pulled, lined, and fretted their fifteen-foot pine dory against the current, not aware that the distance was some forty-two miles longer. Kendrick's boots wore out and he had to put them together with wire; worse was to come as his entry of May 15 describes:

> Started out in the morning with swift water and it kept getting swifter with gravel bars running away out in the river. No help for it but to get out in the water & pull on the rope. Ugh—its cold and to cap it all there is a hurricane blowing making the waves wash over everything & wetting us all over. The sand is blowing so it looks like a heavy snowstorm coming. Often we cannot see the boat. At noon we stopped & consulted about getting dinner & we came to the conclusion that as we had only grub enough for 1 more meal that we had better save it for supper as we might have to travel all day tomorrow without anything.

It was with great relief that they heard the steam whistle of the Denver & Rio Grande late that same day.

Brown's trip down the Green and Colorado was a tragic one. He would allow no life preservers, and his boats were little sturdier than cedar matchboxes, in order, he said, to make portages easier. Brown was drowned in Grand Canyon, a reprisal for carelessness toward the river, and the railroad, it goes without saying, was never blasted out of these narrow canyons.

Eighty-four years later, also in May, we push off into placid water that reiterates the low-horizoned landscape in Renoir reflections. It is 117 miles to the confluence by river, only half that as the hawk flies, and according to Stanton the fall is 176 feet, an average fall of less than one and a half feet per mile, and in some reaches only six inches.

The eternal enticement of water spanking under the bow has led to ambitious attempts to navigate this lower river. In 1891 a thirty-five-foot launch named *Major Powell*, propelled by two six-horsepower engines, left Green River for Moab via the confluence. The first attempt was abandoned because of a broken propeller. Other launches in 1892 were also unsuccessful: the *Undine* and the *Cliff Dweller* both ran aground running upstream on the Colorado side. The promoters requested that Congress appropriate funds for stream improvement, but in 1909, under the River and Harbor Act, investigations showed this to be an impractical venture and the idea of steamboats was forgotten.

We pass under the Denver & Rio Grande Railroad bridge. The Union Pacific to the north was unable to keep up with the demands of a rapidly expanding West and within fourteen years the D. & R. G. bridge spanned the river here. Begun in 1881 and laid as a narrow gage, it was widened to standard in 1890. Just below is a water gaging station established in 1894; measurements used to be made from a ferry that crossed upstream from the bridge; high-water measurements are still made from the railroad bridge.

The river current is relaxed, swirled with small eddies and dimples, scrolling down a gentle gradient. Six phalaropes, small sandpiper-like birds, spin around in a circle on the water like a wind-up toy. Wind kicks out across an open draw and roughens the surface. The water is putty and khaki, reflections laid in looping lozenges and ovals, highlighted with ivory, changing with the magic of a kaleidoscope.

MINERAL DEPOSITS encrust the left bank. Here the Glen Ruby Well No. 1, an oil well drilled in 1935–36, remains only as a pipe stuck in the rock, now called Crystal Geyser. Drilled over 2,500 feet deep, it was abandoned because there was insufficient quantity and quality of both oil and gas. The geyser obtains its energy from trapped carbon-dioxide gas, and when it erupts, spouts a column of odoriferous tepid water that decorates the ground with red, yellow, and gold from the iron oxides dissolved in it. More than five hundred wells have been drilled in the counties contiguous to the confluence of the Green and Colorado, encouraged by an oil seep here or a bituminous outcrop there. None have produced marketable quantities of oil.

Terraces flank the river, describing a time when the river flowed at least eighty feet higher. In the Southwest, warm, dry conditions have existed for the last six hundred years; since 1885 arroyo cutting has become severe, instigated by overgrazing combined with known climatic variations, primarily a change in the frequency of intense rain. Fluctuations of the river's flow are not so much marked in the monumental landscape forms as they are in the smaller alluvial deposits along arroyos and streams in the smaller valleys, and locally in terraces along the big rivers.

Raw, open sand dunes spread over the right bank, white prickly poppy and masses of yellow mustard and sand-verbena blooming across them. They undulate on the horizon, some of the dunes sandy yellow, some with a pink or salmon cast, rising to a crest, falling off steeply. Distant thunder rolls. The sky is sooty blue to the west, and as the pink sands absorb the light, the dunes almost glow. Gray lines streak down from gnarled greasewood bushes hanging on the dunes' flanks. A stab of lightning discharges, remote. The river turns glassy calm.

Dellenbaugh Butte, named for Frederick Dellenbaugh, the young artist who accompanied the second Powell expedition, is a handsome structural landmark faithfully reflected in the river. Dellenbaugh was only seventeen when he made this trip, and he wrote of it with unrestrained and romantic enthusiasm in *The Romance of the Colorado River*, a young man enthralled by both Powell and the river.

The river makes a near-right-angle turn and the current fumes around the outer edge. The San Rafael River slips in from the west. And here we enter Labyrinth Canyon. According to Powell, who named it, Labyrinth runs some sixty-two miles to the head of Stillwater Canyon. On the map, it does indeed seem that the river does not flow downhill but aroundhill. The geologist on Powell's second expedition, Stephen V. Jones, entered in his journal, September, 1871, that the San Rafael was "a stream of about 15 feet wide and 6 inches deep, the water colored nearly white by the soil through which it runs." They found considerable evidence of Indian occupation and the men picked up arrow and lance heads and hundreds of flint chips.

The river is still accessible by road and signs of habitation persist. A dog barks. Rain sheets down ahead, vacuuming up the dryness. Lightning splashes twice on a near horizon. Another dog barks. The sound carries upriver. Two bark together, sounds separating and merging. Two people hoe an alluvial bench; they look like the bronze figures that parade around a Venetian clock, their motions slow, mechanical.

The river is often most beautiful when it rains and I wait with pleasure for the rain to sweep upstream. A quick breeze announces its coming. Rain silvers sky and river, coining circles on the water. The quick, slick sound of rain on the raft, the soft peppering on face and hands—I feel as if I absorb moisture out of the air, like moss on a rock, greening up with its beneficence. The cottonwood leaves along the shore hang heavy, as if made of metal. The vertical cliff faces remain dry, barely changing color, but the streamers of desert varnish begin to gleam. We proceed between two streaming worlds in a cocoon of gray stillness.

We pull ashore at Trin Alcove. A thicket of scrub oak screens the entrance, leaves already infested with galls and leaf miners. Powell described the configuration of its triple alcoves:

The right cove is a narrow, winding gorge, with overhanging walls, almost shutting out the light. The left is an amphitheater, turning spirally up, with overhanging shelves. A series of basins filled with water are seen at different altitudes as we pass up; huge rocks are piled below on the right, and overhead there is an arched ceiling.

It is the left alcove that I follow, guided by walls of Navajo Sandstone that rise far above my head.

Navajo Sandstone is a beautiful rock, rising in walls massive and crossbedded: wind-laid dunes, immortalized in rock. Some of the beds are horizontal but the more dramatic ones lie at a high angle, patterning the wall with a lilt of finely swept lines. The direction of the cross strata indicate that the winds came from the north, with occasional shifts to east and west, at a time when vast deserts extended from southern Wyoming to central Arizona. Each crossbed set represents an individual dune, separated by a gently inclined erosional surface, and the exquisite visible patterns depend upon what segment of the dune is exposed. Crossbedding results from the way in which dunes are formed: wind slides and pushes sand grains up the windward side of the dune to the crest, where they drop over and fall down the lee side, the dune thus moving in the direction of the wind. Sliced through by erosion, the sweeping tangential lines (each a crossbed) are emphasized by changes in grain size, thin layers of larger grains deposited by slightly heavier and more vigorous winds.

A narrow stream bed is cleanly and neatly corrugated from the last runoff. It is firm, crimped with inch-high ripples. At the side of

CROSSBEDDING IN NAVAJO SANDSTONE

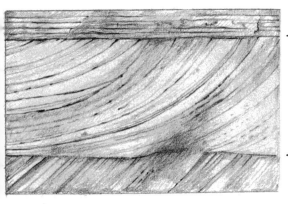

Erosion took place before the succeeding cross set was deposited.

the channel the drier sand is dimpled with recent rain. It seems such a sacrilege to disturb these pristine designs that I skirt them whenever possible. Footsteps make no sound in the velvet silence. I crumble a fragment of sandstone with my fingers, releasing grains of sand, remnants of some sinuous dune, small spheres that under a hand lens consume the vision like frosted moons.

A canyon wren trills, and it is so startling, so sweet, such an unexpected outburst of crystalline song in this alone stillness that I cannot breathe for waiting to hear it again. The song echoes into the silence, flutelike, in the infinity of a sandstone afternoon.

WE MAKE CAMP across from a rosy Navajo cliff, pictured by Robert Stanton in *Down the Colorado*, the original manuscript of which ran some two thousand pages, certainly the longest book ever written on the Colorado River. In the morning, after yesterday's rain, the cliffs look scrubbed clean; colors are fresh and intense. Part of the brilliance of the flowers lies in the quality of the light, and part in the color of the soil weathered out of the Navajo Sandstone. Neither brown nor red, dark nor light, it tends to deepen the colors that bloom

Sandverbena
(*Abronia nana*)

against it. The sand is barely damp, protected by the crosshatch of plant leaves above: bright lavender asters, pure lemon yellow tackstem, and an understory of sand-verbena—small white blooms and thick, red-veined and winged seeds on sturdy three-inch plants.

The river too is all sparkle and charm this morning, sun shooting off ripples in sharp flashes. On this May trip, the boatman runs his three Green River rafts lashed together crosswise. I almost expect to hear someone reading Scott's *Lady of the Lake*, as Powell did with his boats lashed together thus, drifting through Browns Park.

The Navajo Sandstones disappear, and the river slices down to the monumental marker of Labyrinth Canyon: Wingate Sandstone. It rises in a vertical wall along the river, bringing with it a sense of cliffs and canyons. The raft slides in close. Out from this shadow is a sun-bleached river; in this tempered shade I reach out and touch a fluttering reflection on the wall, feeling the granular surface. Wingate Sandstones are composed of extremely uniform fine quartz sands, each grain coated with iron oxide, that provides its vivid rusty color. Iron is abundant in many rocks, and in combination with oxygen, produces stable iron oxides, commonly known as rust. Even an infinitesimal trace of iron gives deep color. Often newly exposed rock surfaces are different in color from those that have been oxidized over centuries of exposure. On fresh break, Wingate Sandstone varies from light red to buff—clear, pale colors seen only in new falls.

Water and wind insinuate into every exposed crevice, gnawing out small handholds and notches, bays and arches, carving friezes and pediments, architraves of rimrock, vast columns and plinths, an architectural vocabulary that is simple and impressive because it is classical. Wingate Sandstones tend to be heavily jointed, the resultant vertical cracks of which form passageways into which rainwater seeps, washing in chemicals that react with the rock itself, forming compounds of greater volume than the original minerals, eventually prying and wedging masses of rock away from the parent cliff. Large blocks lie on the slopes below the cliff, and isolated fingers, the height of the cliff, still stand, a slot of sky between.

Magnificent blind arches also adorn these colossal cliffs. We drift beneath one across from the mouth of Mineral Canyon. The bottom half is heavily darkened with desert varnish, but the top, more protected, is fresher in color, lined with three white streaks. The general consensus is that big arches are not formed piecemeal but that there is, over a period of time, a loss of support beneath and a general loosening of the façade that is triggered in an instantaneous fall. Since no one has ever recorded seeing such a spectacle, it is pleasant to speculate on the birth of such an arch: a muffled rumble, a shimmering of the whole cliff face, a burst of rock violating the river into geysers, ballooning clouds of dust—clearing to reveal an arch implanted in the wall as if by magic.

THIS ARCH faces one of the few access roads in the lower canyons, and in early April, I ride down it with Kent Frost, a guide who has written about and knows Canyonlands like the back of his hand. I have come on this trip in early April to see the river as early in the season as possible since boat trips do not begin until May. It is my first sight of the river for the year. It curves away, an evocative, elegant turning, and a soft hollowing wind whispers of coming summer on the river.

Mineral Canyon is a stage set with Wingate wings. Tumbleweeds, all pale gray, are piled up into the head of a draw, as if the wind had tried to sweep last year's debris out of the way. Sand has blown up into hummocks over a prickly pear cactus; the top spines, porcupine-like, barely emerge. A straight line of badger tracks heads to the entrance of an old uranium mine, a remnant of the mining boom here in the 1950s. Early commercial mining was for radium; not until 1881 were the associated minerals noted, and uranium was described only as "an unknown yellow mineral," not segregated and identified until 1898. Ten tons of ore, shipped out by burro and wagon, sold for $2,600, or about 13 cents a pound.

This mine tapped a belt that lies southwest of the La Sal Mountains. The uranium deposits here are related to the intrusions of magma that raised these mountains. Igneous activity is accompanied by a production of mineralized "juices," that may spread into adjacent rock through ancient stream channels, impregnating them with ore-rich fluids. Stream deposits are continuous enough so that solutions may flow within the lens of the deposit, but lateral dispersal is blocked by the finer materials that define the edges of these lenses. The Chinle and Morrison formations both contain river channel deposits marked by sandstone lenses, and produce over 90 percent of the uranium mined in this area.

Dark red Chinle Formation strata appear at the base of the Wingate cliff as a sloping pedestal. Because of its slabby weathering, it provides

Tansy aster
(*Machaeranthera tanacetifolia*)

pockets of soil for plants, especially golden prince's plume, up to six
feet tall, that grows like so many luminous candles. Some prospecting
has been done here by identifying plant species that indicate selenium,
an ore intimately associated with uranium; these plants are the only
group known to be dependent on the occurrence of a single element
for growth. Among them are prince's plume, several milkvetches,
and rice grass. In addition, many of these desert plants have long root
systems and draw water from moist beds at considerable depth, making them especially effective indicators in semiarid regions, where they
depend more upon ground water than surface water for moisture.

A little farther downriver an old metal ferry boat is beached across
from a small mine opening. The boat is half full of water, rusty, an
angular, awkward thing to begin with and not enhanced by age. Water
standing in it is scummed over and murky with algae. Useless cables
lie looped like tensile snakes. And, being more trouble and expense
to remove than to leave, the ferry rusts itself to dusty death, unfed
on by any scavengers, unuseful, unwanted, unbeautiful.

BELOW MINERAL CANYON the river swings back and around in a
great double loop, flowing in all some nine miles and advancing only
half a mile downstream. Powell's men called it a "bowknot of a river"
and so it is, a striking example of an entrenched meander, where the
river has lowered itself down through nearly a thousand feet of rock.
This meander originated during a previous cycle of erosion, swinging
back and forth across a flood plain of low gradient, through easily
eroded rock. At some point in time, uplift of the Colorado Plateau
accelerated, and its river systems rejuvenated. Downcutting more
quickly, the river preserved the contortions that had evolved earlier,
but why it held to its original curve without lateral cutting is simply
not known. The outer canyons near the confluence were probably
eroded during the last twenty million years, the final mile stripped
off in the last ten million years by a drainage system with little re-
semblance to that which now exists.

In May, three of us get off the rafts for the short, easy climb up
the Chinle Formation ridge separating the upper loop of the horseshoe. As I climb, leaning toward the slope, the heat of the rock radiates up and the heat of the sun presses down, impregnating my backbone with the kind of warmth that will last all winter. Four hundred
feet of Chinle Formation is exposed on this slope, a veritable rain-

Golden prince's plume
(*Stanleya pinnata*)

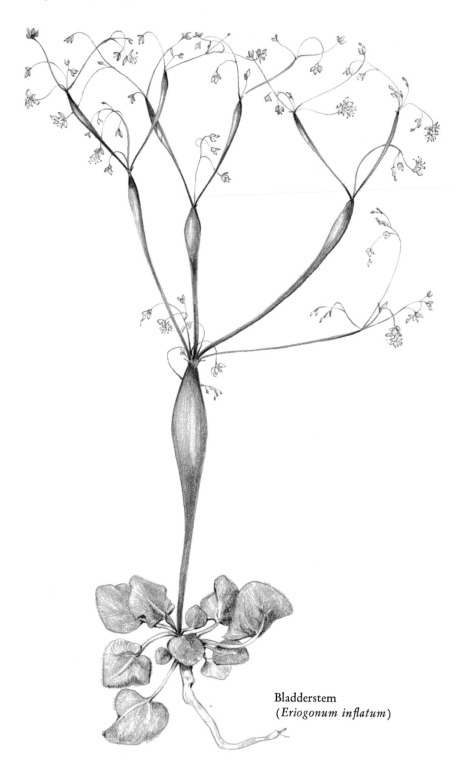

Bladderstem
(*Eriogonum inflatum*)

bow of rock colors: red-brown, green-gray, pale gray, ochre, purple-brown. Maroon shales flake into fragments that slide and cascade underfoot.

I am so absorbed in the variety of rock strewn across the slope that I crest the ridge and see the river on the other side in almost total disbelief. A two-inch-wide river flows below, viscous brown, overlaid with gold netting. An elongated teardrop of an island floats on it. I feel as if I could have kept on climbing for hours and that the finger of Wingate Sandstone, that looked so small from the river and now appears as a thirty-foot silo above me, is but a direction signal indicating the way up.

On top, the ridge is plated with gravel and shale of an extraordinary dark, rich color. Standing astride this two-river world I am eye level with the cliffs across the river. The intense light activates some neurological response: I feel in my shoulder blades what Icarus was thinking and Daedalus knew. The heat from the shale paving the ground sears up through my sneakers, shimmers my horizons. It is a moment of suspended time when one could so easily cross over into another dimension, a feeling neither of exhilaration nor euphoria, but simply of infinite possibilities.

The rafts slide into view below, like silver grains of rice; it is time to traverse the ridge and go down, and it is simply motor reaction that starts me across the saddle. The weird bladderstems seem appropriate to this other world, plants so far apart that each seems a glorious invention. A collared lizard, sunning on a rock, flies off at my approach. Having never seen one before, I am curious. About ten inches long, it holds its tail high as it runs, skimming lightly, bounding up on a boulder where it raises itself as high as possible, stretching and peering about, before lowering to a normal lizard posture. I follow it slowly and it stays just ahead, stopping and watching, waiting, running on ahead without running away. It is graceful, swinging from rock to ground as if without weight or gravity, each time stretching far up off the rock, craning its neck. With care I am within four feet of it. I kneel within three feet. Then two.

It is a dusky gray-green speckled with dark spots on the legs. Its feet are large, spiny and delicate, as sulfurous yellow as if it had been running in pollen. The most distinctive mark is its collar, a black line on either side of a pale tan band inset with brown spots. A slight bluish cast on its flanks is the same as the chalky turquoise of some of the Chinle pebbles. It is a tiny, enameled dinosaur, jeweled, curious,

watchful. It is anthropomorphic and inappropriate to attribute senti-
ence to a small lizard, yet I know, I *know* that it is curious about the
two-legged being that studies it, but that it does not seem to wish to
be thought so. I move closer and violate its perimeters. It dematerializes
with a faint scrabbling sound. I instinctively reach out and touch the
rock where it sat. The rock is too hot to leave my hand on.

I watch for it across the remainder of the saddle. The enchantment
persists, as if on top of this ridge with a river on either side I partici-
pated in another life that belongs to this hot, dry sky-bottomed world.
Something at this moment reaches across genera and order, straight to
the beating of heart, a sense of being so heightened that I walk outside
of myself into another dimension of sunlight.

Climbing up is simple; going down is sobering. Intimations of glory
disappear in the immediate and practical need for footing across
narrow ledges and precarious boulders. One ledge is so confined by
overhanging rock that there is no place to stand or crawl, to hold to,
to sit. After somehow traversing this, lifting through boulders and
sliding downslope is nothing. I reach the bottom out of focus. There
has been no time to sort through, to think out. I look back up at the
saddle just crossed. A human figure, from the river, would be microscopic.

I am glad when we pull off the river for lunch. We noon on a small
terrace at Oak Bottom, edged with scrub oak and perched against a
high cliff where Brown and Stanton camped in 1889. The river must
have been lovely in those years, with only the oaks and willows, un-
tangled with trashy tamarisks. Noon on the river, when the sun is
shining and the breeze is pensive, is peace incarnate. On the underside
of a leaf, an empty bee skin hangs and never quivers. Three-quarters
of an inch long, it is transparent, crisp, with dark brown stripes on
the abdomen, perfect even to the hollow, bristled legs, the empty
antennae, the fragile mandibles. The sonorous buzzing of the flies is
soporific. I prop myself up against a rock ledge and close my eyes
and fall asleep with my mind open.

AN AFTERNOON in Labyrinth Canyon has a panoramic quality, as
if the raft stands still and the landscape is pulled by. The Wingate
cliffs are cut with massive, sharp-edged alcoves and amphitheaters.
The magnificent rock-carved walls of Petra, the ancient city of Jor-
dan, are the only suitable comparison: the same warm rock, the same

sense of structural walls overlaid with designs in relief, the same sense of heat and silence and nonrelatable time. Beneath these cliffs, the river is running so terra cotta in color that reflections only subdue it, the fired clay of some exquisite Indian bowl, slotted with lavender and buff.

We stop off at Hell Roaring Canyon, a wide-mouthed canyon slipping eastward off the river. Neatly pecked into a sandstone ledge, up under an overhang, is "D. Julien" above "1836" and "3 Mai." Perhaps, sheltered under this overhang, M. Julien sat out a gully washer, while the water foamed down the flat-bottomed creek bed below and tore away at the silty bank, and passed the time by chiseling out his name.

Denis Julien was a trapper and trader from St. Louis, but records about him are sparse. His name, with a date of 1831, appears near Antoine Roubidoux's fort on the White River, near where it enters the Green, and Julien may have worked as a guide there. The next inscription in Labyrinth, some twenty miles upstream from Hell Roaring Canyon, is dated the 16th of May, implying that Julien was traveling upstream. But the one at the foot of Cataract Canyon, discovered by Robert Stanton, is the most intriguing: it was chipped into a wall that could only have been reached during high water and by boat, thus making D. Julien the first known boater to navigate what is still, at high water, a whopping good ride.

A slowing of the day begins, not anything I can detail, perhaps only a subtle change in color or angle of light, perhaps nothing more than a slowing of my own metabolism. It is an awareness that becomes marked out of doors, even if only subliminally, more so than in the light-switch world. The emerald willows at Tidwell Bottom stand out with such a greenness as I do not recall seeing before on the lower river. A haze of green gentles the far benches, a verdure that only comes in a wet springtime in these dry canyons.

There is a second blind arch in the Wingate Sandstone, high on the right bank across from Point Bottom, wider and more splayed than the one across from Mineral Canyon. Powell called it an entrance to a monastery—indeed, once beyond that door there would be no turning back. Within the main arch is a vertical setback, like some great metal door, already beginning to move, to clang shut with the sound of epochs. This is not a static arch; it is spreading and stressed, vital, flanked on either side by seated guardian statues like those of the pharaoh Rameses II at Karnak. Far to the left, one massive pilaster with a sculptural weighty capital remains.

I sleep on a low ledge near the water's edge, a bank fragrant with evening-primroses and pale blue amsonia, so I can listen to the sound of the river. A cluster of big boulders shoulder up out of the water; behind them the water periodically backs up, then surges over. Then the sound subsides, the river is momentarily quiet, and then another sequence of fluvial commentary begins. At nine o'clock the day turns and the world stands still. It is neither dark nor light but a hanging balance, an eternal fulcrum of time. Bats loop through the insect-laden air above the river. Crickets liquefy the night air with their singing.

At first light I awake for the fiftieth time, chilled by the dawn breeze. The moon, which rose shortly after midnight, is still bright. Venus tags along just to the left. I am tired, stiff, and damp. My sleeping bag streams with condensation, as if it had been rained on. The river rose during the night and the surges lasted progressively longer in the darkness, and against that rhythm I listened for the tiny lapping sounds that would say the river was flooding this ledge. Water flowing over the rock sounded like a gallon jug held upside down, water guggling out. In addition, a great hollow thumping pounded through the ground, a cavitational shuddering that added nothing to my peace of mind.

The rising water took fresh chunks out of the bank. The river is now halfway up a willow bush. Mats of roots hold most of the soil in the bank firmly, although there is evidence of the river's carving in a tamarisk hanging out over the water by a root thread. It is a six-foot-high tree composed of oversized twigs, topped with two flaccid sprigs of green, a misbegotten upstart, not even good for hanging a wet sleeping bag on.

Yet what I come to remember of that ill-chosen ledge beneath a red sandstone arch is not the discomfort but a mockingbird that sang all night within the moonlight, a wandering sagebrush song, pensive and melodic, haunting and penetratingly sweet.

THE RIVER swings into Fort Bottom, so called because of the Indian lookout on the top of the pinnacle above the river. A small cabin on the bench below, reminiscent of the small homestead cabins all along the river, is said to have been one of the way stations of Butch Cassidy. One of the well-used trails led from Hanksville, on the other side of the river, crossed this remote backcountry, and ended at

Amsonia
(*Amsonia eastwoodiana*)

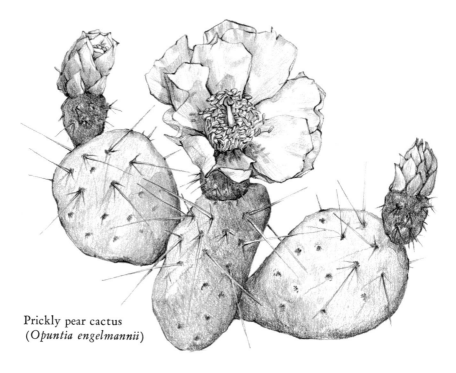

Prickly pear cactus
(*Opuntia engelmannii*)

Brown's Hole or Hole-in-the-Wall. Like Browns Park, this was superb hiding country for those who knew it well, and the high Chinle parapet provides a panoramic view.

At its base are hundreds of prickly pears, vivid with waxy yellow flowers, stained deep pink toward the base, heavily powdered with pollen. The cup of each flower is alive with tiny translucent gray-backed beetles, and all the stamens twitch with their pushing and probing. As I sit drawing, I notice other infinitesimal bugs, thickly clustered on the stems, bodies the same green as the cactus, spiky brown legs and antennae that look like the spines, safe from almost any predator behind a barricade of spines. It has been suggested that the plethora of prickly pears here, which produce edible fruits, is the result of some unintentional agriculture by the Fremont Indians who frequented these canyons.

Some of us walk the dusty path winding up the pinnacle and climb the loose shale slopes, shinnying up the last few vertical feet. The construction is by no means a fort, merely two small connected circular rooms, with a third partially intact. It commands a view both up and down the river, and across the mesas. The flat stones, such as litter the area, were here placed so carefully that they have maintained some semblance of structure over the centuries, even though laid without mortar.

I walk away from the lookout and face upriver. Even with a group, it is possible to have a great deal of time alone with the river. I sit on the edge of the Chinle parapet and dangle my feet over the side. It occurs to me, somewhat vaguely, that I who am normally afraid of heights am sitting comfortably above a large segment of empty space. The cottonwoods below follow the river's curve in an esker of green. The river is brown and the clanking hot shale beneath my hand is gray-green. I should be writing or drawing, recording, but I can only ponder, feeling immobilized by the weight of the sunlight on my back. Rock, tree, sky, a hand shadow on the page, a morning breeze, a sunlight-webbed river: I suppose it is the proportions that count, how much is stone, strong, how much is green, yielding, and how much is river, going on and never coming back.

14

And it sometimes happened that while listening to the river, they both thought the same thoughts, perhaps of a conversation of the previous day, or about one of the travellers whose fate and circumstances occupied their minds, or death, or their childhood; and when the river told them something good at the same moment, they looked at each other, both thinking the same thought, both happy at the same answer to the same question.

HERMANN HESSE, 1951, *Siddhartha*

Tufted evening-primrose
(*Oenothera caespitosa*)

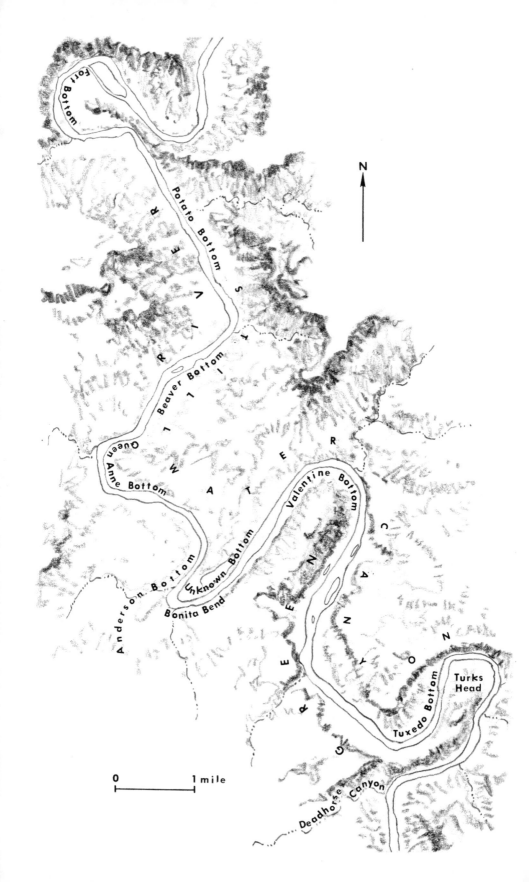

FORT BOTTOM
TO TURKS HEAD

OF ALL THE PLACES on the Green River that have their own character, Stillwater Canyon is the one that remains in the back of my mind as a measure of the meaning of the river. Many sections of the river have, by pure chance, come to be associated in my mind with particular times of the year or day: Lodore will be forever, to me, a foreboding, sense-of-winter canyon; Split Mountain's rapids are always those of a spring morning, even though I have run them more often in the fall. But Stillwater has no temporal annotations. When I think about the river I always come back to Stillwater, my place of *déjà vu*.

Part of the enchantment of Stillwater Canyon lies in its name. Stillwater remains one of the most mellifluous names with which Powell endowed this river, an almost onomatopoetic balancing of syllables, a word of peaceful sound and rhythm, definitive, just as the skyline itself is, defined by White Rim Sandstone. In all its separate parts, it always conveys the same meaning, in a summation that means more than the simple sum of its individual parts.

The surface excitement of rapids does not exist in Stillwater. Those who come to the river only for rapids and who must pass through the slows of Labyrinth and Stillwater to reach Cataract Canyon must find it a nuisance. But those who go on the river just for rapids miss the totality of the river. Rapids are only a part, a very small part of the river. The high of running rapids can remain for a long time, but Stillwater remains longer, the measure behind the running, the peace of the river.

The White Rim rises out of the river at an angle of intent and authority, an angle of progression, sloping upward like the corner angle of the pediment of a Greek temple allotted to a river deity. It is so reminiscent of that pediment angle that the formation might be an old river god fused back into stone, before it was carved into personification. This time the White Rim appears at noon and the day stretches loose on either side, warm, somnolent, walled-in noontime.

The name White Rim derives from local usage; it is a prominent rim visible from land or river or air, a clear, light color against the darker lower beds, the topmost of the formations—White Rim Sandstone, Organ Rock Shale, Cedar Mesa Sandstone—that form the Cutler Group. The White Rim records a persistent quiet marine current that left sand bars built up by offshore currents moving down from the northwest some 225 to 275 million years ago. White Rim Sandstone differs from the wind-laid Navajo Sandstone, for sands laid underwater usually lie at a lower angle of bedding since the angle of repose for water-laid sands is less than that for wind-laid. Wind deposits are also likely to be more multidirectional because of the greater variety of surface winds. White Rim Sandstone also bears symmetrical ripple marks characteristic of those scooped out by oscillating ocean waves rather than the symmetrical ones formed by the wind.

In Labyrinth Canyon, cliffs of Wingate Sandstone darkly define the skyline, and one can see little behind or above them while on the river. In Stillwater, the White Rim is a lower rimrock, variegated with high mesas and buttes. Some bear fanciful names, like Butte of the Cross and Cleopatra's Chair, witness to the sentimental side of Powell's nomenclature. The names are forgettable; it is the changing aspect of the skyline, as one floats downriver, that is memorable—the convexity of rock, the concavity of sky, a view that spills open to high buttes beyond and around, and between which distant storms pace stately pavanes, a panorama constantly rearranged and reunderstood as one drifts downriver. The relationship of one solid to another, seen from passing angles, creates an explanatory landscape of great clarity, and floating through Stillwater Canyon is the same privilege as walking around a piece of great sculpture.

On shore, the White Rim shelves down to the river. Each shelf drops off to the next in a series of broad gentle steps. One shelf is contoured, pitted with shallow holes. Another resembles San Blas Indian embroidery, each thin lamina cut through to a new layer beneath. A scattering of cobbles down a gully look ready to roll at the first wind; in reality they are stable, each firmly mounted on top of a quarter-inch pedestal built by washed-in sand. I pick one up. Its impression in the sand is clear and smooth. A river rock is a work of art in itself, containing the elegant curve of a Brancusi sculpture, the curve of satisfaction, the weight of meaning, the shape of river. I scrupulously replace it as it was.

Farther downriver, the thin beds of the White Rim show edge on. Embedded in the rock are spheres of iron concretions, many haloed by a five-inch brilliant red disk that fades to rust, sometimes enclosed with a thin charcoal-gray line. Although minor features of most sedimentary rocks, nodules are common. They form from materials within the rock, generally after the rock has hardened. They are dense, often precipitating around a nucleus; the most frequent ones are formed of those minerals most common in the rocks in which they occur: silica, calcite, iron oxide. Nodules are often round or oval, and when several form close together they may coalesce into knobs or even into layers.

There are many nodules here, some lying loose to be picked up and weighed in the hand, heavy, dark rust-brown iron pellets the size of hazelnuts and larger. Sometimes the spheres stand above the eroded surface, and sometimes the rock is pegged with nodules that weather out to cylinders pointing toward the river like two-inch sundial handles. Or protrude, like ancient clamps, awaiting a façade not yet carved.

When I am on the river I feel the necessity to check with it before I go to bed, some primeval necessity, I suppose, of obeisance to the river gods. At the river's edge, reedgrass stridulates two feet over my head, dried stalks rattling in the evening wind. The whole patch is

Iron nodules from White Rim Sandstone

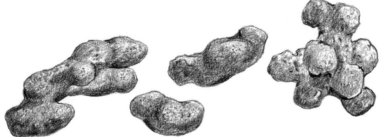

restive, passing on the sound. Some are weathered to gray and darker; last year's stalks are Naples yellow, lined dark at the joints. They are surprisingly tough—years ago they were used by Indians for arrow shafts.

The stars emerge, remote, cool. The night sounds begin, the aural warnings and announcements, the statements and challenges, floating upvalley, across canyon, dimming with distance but not blurred, for the fragile clarity holds in this dry air. The rocks are moon bright. The White Rim glows. It is light enough to write without a flashlight. My sleeve sibilates across the paper, pen making ink sounds, words made audible, loud enough to mask the river's flowing. The river goes so quietly that I hear it only when I stop writing and listen. The big open W of Cassiopeia reflects in the water. I feel caught in some ancient spell, listening to the river, held by some demonic sign of stone and water and approaching solstice.

ANDERSON'S FERRY is one of the few crossings on the lower river. Cattle were once ferried back and forth to Anderson's Bottom across the river, wintering in Moab, brought back each spring. The flotsam of civilization infests the place: a decrepit truck, a disheveled fence, a disintegrating mattress and bedsprings, an ancient refrigerator, the last three in a cave where six of us once sat out an afternoon storm.

A rancher can run cattle and sheep in this country, but there is neither enough grass nor enough moisture, and the land becomes overgrazed so quickly that it soon turns to dust and blows away. The good natural grasses that make nourishing feed are insufficient to support large herds, and now that this is a national park, grazing has been terminated. Anderson's Bottom has fertile alluvial soil, for it is a cutoff meander, a horseshoe of land around which the river once flowed, and then broke through the narrow neck, abandoning its former course but leaving an enriched soil.

Below Anderson's Bottom the White Rim rises farther above the river to become the rimrock of Stillwater Canyon. Within a few miles the next-lower formation of the Cutler Group emerges, deep maroon infused with brown: Organ Rock Shale. Almost as if in response, the character of the White Rim solidifies into an impassable cliff. Where it meets the Organ Rock Shale it becomes concave, scooped back, a *cavetto* arched with shadow, full of seepage lines defined by inky streaks, flanked by white stripes. Spalling leaves fresh areas that are

Longleaf phlox (*Phlox longifolia*)

paler still, creamy white tinged with apricot. Fremont Indian structures are often found in the contact between the two formations, storage cists mostly, tucked into the overhangs, approached by an almost impossible slope of loose, sliding rock. The overhangs are narrow, the structures small, a few dozen pieces of rock, unshaped and rough. Most are windowless, so close to the spirit of the rock that one is looking at them before one registers that they are there, so well protected from weather and sight are they.

The White Rim holds a near-uniform cliff; the dark strata below present a steep slope, striped with broad white panels of talus slumped from the White Rim. This combination of vertical and diagonal produces the particular steplike profile characteristic of arid lands: hard rock verticals, soft rock diagonals. As the softer rock falls away beneath, the undermined harder rock breaks away above, usually on vertical planes of weakness along joints, repeating the configuration of the previous cliff.

AT VALENTINE BOTTOM, the rain begins in isolated circles on the water, and then it comes more quickly and the circles interlock, and then it rains hard and each white drop is answered by a dark peak of water, a constant staccato alternation of dark and light. Everything drips. The wind kicks up a chop that curls on top, contemptuously going against the current. It is November cold, settling down around the head, enshrouding the shoulders. It rains all afternoon and into the evening, darkening the sky by five in the afternoon. Rain firehoses off the cliffs as the notches of dry washes on top of the cliff fill with water and turn into drain spouts. The jets shoot out almost horizontally before they fall. In this climate these dry washes do not carry water often enough to cut canyons to the river level, so they come in high off the cliff, draining the roof of rock that catches the main brunt of the storm.

On shore, the bank is sodden. Looking for a place to stow notebook and sketch pad, I find a few dry inches under a sandstone shelf. Rain drips off its edges and makes rosettes in the sand. The rain has an incessant feel, as if it had rained yesterday and will rain tomorrow. I feel encapsulated in a shimmering wetness that drips off my eyelashes and nose. The sandstone smells dank. It crumbles underfoot, granular, disintegrating, leaving a red residue on my sneakers. It rains even harder and the whole terrace shimmers with a sheet of water. Even as I watch, the trickle of running sand at my feet swirls and feathers into the river, staining it red, creating minuscule vortices opening downstream, the arterial blood of the mesas going downriver.

The storm passes slowly. A double rainbow illumines the still-smoky sky. A last flare from the clearing sky to the west kindles the cliffs. The White Rim is wet and darkened across its entire face except for one illuminated prow that is tender, creamy salmon in the after-glow, a diaphanous, transitory moment. Watching the light, I find the visual experience so intense that I forget about the rain and the chill, about cold, wet sneakers and dissonant voices complaining about wet gear, and concentrate upon locking the resonance of the color in my mind.

The river pulsates all night. At dawn it runs deep terra cotta, rufous. The sky is only faintly blue at first light, creamy on the horizon; the land lies in amorphous shadow. Last evening's storm must have cleared off the mesas and scoured the sandstones, for there is a great deal of flotsam on the surface. Debris brocades the water. Islands of foam four and five inches across saucer and wheel in the current. Brief rainstorms such as these transport most of the sedi-ment into the lower river; they pull away more sediment over a period of time than the rare major storms that occur infrequently and, while torrential, last only a short time. These summer storms that come frequently are responsible for the main erosion on this semiarid and arid land; they need not even be massive cloudbursts—a large proportion of the sediments are picked up by rainfalls of less than one inch.

Sunlight begins to pick out forms, to light patches of green. Distant mesas are still cool and flat. Water vapor coming off the warm river condenses into opaline mists. By the time the raft is loaded and we are ready to leave, the sun is well up, the mists gone. A hot stillness settles on the river. The chill and rain are but a memory. Only the color of the river, like a slashed jugular, tells of swift runoff and gnawing erosion, and a rainstorm that pared off the mesas and buttes.

BY TURKS HEAD, Cedar Mesa Sandstone flanks the river, and Fremont petroglyphs have been cut into a wall of it set above a mud-caked alluvial flat. This is one of the fertile places on the river. Perhaps a little corn or squash was grown here, seeds poked into the ground with a planting stick. In other settlements places of habitation were quite separate from rock art, and there is no reason to think otherwise here. On the east side of the Green River, where Fremont Indians did not live, their pictographs and petroglyphs have been found in situations that suggest that they might have been used as trail markers on migration routes.

The petroglyphs here are almost hidden behind a slab of outcrop, shadowed in the wall. Cedar Mesa Sandstone is a very hard rock; to chip out such symbols takes time and effort, and this implies intent. One may doodle with a pencil and paper or a stick in the dirt, but this is not true of a near-perfect circle, ten inches in diameter, with four others laid inside, each a finger width wide, pecked a quarter inch deep into the sandstone. The circles appear again, like pebbles dropped into the water: a smaller and two larger ones, the latter all chipped out in the center, the first elaborated with ten, the second with nine spokes radiating outward. The third circle is quartered, with only some of the rays completed.

When I recall Fremont drawings, it is these circles that I remember. A circle is the first shape perceived, depending upon the way in which neurological reactions take place in the brain. It has nothing to do with culture or heredity. It is simply the expression of brain structure. The simplest arm movement is a rotational one, out of the ball and socket of the shoulder, and circles are the first shapes drawn by children. A circle is perfect and complete, therefore a shape that attracts the eye, but it is also ambiguous: is it a hollow ring, a flat disk, or a round sphere? Overcoming that ambiguity is the next step, and this is also a universal one, that of combination, such as the addition of radiating lines—the repetition of sunwheels in many cultures, like those of children's drawings, reflects a basic human expression using pictorial forms. Shields, a more sophisticated use of the circle, are often represented in Fremont drawings, shown covering all but rudimentary head and stick limbs. Huge shields, which would have covered most of the body, have been found and identified as Fremont, giving these drawings a strong realistic flavor. Although only a few basic lines are used in all these representations, the conception has reached a high level of complexity, based on acute observation.

Some anthropologists feel that these drawings have little symbolic or narrative significance for the modern observer, and, from a Renaissance fixed-point-perspective outlook, which puts heavy emphasis upon naturalism, this may be so. But this kind of observation has profitably been ignored by many cultures, such as that of ancient Egypt, and by modern artists, such as Paul Klee and Marc Chagall, who enrich ordinary visual experiences by just such free-wheeling conceptions of spatial relationships. Fremont petroglyphs are remarkable. A few selected lines are able to conjure up a recollection of complex objects and ideas; a keen eye and a disciplined hand are coupled to present a fresh view of reality, fulfilling one of the criteria of a work of art.

WITH THE RIVER so high this spring, and level sleeping space at a premium, a leaf-covered triangle seems like very good luck. A thatch of dead branches still attached to the sheltering scrub oak needs to be put aside. I pull each branch back, one by one, beside a big boulder. After I have nearly finished I realize that on top of that boulder is a coiled piece of diamond-patterned rosy-brown rope that has two eyes. It has given no warning, no sound; its head is turned slightly away, but it watches. I am amazed to find that I am neither afraid nor repelled, only extremely curious and exceedingly cautious.

The paucity of sleeping places decides me. I pitch my tent as planned and keep it zipped tight. We do not disturb each other. When I get up in the morning it is still here, whirring softly at a hand shadow passed in front of it. It is gone by the time we leave.

UNDER THE SPIRE of Turks Head, in the Organ Rock Shale, there is a splendid two-foot-thick seam of jasper. Indians were known to travel many miles to areas where superior flint could be collected or quarried; these areas may well have been neutral grounds. Shattered pieces of jasper lie in the sun, hot in the hand. Jasper is almost pure silica, mineral matter precipitated out after the sandstone formed. This vein is brick-red, subtly mottled with other warm colors—Indian red fused with liver, pale salmon shading to warm gray.

Although it was valuable as a utilitarian rock, in this land of abrasive granular sandstones and unreliable sliding shales, it is somehow also a sensuous stone. It has a soft peculiar smell from lying in the dirt. Jasper does not change color, like so many rocks, when wet or weathered. A piece of jasper in the hand is a talisman, and with skill, the flaking is predictable, leaving conchoidal fractures and a knife edge. On the other side of the river, a ledge of White Rim Sandstone slopes into the sandy ground, and I found, at its base, a handful of similar jasper chips, tomato red, scattered in the sand. The sandstone lay at a good slant for pressure flaking; it would have been impossible to break off such uniformly small bits without control. The color of the chips was beautiful and pure. And a point made from such perfection of material must have been exquisite, translucent on the moon-shaped edges, rich red in the center.

ONE OF THE DELIGHTS of a river evening, especially after chinning up sandstone and shale ledges and poking around dry, silty terraces, is a rinse in the river. There is a place below Turks Head which, at high water, fulfills the requirements of privacy and a safe place out of the current. The water temperature in May is hardly tepid, at 62° F., but the air is warm. There are two table rocks, firm sandstones, upon which I can stand and safely submerge, letting the water swirl around me. In water that is so opaque, it is a matter of some faith to sit down. The current nudges but little in this back eddy, yet it is still easy to feel the erosive power of a big springtime river. The river sounds ear close. Seated eye level with the surface, I feel like an apprentice Lorelei, learning the siren sounds of the river.

The silt wells and fumes, voluminous and soft, just beneath the surface. It is fascinating to discover that by moving a hand just under water I can evoke all kinds of kaleidoscopic patterns. This silt settles out of a container of river water within twenty-four hours, but the remaining water looks like clam juice, colored by finer particles that do not precipitate as quickly in response to gravity. These extremely small particles are colloidal; since they have more surface compared to their volume, and so a specific gravity less than that of water, they remain in suspension almost indefinitely, settling out only if they clus-

Jasper flakes

ter together to form larger particles. Gravels in a stream may fall out in less than a second when the velocity drops; colloidal particles may remain for decades.

The Green River, at this time of moderately heavy runoff, is probably carrying more than half its silt load for the year. The average load held in suspension by the river is estimated at 19 tons a year, plus 2.5 million tons dissolved. The silt content near the mouth of the Green, by volume, was once estimated at 0.5 percent; it seems a minute amount, but evenly distributed by the current it forms an effective screen, creating the year-round turbidity in the river from the Gates of Lodore south.

The sandpaper surface of the rock, unslicked by algae, provides a sense of stability in a flowing, swirling, moving world. How to explain the pure delight of being here—some of it no doubt stems from the fact that, after a day of unrelenting sunshine, almost any kind of ablution feels welcome. But there is an ineffable sybaritic pleasure beyond the necessity. The cool slide of water slips down the back of my neck, down my arm, drips off my elbow, picks patterns on the river's surface. The water that tugs around my ankles is pure hedonistic enticement, issuing a reminder of downriver delights in a branch that bobs by, on its way to other appointments.

After seeing ruins all day, I am extremely conscious of those who came here before me. So too, on a warm spring evening, a thousand years ago, someone must have stood like this, soothing calloused feet, cactus-scratched legs. I feel no time interval, no difference in flesh between who stood here then and who stands here now. The same need exists for the essentials of food and shelter, the same need to communicate and to put down symbols for someone else to see, and, so I cannot help but believe, the same response to cool water and warm sun and heated rock and sandstone on bare feet.

The last rays of the sun keep it warm enough to air dry. The sun hangs for a moment above the cliff. As it disappears behind the rim, the air cools. And yet it is not cold; maybe time to robe and leave, but not yet, not cold yet. As long as I can stand, ankle deep, without civilization, without defense, going back to self, as long as there is yet enough warmth in the air to respect needful body temperature, so long as possible I stand here, submerged physically only to the ankles, psychologically to the base of being.

15

Hurra! Hurra! Hurra! Grand River came upon us or rather we came upon that very suddenly and to me unexpectedly 5½ P.M. Had been running all day through higher walls, mostly vertical, but the river was smooth though in some places more rapid than for two days. The cañon looked dark and threatening but at last without warning, no valley or even opening unusual, in broke the Grand with a calm strong tide very different from what it has been represented. We were led to expect that it was a rushing, roaring mountain torrent which when united with the Green would give us a grand promenade across the mountains. The rock is the same old sand-stone underlaid for the last 20 miles with limestone containing marine foccils and at the junction of the two rivers, strangely curved and broken.

GEORGE Y. BRADLEY, July 16, 1869, *Journal*

Monday, November 15, 1909

The strenuous effort, the chance of failure, and the eager stimulation a difficult task inspires—all are ended. And yet, strange to say I feel no sense of elation.

JULIUS STONE, 1932, *Canyon Country*

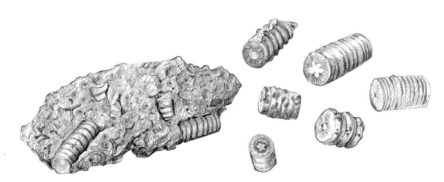

Crinoid stems, Hermosa Group

N

COLORADO RIVER

Turks Head

Horse Canyon

Jasper Canyon

Shot Water Canyon

GREEN RIVER

0   1 mile

TURKS HEAD
TO THE CONFLUENCE

BELOW TURKS HEAD the White Rim breaks back from the river. According to my sense of river and aesthetics, Stillwater Canyon loses its essence when the White Rim disappears, when the Organ Rock Shale slips out of sight, and Cedar Mesa Sandstones become the skyline rock, even though, according to Powell, Stillwater Canyon continues to the confluence. Stillwater Canyon is so characterized by the White Rim that if it begins with it, it should end with it. After the White Rim retreats, the whole character of the canyon changes. The formations are different in form and color, in aspect, a restless preparation for the confluence and the big rapids of the Colorado.

By Horse Canyon, the Cedar Mesa cliffs are formidable, reaching up thirteen hundred feet above the water, notched by tributary canyons, topped by rounded domes and spires. The once-smooth White Rim of Stillwater is replaced by fanciful shapes and fantastic phalanxes; content overrides form. Grotesque heads peer over serrated parapets. Corteges of deformed animals cross the skyline, bawling who knows what brayings and barkings that are sheared away by the high wind. The Cedar Mesa Sandstone weathers rough, almost a magnified representation of the turreted soil lichens that castellate the fragile dust.

The Elephant Canyon Formation rises above water level about sixteen miles upstream from the confluence, near Horse Canyon; seven miles farther downriver, the uppermost layers of the Hermosa Group appear. Both outcrop in steep, ledgy slopes. Their surface character is

273

responsible for the sense of unrest in this lower canyon—broken, interrupted, rough of surface, tumbled gray forms as fragmented as a Monet study of a Gothic façade, small forms casting small shadows, almost a pointillist surface.

The source of these limestones, as of the Organ Rock Shales, must have been the massive Uncompahgre Uplift of the Ancestral Rocky Mountains. The coarseness of grain, the thick, irregular bedding and crossbedding indicate that these formations were deposited rapidly by rivers dropping into the edge of a sea. Envision a plain sloping westward from highlands in western Colorado, the lower edge of which is periodically invaded by encroaching seas; it was on such a plain, that lay in an alternating marine and continental environment, that these sediments fell.

The slope rises in large steps, and on these, fossils lie scattered. At first one sees nothing, and then a more regular shape or a fine fluting catches the eye, and once one is seen and the eye adjusts, they appear just frequently enough to lure one up to the next step, and the next. Many fossils lie entrapped in the stone but some are weathered out, lying loose on the slope. The original shells are often replaced with chert, a form of pure silica, here a handsome cinnabar color, or sometimes black. Marine fossils dominate, especially brachiopods, but there are also bryozoans, crinoids, corals, and fusulinids—infinitesimal shells that are valuable as index fossils and exist in astronomical numbers.

Brachiopods resemble plump cockle or scallop shells; the animal inside was anchored to the mud bottom by a "stem" that extended through an opening in the base of the shell, and its relative immobility may have been one reason for its decrease in species—only a few exist today. Crinoids, or sea lilies, of which also a few species still exist, had a base anchored in the sand or mud, connected by a long,

Brachiopods, Hermosa Group
(*Neospirifer cameratus*)

stemlike column to a head made up of five (or multiples thereof) plates. Most often preserved were the disks, series of which formed the columns. These lying on the slope measure between a quarter and a half inch in diameter, like small Sumerian seals making signatures in the dust. Often encrusting other shells and crinoid stems with a fine reticulation are bryozoans, minute colonial animals. Generally there are only bits and pieces of fossils, but once in a while a whole brachiopod weathers out, dense and heavy. Each growth line, each rib, is there in plicate perfection. It lies in my hand with the contour of eternity, and I relinquish and replace it with reluctance.

WATER CANYON, steeped in deep green growth, enters on the right. The bottom of the draw is thick with trees and squawbush, always damp and verdant when other canyons are dry, no matter what time of summer. The only place to walk is halfway up a loose-rocked rim, a path picked out between rock outcrops, cactus, and treacherous scree. In contrast to the lushness below, the canyon wall is dry and every footstep fumes with a fine gray powder. The limestones that make up the canyon wall are hostile rocks, coarse, sharp as coral. Brushing up against one ensures a bloody scrape. Many of the rocks are full of fossils; I pass a pale gray boulder studded with the black chert cylinders of crinoid stems, shiny and smooth against the rough matrix.

The small Indian ruins, scrubbed out of the shattered stone, are built around the bend, out of sight of the river. A cist is tucked up beneath an overhang, slabs of stone laid without any adhesive mortar, top stones fallen in. The stones are neither chipped nor dressed, about twice as wide as a brick and as long, of irregular thickness, laid in

horizontal courses. A snail-shaped wall stands on a slight peninsula of rock, built with a curving entrance into a small chamber between four and five feet wide. The walls remain but waist high, yet with a surprising stability for a free-standing structure. Originally it may have been roofed with poles overlaid with brush and bark, perhaps a temporary habitation, a migration way station. Whatever it was, it looks out across the top of such a dreamlike greenness of grass and trees and coolness as one seldom finds on the lower desert-wrapped Green River.

From Water Canyon less than five miles remain to the confluence. Powell, who reached it on July 16, 1869, describes a different river from the one I know: "Late in the afternoon the water becomes swift and our boats make great speed. An hour of this rapid running brings us to the junction of the Grand and Green, the foot of Stillwater Canyon, as we have named it. These streams unite in solemn depths, more than 1,200 feet below the general surface of the country." The river now could hardly be called fast, and yet I would have it go more slowly. The cliffs that bind our going tower over a thousand feet high. There is no repose for the eye, no restful pause. The first time I see this junction of the two rivers, I feel as Powell felt: a sense of anti-climax. At least there should be trumpets. And geologically and historically and technically speaking, I know that it is the Grand (*not* the Colorado) River that enters on the left, and the Green (*not* the Colorado) River that goes on downstream.

Originally, the Green (on the west) and the Grand (on the east) met to form the Colorado River. The Green River extends northward from this confluence over 700 miles; the Grand, roughly 340 miles. The Green River drains 45,000 square miles; the Grand, 26,500 square miles. The Green River is the master stream. (The runoff of the Grand may exceed that of the Green River but only because the latter runs through so many more miles of desert country.) The Grand River gave its name to places in both Colorado and Utah: Grand Lake, Grand Junction, Grand County. "Colorado" was applied only to the lower part of the river, the Spanish designation for a river that ran red.

But this practice of a different name for every branch of a river was precisely what the Board on Geographic Names, established in September, 1890, was created to avoid. Several government offices were concerned with the proliferation and repetition of place names, among them, the Geological Survey, the Coast and Geodetic Survey, and the

Post Office Department. The board was empowered by executive order to bring some order out of chaos, with final power over naming, and to establish some guidelines for future naming.

The confusion about the naming of the stretch of the river between Grand Lake and the confluence began innocently enough. It was common practice for a territory to take its name from a prominent river, hence the Colorado Territory. But when the surveys were completed for the new state, the Colorado River was nowhere to be found within its boundaries. Over the decades this so chafed the Colorado legislature that, in a flurry of chauvinism, they decreed in 1921 that the river that *did* run through the state and connected with the Colorado River in Utah was indeed and should therefore be called the Colorado River too. This left eighty miles of the Grand River still running in Utah.

It was one of those embarrassingly thorny problems that have the potential to undo a government bureau. On one hand, the board had specifically stated that it was against the repetition of names, and there were already too many "Grands" scattered across the country. On the other hand, the board approved of maintaining traditional names wherever possible, and also declared that the longer branch of a river should be considered the main one, and the river in its entirety should assume that name. By that standard, it was either the Green or the Colorado that began in the Wind River Range and went to the Gulf of California, and whatever came out of Grand Lake was neither. The board weaseled out of the dilemma by giving mild approval to the older name of Grand River. Colorado took the case to Congress. Utah raised no objection to the change. Congress, after considerable debate and questionable authority, passed a resolution on the 25th of July, 1921, stating that the river was indeed the Colorado River all the way from Grand Lake, Colorado, to the Gulf of California, in the face of common usage, geographical and geological definition.

A SAND BAR marks the turn of the inner cliff, rimmed with an abatis of tamarisk below a loose gray limestone slope. I work up the steep incline, slipping and grabbing, mostly air. There is little to hold to and often, in sneakers, two steps up are succeeded by three steps down. The slope is surfaced with treacherous scree and the limestone is hard on the hands. There are many crinoid stems all over the ground, each slightly different, serrated or smooth, centered with a round channel

or a five-lobed one, each of which deserves to be minutely examined
before being returned to its impression in the dirt. Attaining the high
ledge above me becomes a test, a race against time, while the light
holds, before this day drifts downstream. The ledge, when I reach it,
is just wide enough to hunker on, back against the slope. Facing the
paired cliff across the river, I feel like some small animal, protected,
nestled safely above predator below. But a sense of uneasiness assails
me as a hawk drifts over and then comes in lower for a second pass.

I am sad, depressed. These are feelings that do not come often on
the river. I remember the next to the last trip for this book, down
Desolation Canyon. I awoke at first light with foreboding, torn un-
willingly out of sleep by the carping of a magpie. As the sky grew
light, I unzipped the tent fly and clipped it back. The big bird teetered
on a beached snag, switching its long tail, voice harsh and wheedling.
Across the river, the east-facing cliffs caught first light—pale peach,
the color of the inside of a conch shell. As I watched, the color warmed
faintly, and the river carried cream and gold and apricot in thin undulating lines. For the first time I felt out of phase with the light, with
the clarity of a river morning.

I took extra time with the tent, wiped it more carefully than usual,
wedged the damp sand out of my boot cleats, took solace in quiet tasks
and busy hands. And, when all these things were done, I turned my
back on the river and walked the sand bar. It lay wide, sprigged with
thousands of green tamarisks two or three inches high. Where silt had
dried, it curled up in uneven plates. A last sunflower bloomed, knee-
high, with frost spots on the petals. Facing the sun for whatever
warmth there was, I wished it to soothe and heal. The furze of
tamarisks shimmered with dew, but walking toward the sun, I was
Die Frau ohne Schatten.

Without shadow—without all the familiar framework of my other
world, in the self-imposed isolation of wilderness, I had found moments of nonrecordable time: the discovery of sinuous beauty in a
point bar, the elegance of a meander, the challenge of running a rapid
myself. The river had brought moments of elation that had come so
unexpectedly that I could not breathe for the delight: a mockingbird
at midnight in a quiet-rimmed canyon; the constellation Orion wheeling up at four in the morning, striding a misty sky over a misty river;
the moon rising in a cool sidereal light, locked in star patterns, over an
October-frosted sand bar; a rim of white sandstone turning rose in
afterglow. I admitted this necessity of solitude. When I turned to walk

back to camp, I gained a shadow. It went before me, outlined by an opalescent aura of sun catching in prisms of dew. I walked into a glowing mandorla of aloneness, toward the river.

Now, below me, the gentle curve of the sand bar at the confluence stretches to velvet smoothness, a boomerang held tightly between cliff and river. At noon the light on this slope is so bright that I cannot look at the water without squinting, and the ripples shoot out flashes of retina-shattering light. The midday brilliance washes out colors and consumes shadows. But the light softens in late afternoon, gentles the wide-open dazzle of this landscape. It lessens the demands on eyesight and so brings an easing of muscle and mind. Even the river seems slower in its going as it creams into vortices and piles downstream, an optical illusion brought on by my own slowing metabolism. Human warmth slips out of skin into sand and only residual warmth in the rock preserves the bone against chilling. The river runs with soft ochre and evening reflections.

Across the river the matched cliff rises, split by an unconformity that represents millions of years of lost time. Some part of mental discipline notes the logic of rock layers and light intensity and vortices of time and space, but something slips with the river's going. Logic time crosses over to river time. Time is only today on the river and tonight on the sand bar. Days of the week have no meaning. Nor do eons or epochs. The cliff across the river is as durable as the sand bar below, and the sand bar lasts as long as the morning light on the cliff. I remember how the river sounds as it melts six-spoked silt-free crystals to pellucid drops, once oxygen and twice hydrogen. And, as it rose in rock, so it ends in rock, not in the hard, shattered gray granites, but the sediments from more ancient mountains, layered, worked, reworked, laid in witness layers.

A cliff swallow makes a last sweep of the sky, then shafts like an arrow downstream. The wind stills. It is too quiet.

I do not want to hear the river ending.

NOTES

1   THE SOURCE TO PEAK LAKE

UNITED STATES GEOLOGICAL SURVEY quadrangle for this chapter is Gannett Peak, Wyoming. Maps are listed by chapters; all are 7.5-min. series unless otherwise noted.

The source and first 12 miles of the Green River lie within the Bridger Wilderness. Set aside as a primitive area in 1931, it was given wilderness status by Congress in 1964; an additional 50 miles of the Green River were included in the original draft of the Scenic Rivers Act (Public Law 90–542) but unfortunately were not included when the act became law.

page

4   Ralf R. Woolley, *The Green River and Its Utilization*, U.S.G.S. Water Supply Paper 618 (Washington, D.C.: Government Printing Office, 1930), p. xi, gives mileages, and was the first comprehensive description of the Green River written. Washington Irving, *Captain Bonneville, U.S.A.* (New York: G. P. Putnam, 1868), 258–61; and John Wesley Powell, *The Exploration of the Colorado River and Its Canyons* (New York: Dover Publications, reprinted 1961), p. 17, for the source of the Green. Absence of good maps caused part of the earlier uncertainty as to source. L. G. Westgate and E. B. Branson, "Later Cenozoic History of the Wind River Mountains," *Journal of Geology* 21(1913):143, complained that the "Fremont quadrangle is the only topographic sheet published by the U.S. Geological Survey which covers any part of the Wind River Mountains," and those of the Hayden Survey were "too generalized for our uses." Those issued by the U.S. General Land Office, October, 1886, would have been equally inadequate, being drawn to a scale of 18 miles to 1 inch. See also E. C. LaRue, *The Colorado River and Its Utilization*, U.S.G.S. Water Supply Paper 395 (Washington, D.C., 1916).

Because Mammoth Glacier, southwest of Gannett Peak, is larger than other contributory glaciers of the Green, it has been mistakenly assumed to be the source, and was on some maps labeled "Green River Glacier"—e.g., M. F. Meier, "Recent Eskers in the Wind River Mountains of Wyoming," *Iowa Academy of Science* 58(1951):291. Orrin and Lorraine G. Bonney, *Field Book: The Wind River Range* (Houston: Orrin H. and Lorraine G. Bonney, 1968), p. 85: "Gannett is the only peak in the Wind River Range to which the beginnings of the Green River can thus be tied." However, Wallace R. Hansen, head of the Environmental Geology Group, U.S.G.S., Denver, *personal communication,* says that drainage basin is the essential criterion; at every intersection down to Wells Creek, the stream that heads in the valley of Stroud Glacier is the longer and therefore master stream; Wells Creek, coming off Mammoth Glacier, drains only a single valley and is a tributary to the Green, as are other creeks down the line. H. M. Townsend, Chief, Branch of Cartography, Topographic Division, U.S.G.S., Denver, *pers. comm.*, also locates the source of the river "in the drainage basin defined by Split Mountain, Twin Peaks, Winifred Peaks, Sulphur Peak and Brimstone Mountain." (N.B., there are two Split Mountains on the Green River.) The theory of drainage order upon which this conception of source is based was developed by R. E. Horton, "Drainage basin characteristics," *Transactions of the American Geophysical Union* 13(1932):350–61. Excellent discussions exist in the following, upon which I have also drawn extensively for this book: Marie Morisawa, *Streams: Their Dynamics and Morphology* (New York: McGraw-Hill, 1968); H. B. N. Hynes, *The Ecology of Running Water* (Toronto: University of Toronto Press, 1970); and most especially, Luna B. Leopold, M. Gordon Wolman, and John P. Miller, *Fluvial Processes in Geomorphology* (San Francisco, W. H. Freeman, 1964), the definitive text on this subject.

4–5 Donald J. Orth, Executive Secretary for Domestic Names, Board on Geographic Names, *pers. comm.*

6 Flow of the Green is directly dependent upon glacial runoff in the Wind Rivers; pioneer work in Rocky Mountain glaciation is Eliot Blackwelder's "Post-Cretaceous History of the Mountains of Central Wyoming," *Jour. Geol.* 23(1915):97–115, 193–217, 307–40, and "Pleistocene Geology: The Green River Basin," Wyoming Geological Association Field Conference in Southwest Wyoming, *Guidebook* (1950):81–85.

7 Bonney and Bonney, *Wind Rivers*, p. 69: William J. Stroud, for whom the glacier and mountain were named, "lived by himself in run-down quarters in Rock Springs. He always wore the same business suit and hat whether conducting business affairs, visiting friends, or climbing rugged peaks. His dusty pockets were always filled with hard candy for the children who gathered round . . ." The middle fork of the Green has been labeled on some older maps as "Stroud Creek"; see Kenneth A. Henderson, "Wind River Range of Wyoming," *Appalachia* 19(1933), no. 204–27, and no. 3:354–75.

10 J. H. Moss, "Late Glacial Advances in the Southern Wind River Mountains," *American Journal of Science* 249(1951):868, indicates 23-foot snowfalls.

11 Water confined in a crack and freezing increases its volume 9 percent, theoretically capable of creating pressures up to 2,100 tons per square foot; although that is seldom if ever reached in nature, pressures are nevertheless considerable; see Arthur L. Bloom, *The Surface of the Earth* (Englewood Cliffs, N.J.: Prentice-Hall, 1969), pp. 19–20, a well-illustrated paperback on geomorphology. Talus slopes steeper than 40° are rare; they more commonly lie near 36½°; see C. H. Behre, Jr., "Talus Behavior Above Timber in the Rocky Mountains," *Jour. Geol.* 41(1936):622–35, and H. T. U. Smith, "Physical Effects of Pleistocene Climatic Changes in Nonglaciated Areas: Eolian Phenomena, Frost Action, and Stream Terracing," *Geological Society of America Bulletin* 60(1949):1485–1516.

J. C. Frémont, *The Exploring Expedition to the Rocky Mountains, Oregon and California* (Buffalo: Geo. H. Derby, 1851), p. 97. In 1842 Frémont crossed into the Green River drainage via South Pass at the southern end of the Wind River Range; that August his journal records his ascent of the peak that now bears his name.

Dr. Richard Beidleman of the Zoology Department, The Colorado College, tells me that these are mountain midge larvae of the family Deuterophlebiidae.

15 Bloom, *Surface of the Earth*, pp. 14 ff., concerning the hydrologic cycle; also Hynes, *The Ecology of Running Water*, pp. 1–2. Only a small amount of the world's water occurs on land, and of this a large amount is locked up in glaciers and ice caps, and at any given time, only 0.0001 percent is in river channels. Of the 30″ of average annual rainfall in the U.S., about 9″ goes into streamflow. See also Leopold, Wolman, and Miller, *Fluvial Processes*, pp. 51–52.

2 PEAK LAKE TO LOWER GREEN RIVER LAKE

Quadrangle maps: Gannett Peak, Squaretop, and Green River Lakes, Wyo.

17 The points were found by Perry Binning.

19 For descriptions and illustrations of fast-stream biota, see John Bardach, *Downstream:A Natural History of the River* (N.Y.: Harper & Row, 1964); Robert E. Coker, *Streams, Lakes, Ponds* (Chapel Hill: University of North Carolina Press, 1954); and Hynes, *The Ecology of Running Water.*

23 For the information about Gottfried Rahm I am indebted to Connie and Perry Binning, who kindly shared their knowledge of the countryside and its history.

25 Irving, *Bonneville,* pp. 258–59: "Whichever way he looked, he beheld vast plains glimmering with reflected sunshine. . . . For a time, the Indian fable seemed realized; he had attained that height from which the Blackfoot warrior, after death, first catches a view of the land of souls, and beholds the happy hunting grounds spread out below him, brightening with the abodes of the free and generous spirits."

John W. Marr and Beatrice E. Willard, "Persisting Vegetation in an Alpine Recreation Area in the Southern Rocky Mountains, Colorado," *Biological Conservation* 2, no. 2(1970):97–104, is the result of 5 years' study; the authors concluded that informal trails developed because regular trails were poorly routed and/or constructed, and were one of the major sources of damage to natural ecosystems because they progressively damaged areas adjacent to regular paths.

27 As 19th-century accounts indicate, elk were once more plentiful at lower elevations. Olaus J. Murie, *The Elk of North America* (Harrisburg, Pa.: Stackpole, 1966), p. 53, says elk have always been at home both in mountains and on plains, but that on the latter they were more accessible to hunters, and therefore were destroyed or forced to migrate into higher altitudes. T. A. Larson, *History of Wyoming* (Lincoln: University of Nebraska Press, 1965), p. 385, credits the spread of ranching and fencing in the upper Green River valley, coupled with a hard winter 1909–10, with the legislative decision to introduce large-scale winter feeding; the big herd in the Wind Rivers survives only with such a program on state-owned lands. N. Allen Binns, *An Inventory and Evaluation of the Game and Fish Resources of the Upper Green River in Relation to Current and Proposed Water Development Programs* (Wyoming Game and Fish Commission, 1972), identifies two major herds, one on each side of the Green River Basin, each with some 2,000 elk. Summer range is generally restricted to mountainous national forest lands, with traditional winter range in the desert areas in the southern part of the basin. About 75 percent of the elk winter in the feed grounds, while others remain on protected mountain ridges. The largest feed ground is located at Black Butte, near the Green River.

28 Leopold, Wolman, and Miller, *Fluvial Processes in Geomorphology,* p. 165, estimate that at high stage, velocities in most streams average between 3 and 6 ft/sec. Timing the rate of travel and multiplying by a factor of 0.8 gives fairly reliable results. Hynes, *The Ecology of Running Water,* suggests using an orange because it floats and is easily visible (it may also be lunch, a practical consideration not lost on backpackers). For glacial streams, see Robert K. Fahnestock, *Competence of a Glacial Stream,* U.S.G.S. Professional Paper 424–B (Washington, D.C., 1961).

29 See Morisawa, *Streams,* p. 67–69, for cavitation.

32 Bardach, *Downstream,* p. 44, gives comparative figures on fish production.

The Green River Lakes and environs have been studied by C. L. Baker, "Geology of the Northwestern Wind River Mountains," *Geol. Soc. Am. Bull*, 57(1946):565–96. Work on high-altitude lakes has been done by Robert Pennak, "Comparative Limnology of Eight Colorado Mountain Lakes," *University of Colorado Studies*, Series in Biology, No. 2 (Boulder: University of Colorado Press, 1955), and Paul S. Welch, *Limnology* (New York: McGraw-Hill, 1952). Rainbow trout from both wild and hatchery stock are the principal game fish here; brown trout were introduced in the mid-1960s and are now established; brook and cutthroat are present in lesser numbers and neither are stocked; see Binns, *Inventory*.

3   LOWER GREEN RIVER LAKE TO KENDALL WARM SPRINGS

Quadrangles: Green River Lakes, Big Sheep Mountain, Klondike Hill, and Dodge Butte, Wyoming.

37 Data about the upper river is from Dr. Binns' thorough *Inventory and Evaluation*.

39 Dr. Binns, *pers. comm.*, concerning Green River cutthroat.

42 J. W. Powell, *The Exploration of the Colorado River and Its Canyons*, p. 160.

43 The differentiation and correlation of terraces and moraines has been attempted only in isolated areas; see Luna B. Leopold and John P. Miller, *A Post-Glacial Chronology for Some Alluvial Valleys in Wyoming*, U.S.G.S. Water Supply Paper 1261 (Washington, D.C., 1954). For a basic and lucid discussion of terraces (and other matters of hydrology), see Luna B. Leopold, *Water: A Primer* (San Francisco: W. H. Freeman, 1974). For their formation, Blackwelder, "Pleistocene Geology," p. 85: "From the relation of the terraces to the glacial moraines and also to the valley sides, it seems probable that the excavation of the Green River Valley took place in the Pleistocene epoch and largely in the latter half of it. Although downward erosion was the prevailing tendency, it appears to have been interrupted by rather long episodes of stability during which the plantation widened the valley bottoms extensively. Intervals of stream aggradation—probably associated with glacial ages—must have been rather short." Blackwelder places the height of "Little Ice Age" terraces at 5–11 feet, Pinedale moraines, 35–42 feet, Bull Lake moraines, 70–90 feet. C. L. Baker, *Wind Rivers*, p. 595, observes that the terrace at the 8,300-foot level is very prominent for 6 miles above and below the mouth of the Roaring Fork.

Dr. Binns, *pers. comm.*, cites a sandhill-crane study of June, 1973, that estimates 10,000 to 15,000 birds near the Green.

44 Besides Leopold, *Water*, see G. K. Gilbert, *The Transportation of Debris by Running Water*, U.S.G.S. Profess. Paper 86 (Washington, D.C., 1914), very readable and of special historical interest because of Gilbert's connection with Powell. Leopold, Wolman, and Miller, *Fluvial Processes in Geomorphology*, p. 212: "Thus the gravel bar is made up of particles that lodge on the bar only temporarily; yet the bar is an entity that may change shape or position. The gravel bar, then, may be regarded as a kind of kinematic wave in the traffic of clastic debris. A kinematic wave is a wave consisting of a concentration of units, particles, or individuals, but through which these units may move. A concentration of cars on a highway is an example. A concentration of cars behind a traffic signal is a wave through which individual cars move. The wave, or zone of traffic concentration, may move in the same or opposite

direction as the traffic, or may remain fixed in space." See also W. B. Langbein and L. B. Leopold, *River Channel Bars and Dunes—Theory of Kinematic Waves,* U.S.G.S. Profess. Paper 422–L (Washington, D.C., 1968). Leopold, Wolman, and Miller, pp. 281–82, find that channels are seldom straight longer than a distance that is about ten times the channel width, and even when straight, the line of maximum depth wanders back and forth from one bank to the other: "In an idealized sense, flow and depositional pattern seen in the plan view is similar in straight and meandering patterns." See also L. B. Leopold and M. G. Wolman, *River Channel Patterns: Braided, Meandering and Straight,* U.S.G.S. Profess. Paper 282–B (Washington, D. C., 1957).

45 Tosi Creek was once known as Little Gros Ventre River. As to how Beats the Hell Out of Me Creek got its name, Dr. Binns wrote me that he was processing a batch of fish from the creek for a Wyoming Game & Fish study; the man who was recording data asked the name of the creek. Having been unable to discover its name, Dr. Binns answered, "Beats the hell out of me!" and that is what was entered on the record sheet.

46 Robert McNair, *Basic River Canoeing* (Martinsville, Indiana: American Camping Association, 1968), has good diagrams and explanations. It's how I learned.

48–49 The terms "marl," "travertine," and "tufa" are used to describe deposits of recent age consisting of a large proportion of calcium carbonate or bicarbonate; confusion arises because the terms are sometimes used interchangeably. Tufa is defined as a spongy, porous rock that forms thin surface deposits around springs and seeps by the evaporation of spring and river water; marl is a descriptive term for deposits of 35–65 percent calcium carbonate; travertine is more massive and considered a variety of limestone, made up of many thin, often very colorful, layers. See Welch, *Limnology,* pp. 100, 194; Harvey Blatt, Gerald Middleton, and Raymond Murray, *Origin of Sedimentary Rocks* (Englewood Cliffs, N.J.: Prentice-Hall, 1972), pp. 450–52; William R. Keefer, *The Geological Story of Yellowstone Park,* U.S.G.S. Bulletin 1347 (Washington, D.C., no date).

The fauna of Kendall Warm Springs is not the highly distinctive fauna found in extremely hot or cold springs; all species I found were common. Most interesting was the soldier fly larva, described by Harold Oldroyd, *The Natural History of Flies* (New York: W. W. Norton, 1966), pp. 116–17; he knows of no possible function for the deposition of calcium carbonate in the cuticle of these larvae unless it is "possible that this calcareous layer is a sort of built-in cocoon with the aid of which the larva, during its long life, can retire from the adverse conditions in the world outside." For the endemic Kendall dace, *Rhinichthys osculus thermalis,* see Galen Boyer, "Kendall Dace," *Wyoming Wildlife 35,* no. 4(1971):14–17, and George T. Baxter and James R. Simon, *Wyoming Fishes* (Cheyenne: Wyoming Game & Fish Dept., 1970), pp. 75–76.

50 Julius Stone, *Canyon Country* (New York: G. P. Putnam, 1932), who ran the Green and Colorado Rivers in 1909, wrote (p. 85) that he was looking forward to "an adventure," but that one "may only have an adventure if through oversight or lack of information inadequate preparation is made for whatever is to be undertaken. If he then meets with unforeseen difficulty, an adventure may result . . . [but] having an adventure is proof of incompetence." A week after we ran Kendall Rapids, two experienced white-water canoers wrapped their aluminum canoe around a rock there. Perry's fiberglass canoe, at the end of the trip, was gouged and scratched, but only needed a fresh coat of epoxy.

Quadrangles: Dodge Butte and Warren Bridge, Wyoming.

55   The Bridger National Forest folder places the opening of the tie camp at 1868 and says that fairly large-scale operations continued until 1956. The graveyard marker was placed by the Sublette County Historical Society. See also Myra Cooley, *Meet Me on the Green* (New York: William-Frederick Press, 1960), a charming book of local history.

56   Dr. Binns, *Inventory*, pp. 118–20, Green River upstream from Fontenelle Reservoir contains important nesting populations of Canada geese; duck broods are common, sandhill cranes nest in marshes along the river. Very few birds overwinter here because of harsh winter conditions, although a few may stay late in isolated open-water areas, such as near warm springs or in Fontenelle Reservoir tailrace. Mallards are most numerous; also here are gadwalls, pintails, shovelers, green-wing teal, goldeneye, bufflehead, and redhead ducks; white-fronted geese and coots; trumpeter and whistling swans may occasionally be sighted during migration. Binns estimates that 27,000 ducks make up the breeding population, and 64,000 of all species use the drainage as a whole during migration.

57   W. H. Bucher, "On Ripples and Related Sedimentary Surface Forms and Their Paleographic Interpretations," *Am. Jour. Sci.* 47 (4th series, 1919):149–210, 241–69. F. J. Pettijohn, Paul E. Potter, Raymond Siever, *Sand and Sandstone* (New York: Springer-Verlag, 1972), p. 3, isolate a characteristic of sand not shared by coarser or finer materials, the quality of self-accumulation, "of utilizing the energy of the transporting medium to collect their scattered components together in definite heaps, leaving the intervening surface free of grains." The common mode of sand transport is by the migration of such heaps in dunes, whether they be subaerial or subaqueous.

Ripples and dunes are characteristic of low velocities; when velocity increases, as it does in the Green during rapid runoff and flood stage, ripples and dunes disappear, the bed flattens momentarily and blurs with moving sand, and then antidunes form, when the amplitude of the water waves becomes greater than the amplitude of the sand waves. Antidunes (a term coined by W. K. Gilbert in 1914) travel upstream and are in phase with the water waves, unlike the lower-velocity forms. Large quantities of sand and silt are kept kept suspended in the water, and because of the amount of turbidity at this high level of flow, antidunes themselves are nearly always invisible, but the waves they generate are unmistakable.

58–59   L. B. Leopold and W. B. Langbein, "River Meanders," *Scientific American* 214, no. 6(1966):60–70, describe a meander as a "sine-generated curve," or one that differs from other familiar geometric curves "in that it has the smallest variation of the changes of direction." They suggest that such a curve can be created by holding a strip of spring steel firmly at two separated points and bringing the hands together (a strip of heavy paper works also); the strip assumes a shape in which the bend is as uniform as possible; "meanders are not mere accidents of nature but the form in which a river does the least work in turning, and hence are the most probable form a river can take." A curved section of river, 100 feet wide, averages 8 to 10 curves per mile. See also Leopold and Wolman, *River Channel Patterns*.

60   For moose on the upper Green, see Binns, *Inventory*, pp. 94–95. Antelope (pp. 111–13) now are widespread in the Green River drainage, having

greatly increased since they were nearly exterminated in the early 1900s. Summer range has historically included a large area in the Green River Basin, extending over into the Snake River drainage; winter range is limited, lying predominantly in the V formed by the confluence of the Green and New Fork rivers.

61   The first irrigation rights on the upper Green were granted in 1882, the oldest and most extensive irrigation system in the U.S. In 1951, 245,000 acres were irrigated here. See W. B. Freeman and R. H. Bolster, *Surface Water Supply of the United States, 1907–8,* IX, Colorado River Basin, U.S.G.S. Water-Supply Paper 249 (Washington, D.C., 1910) and Albert N. Williams, *The Water and the Power* (New York: Duell, Sloan and Pearce, 1951).

62   Irving, *Bonneville,* p. 267.

63ff. For beaver trapping and the fur trade, see Robert Cleland. *This Reckless Breed of Men* (New York: Knopf, 1963); Bernard DeVoto, *Across the Wide Missouri* (Boston: Houghton Mifflin, 1947), and especially LeRoy Hafen, ed., *The Mountain Men and the Fur Trade of the Far West,* 10 vols. (Glendale: Arthur H. Clark, 1965–72).

64   W. A. Ferris, *Life in the Rocky Mountains, A Diary of Wanderings on the Sources of the Rivers Missouri, Columbia, and Colorado from February, 1830, to November, 1835,* ed. Paul C. Phillips (Denver: Old West, 1940), p. 144; Ferris was a trapper for the American Fur Company and kept a priceless journal of these years. For trappers' equipment, Carl P. Russell, *Firearms, Traps, & Tools of the Mountain Man* (New York: Knopf, 1967), is well researched and illustrated, and in a way gives a truer feeling for the period than conjectural description. See also Robert L. Williamson, "The Muzzle-Loading Rifle: Frontier Tool," in *Essays on the American West* (Austin: University of Texas Press, 1969), pp. 66–88. For a contemporary account, Dr. F. A. Wislizenus, *A Journey to the Rocky Mountains in the Year 1839* (St. Louis: Missouri Historical Society, 1912), pp. 122–23: ". . . one gets habituated to his rifle as to a trusty traveling companion. During the march the gun lies across the saddle; when one rests it is always close at hand. One never leaves camp without taking it as a cane; and at night it is wrapped in the blanket with the sleeper, to be ready for use at the first alarm." Arthur Woodward's special interest was the Green River knife: "Those Green River Knives," *Indian Notes* 4, no. 4(1927):403–18; "Up to Green River," *Brand Book* (1948):141–46; "Green River Knives," *Western Folklore* (1950):56–59. Handsome reproductions of these knives are sold at the re-enactment of rendezvous on the second Sunday in July, at the rendezvous site near Pinedale, Wyoming.

68–69 Woolley, *Green River,* pp. 168–69: in the late 1880s and early 1890s many large irrigation enterprises were "undertaken by promoters who hoped to make big profits from increased land values created by irrigation. This enthusiasm was not tempered with the proper amount of reason, and the settlers were not always apprised of the conditions to be met. Consequently many of the projects were failures, and a period of inactivity followed this boom." William C. Darrah, "Powell of the Colorado," *Utah Hist. Quar.* 28(1960):222–31 New York *Tribune* quote, p. 225. Wallace Stegner, *Beyond the Hundredth Meridian* (Boston: Houghton Mifflin, 1954) should be required reading for those who persist in the assumption that there is ample water in the arid West for all needs. For background on the Homestead Act as it applied in the West, see Richard A. Bartlett, *Great Surveys of the American West* (Norman: University of Oklahoma Press, 1962); Larson, *History of Wyoming,* and pertinent articles in U.S.D.A. Yearbook on *Water* (Washington, D.C., 1955).

When Powell retired as U.S.G.S. director, approximately one-fifth of the country had been surveyed and mapped; in 1884–85 he estimated that the maps could be produced in 24 years for $18 million (Stegner, p. 280). By 1952, costs were approaching $100 million and about 60 percent of the country was mapped. James Keogh, U.S.G.S., Denver, *pers. comm.*, says that as of 1974 about 86 percent of the U.S. is mapped and production cost is not available; some 30,000 7.5-minute and 3,600 15-minute quadrangles are in print.

69–70   Four reservoirs are under consideration for the Green River Basin, two of which are on the Green itself—Kendall and Lower Green (just above the town of Green River)—and two on tributaries of the Green, the New Fork Narrows Dam and the Plains Reservoir, across the drainage between the Green and Big Sandy. Water would be carried by canal and/or pipeline, mostly east and northeast to the Great Divide Basin or the North Platte River Basin. Primary use for this transbasin water would be for power, coal mining, coal gasification, and hydraulic transport of coal—i.e., liquification of coal so that it can be shipped by pipeline as a slurry, requiring about one ton of water for one ton of coal, power and coal both largely going out of state. From an engineering point of view, the higher elevation of the Kendall Reservoir would allow for gravity flow in a proposed canal to run along the southwest flank of the Wind Rivers; water from the Lower Green Reservoir would require pumping, but, being farther downstream, would drain a larger area (see p. 122).

Pressures for these reservoirs are formidable, and persistently call upon the closure argument of "use it or lose it": Frank Trelease III, "Green River Water Development Plans," *Wyoming Wildlife* 35, no. 4(1971): 14: "Without additional reservoir storage in the Green River Basin, Wyoming will likely forfeit from 177,000 to 345,000 acre-feet per year of beneficial consumptive use to which the State is entitled under interstate compacts." State of Wyoming, Department of Economic Planning and Development, *Engineering Report on the Development of Presently Unused Water Supplies of the Green River Basin in Wyoming* (Denver: Tipton and Kalmbach, October, 1972), preface, anticipates water shortages in the Lower Basin as early as 1985, to become major by the end of the century: "In these circumstances, and notwithstanding the presumed protection afforded by language contained in the Colorado River Compact regarding minimum delivery to the Lower Basin and preservation of rights to water use, it is essential that Wyoming take steps to expeditiously develop and put to beneficial use the supplies to which it is entitled."

Water from the Colorado River was divided among upper and lower basin states by the Colorado River Compact of 1922, the upper basin to receive 7.5 million acre-feet yearly. Problems have arisen because the amount of available water was overestimated. A second compact, among the states of the upper basin, signed in 1948, allot Wyoming 14 percent of approximately 1 million acre-feet/year. However, Frank Trelease, Director of Wyoming Water Development Plan, *pers. comm.*, says that although Wyoming is guaranteed the water in perpetuity from the 1922 compact, "Wyoming is not guaranteed a share of the 7.5 million acre feet." But water from the 1922 compact *is* guaranted in perpetuity and *cannot* be forfeited by non-use, and the "use it or lose it" propaganda is as fallacious as "rain follows the plow" of a century ago. A state official also involved with water planning, who would not be quoted, assessed the Wyoming administration view of the situation within the Upper

Colorado River Basin as a political one. He feels that as other states develop their water supplies, and as other problems (such as the river's salinity) receive more attention, there will be less and less probability of Congress authorizing projects for Wyoming if it appears other more heavily-populated states with more political leverage (e.g., Arizona, California) would be adversely affected. The "use it or lose it" pressure is an attempt to justify selling Green River water to industry in an area where there is considerable resistance to loosing a free-flowing Green River. I am much indebted to Dr. Luna Leopold for a cogent description of this complex political, economic, and environmental situation.

The most comprehensive presentation of the various projects under consideration is Bureau of Reclamation, *Alternative Plans for Water Resource Developments, Green River Basin, Wyoming,* May, 1972. The State Engineer's office has two publications (besides that cited above): *State Water Plan Report No. 3, Water & Related Land Resources of the Green River Basin, Wyoming,* September, 1970, and *The Wyoming Framework Water Plan—A Summary,* May, 1973. The entire April, 1971, issue of *Wyoming Wildlife,* published by The Wyoming Game & Fish Commission, was devoted to the upper Green; of special note is an article by Kenneth Diem, "Green River Statement," for preserving the upper Green as free flowing. *High Country News,* May 10, 1974, focused on water problems of the West. Editor Tom Bell wrote: ". . . like the shortage of fuel and energy, it seems likely that uncoordinated use of such a finite resource will undoubtedly lead to shortage of water. . . . Worse yet, the best laid plans of men do not take into account the vagaries of nature. Cliff dwellings in the Southwest are mute testimony to the recurring patterns of drouth. Society is dependent upon the basic natural resources of land, water and air. When extraordinary reliance is put on any one of these resources, as it is now being placed on water in the West, then society is placing itself in jeopardy."

5   WARREN BRIDGE TO REARDON DRAW

Quadrangles: Warren Bridge, Signal Hill, Daniel Junction, Cora, and Mount Airy, Wyoming.

76–77   Bonneville's letter to Macomb, *The Adventures of Captain Bonneville, U.S.A., in the Rocky Mountains and the Far West,* ed. Edgeley W. Todd (Norman: University of Oklahoma Press, 1961), p. xxv. Bonneville's original journal, that he gave to Macomb in Washington, November, 1835, is missing; Irving saw this journal but did not have it to write from. Kenneth Spaulding, ed., *On the Oregon Trail, Robert Stuart's Journey of Discovery* (Norman: University of Oklahoma Press, 1953), thinks Irving lifted passages bodily from Stuart's journals. DeVoto, *Across the Wide Missouri,* pp. 58–59, believes Bonneville was sent west to keep track of the Hudson's Bay Company and British activities in Oregon. Federal Writers' Project, W.P.A., *The Oregon Trail* (New York: Hastings House, 1972), pp. 24–25: ". . . judged by the maps and reports he made and by recently discovered pay-roll records, actually [he went] as a United States secret intelligence officer." Irving, pp. 60–61, quotes Bonneville's comments about wood drying; Fontenelle's train, that Bonneville met the summer of 1832, was using mules; Sublette had taken wagons only as far as the eastern end of the Wind River Range in 1830. H. V. Hayden, *Eleventh Annual Report of the United States Geological and Geographical Survey of the Territories embracing Idaho and Wyoming, Being a*

Report of Progress of the Exploration for the Year 1877 (Washington, D.C., 1879), pp. 708–10, contains Gannett's remarks. Bonneville's "A Map of the Sources of the Colorado & Big Salt Lake, Platte, Yellow-stone, Muscle-shell, Missouri & Salmon & Snake River, Branches of the Columbia River," was an odd 23.3 miles to the inch.

77–79 Harrison C. Dale, *The Ashley-Smith Explorations and the Discovery of a Central Route to the Pacific, 1822–1829, with the original journals* (Cleveland: Arthur H. Clark, 1918); Dale L. Morgan, *Jedediah Smith and the Opening of the West* (Indianapolis: Bobbs-Merrill, 1953) and *The West of William H. Ashley* (Denver: Old West, 1964); Harvey L. Carter, "William H. Ashley," in LeRoy Hafen, ed., *Mountain Men,* 7:23–34, and LeRoy Hafen, "Étienne Provost," *ibid.,* 6:371–85. Little is known about Provost; he trapped out of Taos and was probably in the Uinta Basin as early as 1823–25; he was with Fontenelle's supply train that Bonneville met in 1832, and was portrayed by Alfred Miller in "Catch Up," painted at the 1837 rendezvous (Walters Art Gallery, Baltimore).

The myth of the San Buenaventura was much in the air; see Dee Linford, "Wyoming Stream Names," *Wyoming Game & Fish Department Bulletin* No. 3, 1944. By the time Ashley came to the Green River in 1825, he had met Peter Skene Ogden's Snake Country Expedition, which assured him that there was no such river as the San Buenaventura. Morgan, *Jedediah Smith,* p. 151, suggests Ashley knew that "he was on the Rio Colorado of the West" by the time he reached Desolation Canyon (O. Dock Marston, *pers. comm.*, says Ashley took out near Sand Ferry). Ashley continued to search (*ibid.*, pp. 152–55): "The waters of the Buenaventura, on which he found himself, after crossing the divide, are the tributaries of Weber River. The drainage area is indeed complicated, and he must have been confused by the various directions the stream pursued. . . . The mighty Buenaventura, which according to tradition entered the Pacific in the vicinity of San Francisco, has now dwindled to the rather insignificant Weber."

79 "Seedskadee" is modern usage; it was also spelled Shetskedee, Seeds-ka-day, Seeds-kee-dee, Seedskeeder, Siskade, Sisedepazeah, and Seedskedeeagie, among others. According to David Lavender, *The Rockies* (New York: Harper & Row, 1968), p. 84, Ashley called "the river Seeds-kee-dee until Provost told them the Spanish name was Verde, after the brush that shone so brilliantly along its banks in that gray-red, blasted country." Hubert Howe Bancroft, *History of Nevada, Colorado, and Wyoming, 1540–1888* (San Francisco: The History Co., 1890), Vol. 15, p. 786: "Green river, named after a member of Ashley's expedition of 1823, and not on account of its color as is commonly asserted," was echoed by C. B. Coutant, *The History of Wyoming from the Earliest Known Discoveries* (Laramie: Chaplin, Spafford & Mathison, 1899), p. 123, who says that Ashley "pushed forward to the Spanish River, the name of which he promptly changed to Green River, after one of his St. Louis partners." See also Linford, "Stream Names"; Rufus W. Leigh, "Naming of the Green, Sevier, and Virgin Rivers," *Utah Hist. Quar.* 29(1961):136–47; and especially C. Gregory Crampton, "The Discovery of the Green River," *Utah Hist. Quar.* 20 (1952):299–312, and Crampton and Gloria Griffin, "The San Buenaventura, Mythical River of the West," *Pacific Historical Review* 20(1956):163–71. For further on the San Buenaventura, see Chapter 11

A first-hand account of how to build a bullboat is Gwinn Harris Heap, ed. LeRoy R. and Ann W. Hafen, *Central Route to the Pacific* (Glendale: Arthur H. Clark, 1957), pp. 203–15.

80   On March 19, 1824, a group of Ashley's men reached the Green, probably near the mouth of Big Sandy; they divided, arranging to rejoin in mid-June on the Sweetwater River. John Sunder, *Bill Sublette, Mountain Man* (Norman: University of Oklahoma Press, 1959), pp. 52–53: this was "the forerunner of many important rendezvous." Cleland quotes Sublette's 1825 diary, *This Reckless Breed,* pp. 19–20: "The place of deposite as aforesaid, will be the place of randavoze for all our parties on or before the 10th of July next & that the place may be known—Trees will be pealed standing the most conspicuous near the junction of the rivers, or above the mountain as the case may be—should such point be without timber I will raise a mound of earth five feet high or set up rocks the tops of which will be made red with Vermillion."

81   Irving, *Bonneville,* p. 345. Prices are from Cleland, *This Reckless Breed,* pp. 24–25; DeVoto, *Across the Wide Missouri,* p. 103–104; Gerald C. Bagley, "Daniel T. Potts," in Hafen, *Mountain Men,* 3:249–62; and W. A. Ferris, *Life in Rocky Mountains,* entry of May 27, 1834.

82   John K. Nuttall, botanist at Harvard, urged Townsend to come; Townsend was to collect birds and other fauna for the Academy of Natural Sciences at Philadelphia. Townsend, *Narrative of a Journey across the Rocky Mountains, to the Columbia River,* in Reuben Gold Thwaites, *Early Western Travels* (Cleveland: Arthur H. Clark, 1905), Vol. 21, pp. 190–91: "About half an hour's hard riding brought us to the edge of [the Green River], and I observed that the horses had here entered. I noticed other tracks lower down, but supposed them to have been made by the wanderings of the loose animals. Here then seemed the proper fording place, and with some little hesitation, I allowed my nag to enter the water; we had proceeded but a few yards, however, when down he went off a steep bank, far beyond his depth. This was somewhat disconcerting; but there was but one thing to be done, so I turned my horse's head against the swift current, and we went snorting and blowing for the opposite shore. . . . I did not regret my adventure, however, and was congratulating myself upon my good fortune in arriving so seasonably, when, upon looking to my saddle, I discovered that my coat was missing . . . it contained the second volume of my journal, a pocket compass, and other articles of essential value to me. I would gladly have relinquished every thing the garment held, if I could have recovered the book; and although I returned to the river, and searched assiduously until night, and offered large rewards to the men, it could not be found." Nuttall gave Townsend his notes, surely one of the most generous gestures imaginable.

Bridger is quoted, among others, by DeVoto, *Across the Wide Missouri,* p. 230. Marshall Sprague, *Gallery of Dudes* (Boston: Little, Brown, 1967) includes a witty account of Stewart. Bridger guided the group up the Green River to the Green River Lakes, around Squaretop to Green River Pass and Stonehammer Lake; part of the trip must have followed what is now the Highline Trail.

82–83   Matthew Field, *Prairie and Mountain Sketches,* collected by Clyde and Mae Reed Porter, ed. Kate L. Green and John Francis McDermott (Norman: University of Oklahoma Press, 1957), p. 150. The date given of August 15, 1843, is of course 5 years too late.

83–84   LeRoy Hafen, "Robert Newell," in Hafen, *Mountain Men,* 8:269. Father de Smet arrived with the Bidwell-Bartleson party in 1840, reaching the Green River June 23; a marker near Mt. Olivet cemetery, above Horse Creek and the Green, commemorates this rendezvous.

85–86   Leopold, Wolman, and Miller, *Fluvial Processes,* p. 328, estimate that a river swings laterally across its flood plain no oftener than half its width every 80 years; individual sediment particles may remain at rest for a thousand years or more before being picked up and retransported.

Gannett, in Hayden, *Eleventh Annual Report*, pp. 675–79, lists stations and measured angles.

Leopold and Wolman, *River Channel Patterns*, combine a feel for a river and a knowledge of history that make pleasurable technical reading. See also S. A. Schumm, *The Shape of Alluvial Channels in Relation to Sedimentary Type*, U.S.G.S. Profess. Paper 352–B (Washington, D.C., 1960), pp. 17–30, and H. T. Ore, "Characteristic Deposits of Rapidly Aggrading Streams," Wyoming Geological Association Field Conference *Guidebook*, 1965, pp. 195–201.

87–89   For formations of the Green River Basin, see W. H. Bradley, *Geology of the Green River Formation and Associated Eocene Rocks in Southwestern Wyoming and Adjacent Parts of Colorado and Utah*, U.S.G.S. Profess. Paper 496–A (Washington, D.C., 1964); Glenn R. Scott, "Nonglacial Quaternary Geology of the Southern and Middle Rocky Mountains," in H. E. Wright, Jr., and David G. Frey, ed., *The Quaternary of the United States* (Princeton: Princeton University Press, 1965), pp. 243–54; and J. D. Sears and W. H. Bradley, *Relations of the Wasatch and Green River Formations in Northwestern Colorado and Southwestern Wyoming*, U.S.G.S. Profess. Paper 132–C (Washington, D.C., 1924).

88   On the upper Green, water level is raised by weirs that channel water into a canal system; water is returned to the river via an escape weir at the downstream end of the system.

6   REARDON DRAW TO FONTENELLE DAM

Quadrangles: Mount Airy, Mesa Springs, Ross Butte, Big Piney East, Milleson Draw, La Barge SE, La Barge, Names Hill, Fontenelle Reservoir SW, and Fontenelle Reservoir SE, Wyoming.

95   Mosquitoes are an unavoidable fact of life on the river; curiosity is one means of survival. See Marston Bates, *The Natural History of Mosquitoes* (New York: Macmillan, 1949); R. F. Chapman, *The Insects: Structure and Function* (New York: American Elsevier, 1969), and Oldroyd, *Natural History of Flies*.

96   In former days ranchers often dragged dead cattle onto the ice for spring runoff to dispose of; responsible modern ranchers are too aware of the pollution potential to continue this practice.

97   See two articles in U.S.D.A. *Water:* Milton Fireman and H. E. Hayward, "Irrigation Water and Saline and Alkali Soils," pp. 321–27, and Guy D. Smith and Robert V. Ruhe, "Water and Our Soil," pp. 121–26. Larson, *History of Wyoming*, p. 3: salt accumulations reduce the value of perhaps 1 million acres of Wyoming's alluvial soils.

100   A. C. Veatch, *Geography and Geology of a Portion of Southwestern Wyoming*, U.S.G.S. Profess. Paper 56 (Washington, D.C., 1907), and William J. Ghent, *The Road to Oregon, A Chronicle of the Great Emigrant Trail* (London: Longmans, Green, 1929), p. 188. The Lander Cutoff was the only improvement or extension of the Oregon Trail that ever got a cent from the Federal Government. Scale of Lander's map was 1:600,000, published in the *Report of Pacific Wagon Roads*, 1859, and was the first to give definite information on the area between the Green and Bear rivers; it was used until Gannett's maps were published some 20 years later. The famous artist Albert Bierstadt

accompanied Lander. An account of this trip is in Marshall Sprague, *The Great Gates* (Boston: Little, Brown, 1964), pp. 192–96.

101 Lime is calcium oxide which combines with water to form calcium hydroxide, a soluble salt (along with some other mineral salts) detrimental to most crops.

101–104 W. H. Bradley, "Limnology and the Eocene Lakes of the Rocky Mountain Region," *Geol. Soc. Am. Bull.* 59, no. 7(1948):635–48. Dr. Bradley was kind enough to check this section of the manuscript, and wrote nostalgically that he looked forward to seeing if my Green River corresponded to his. Even a few of Dr. Bradley's publications pertinent to this chapter show the scholarly variety that springs from a fertile and wide-ranging mind: "Fossil Caddice Fly Cases from the Green River Formation of Wyoming," *Am. Jour. Sci.* 7(1924):310–12; *The Varves and Climate of the Green River Epoch,* U.S.G.S. Profess. Paper 158-E (Washington, D.C., 1929); *Origin and Microfossils of the Oil Shale of the Green River Formation of Colorado and Utah,* U.S.G.S. Profess. Paper 168 (Washington, D.C., 1931). The Wyoming Geological Association Fifth Annual Field Conference *Guidebook,* 1950, focused on southwest Wyoming and contains a variety of pertinent articles plus road logs.

Platanus leaf, Department of Geology and Geophysics collection, University of Utah, found in Green River Formation northeast of Bonanza, Utah; fish fossil, Utah Fieldhouse of Natural History, courtesy G. E. Untermann.

106 David M. Potter, ed., *Trail to California: The Overland Journal of Vincent Geiger and Wakeman Bryarly* (New Haven: Yale University Press, 1945), pp. 155–56.

107 N. Allen Binns, *pers. comm.* about Green River cutthroat; he adds that these oil spills are a fairly common occurrence here, and have been so for years.

108 Thurman Wilkins, *Clarence King* (New York: Macmillan, 1958), pp. 50–51.

109 Joseph E. Ware, *The Emigrants' Guide to California,* ed. John Caughey (reprint, Princeton: Princeton University Press, 1932), pp. 25–26; mileages were based on Frémont's maps. See also Sunder, *Sublette,* pp. 91–92. Potter, ed., *Bryarly,* pp. 132–33, describes the Green River crossing. Leander V. Loomis, *A Journal of the Birmingham Emigrating Company,* ed. Edgar M. Ledyard (Glendale: Arthur H. Clark, 1928), pp. 55–56, describes an ingenious solution: "Awhile after sunrise we awoke, and found ourselves on the bank of green River to high to foard, by enquiries we learned that our feriage would be $7,oo pr waggon and $1,oo pr head for horses, this we thought to mutch, and, conciquently riged our Boat bed, and ferried our selves and swam our horses, we began to ferry about 10 o clock and by 10 o clock at night we had every thing, horses and all, safely landed on the opposite shore, without meeting with the least accident of any kind— . . . Green River is a fine stream, about 20 rods wide, with a very swift currant, comes down from among the rocky mountains."

110 Potter, ed., *Bryarly,* pp. 134–35, quoting McIlhany, another member of the company.

110–11 Bardach, *Downstream,* p. 217, cites an estimated rate of fill of 2.3 percent per year in small reservoirs in Illinois (where there is less erosion); Lake Mead contains sediments over 100 feet deep immediately above the dam. Quote from Leopold, Wolman, and Miller, *Fluvial Processes,* p. 457. Hayden, *Eleventh-Annual Report,* p. 517. Coker, *Streams, Lakes, Ponds,* pp. 130–31: the inevitable function of small reservoirs "as settling basins leads to their gradual filling, as occurs generally in lakes and ponds, but sometimes in impounded waters at a much more rapid rate. . . . A particular difficulty encountered with reservoirs having storage functions, as most of them do, is the extreme fluctuations of level incident to use of the stored water for power or irrigation and sometimes damaging to life within the reservoir." See also J. K. Neel, "Impact of Reservoirs," in D. G. Frey, ed., *Limnology in North America* (Madison: University of Wisconsin Press, 1963), pp. 575–93. As to the lack of wildlife, Robert Wiley, "The Fish and Wildlife Resource and the Development of the Environment," *Wyoming Wildlife*, 38, no. 4(1974), p. 3: "The use of land and water resources for development of industry and extraction of energy resources is, perhaps, inevitable. The associated loss of a few trout or game animals does not appear to represent a prelude to doomsday. However, the negative significance of these losses can not be overstated when attrition of the total resource is considered. Such attrition can be thought of as a mortgage on a legacy; when the legacy is gone, there will be nothing left . . . and when an area no longer supports fish or wildlife it has lost much of its livability for people as well."

7 FONTENELLE DAM TO GREEN RIVER, WYOMING

Quadrangles: Fontenelle Reservoir SE, Fontenelle, McCullen Bluff, Thoman School, Lombard Buttes, Big Island Bridge, Stevens Flat, Austin Ranch, Peru, and Green River, Wyoming.

115   For two of many newspaper accounts, see *Deseret News*, 4 September 1965, and Cheyenne *Tribune*, 6 September 1965. David Crandall, Regional Director, and E. B. Bywater, Upper Colorado Regional Office, *pers. comm.*: leakage runs 2 to 3 cfs. Dr. Binns and Robert Wiley provided much background information on Fontenelle Dam.

115–16   The first U.S.G.S. gage on the Green is at Warren Bridge; others are near La Barge, below Fontenelle Dam, and near the town of Green River, Wyoming, and at Jensen and Green River, Utah. Number of gages, *pers. comm.*, Dr. Luna Leopold.

116   Study on decreased flow: Roger L. Banks, James W. Mullan, Robert W. Wiley, and David J. Dufek, *The Fontenelle Green River Trout Fisheries Considerations in Its Enhancement and Perpetuation including Test Flow Studies of 1973* (U. S. Department of the Interior, Bureau of Sport Fisheries and Wildlife, and Wyoming Game & Fish Commission, March, 1974). See also Rock Springs *Rocket*, 2, 6, and 17 October 1973, and Green River *Star*, 15 March 1972.

The environmental studies, letters of inquiry and protest, and answers to same, and the proposed contract are published in Department of the Interior, *Final Environmental Statement, Proposed Contract for Sale of Municipal and Industrial Water from Fontenelle Reservoir Seedskadee Project*, Sept. 5, 1974. The state presently sells 35,000 acre-feet to Pacific Power & Light for the Jim Bridger Plant northeast of Rock Springs, and 25,000 to Sun Oil Company (*High Country News*, 10 May 1974). A folder (courtesy Bev G. Godec, Colorado Springs Utilities Dept.) printed by Idaho Power Co. and PP&L (Idaho receives all the power from the one generator now in operation), "The Jim Bridger Steam-Electric Project," projects a production of 1,500,000 kilowatts when completed, with an estimated water consumption of 29,000 acre-feet. PP&L is requesting an additional 30,000 acre-feet (p. 19) along with other industrial users (two trona plants, but mainly energy producers) to total 224,000 acre-feet. Article 9 of the proposed contract declares the 50 cfs minimum flow which the city of Green River (p. 130) says will jeopardize "the water supply of Green River and the surrounding communities that depend on the Green for portable water." Billings *Gazette*, 2 May 1973, reported that Governor Hathaway, in response to the request for a guaranteed 300 cfs minimum, "called this unreasonable and there would not be much water in storage for sale if this was the position." Environmental impact summary, p. i: "The proposal would expedite development of the industrial potential of southwestern Wyoming with the addition of heavy industry and development of existing mineral resources. Along with the development of the area would be changes in land use from grazing to industrial use, a decrease of air quality, added people in the cities of Green River and Rock Springs, a decrease in water quality of the Green River below the diversions. Since Fontenelle Reservoir has not been fully utilized for the authorized purposes, there would also be a reduction in flows available for fisheries below the points of diversion from that flow which has been available since construction of Fontenelle Dam and Reservoir. The proposal would also forestall the construction of additional storage facilities within the Green River Basin."

117   Banks *et al., Trout Fisheries,* pp. 15–17, describe the situation in the Fontenelle tailwaters. The experimental farm was operated by the Bureau of Reclamation with the University of Wyoming and "other interested agencies" until December 31, 1971; see University of Wyoming, Agricultural Extension Service, *Seedskadee Development Farm Progress Report 1964–1969,* Bulletin 506, January, 1970. No irrigation water from Fontenelle, E. G. Bywater, *pers. comm.;* contemplated acreages, Frank J. Trelease, *pers. comm.;* one of the reasons that water is now available for state purchase is that none is used for irrigation.

118   Irving, *Bonneville,* p. 48.

121   John Boardman, "The Journal of John Boardman," *Utah Hist. Quar.* 2, no. 4(1929), pp. 106–107.

121–22   Like rendezvous, early commercial crossings of the West were short-lived, colorful, and unique, largely terminated by the arrival of the railroad in 1869. See Mae Urbanek, *Wyoming Place Names* (Boulder, Colorado: Johnson Publishing, 1967); Edward R. McAuslan, "The Overland Trail in Wyoming," Wyo. Geol. Assoc. *Guidebook,* 1961, pp. 324–28; Trent, *Road to Oregon,* as well as individual journals. Willis T. Lee, Ralph W. Stone, Hoyt S. Gale, and others, *Guidebook to the Western United States. Part B., The Overland Route,* U.S.G.S. Bulletin 612 (Washington, D.C., 1916), p. 66: "The scattered 'bunch grass,' which looks so meagre and dry, is in fact excellent forage, curing into hay where it grew and having a high nutritive value . . . with the first heavy snowfall [the sheep] are driven from the foothills to spend the winter in the open, where they find pasture in the spaces cleared of snow by the wind. The winds are not tempered here, but neither is the lamb shorn, and Wyoming winter winds make heavy wool when shearing time comes."

123–24   For various facets of land management during this period, see G. R. Salmond and A. R. Croft, "The Management of Public Watersheds," in U.S.D.A. Yearbook *Water,* pp. 191–98; Larson, *History of Wyoming,* pp. 3, 385; Stegner, *Beyond the Hundredth Meridian,* p. 224–26, and Woolley, *Green River,* pp. 169–71.

125   Tipton and Kalmbach, *Engineering Report on Development,* is a feasibility report for this and the Plains Reservoir. A dam here would be built about 4 miles up from Green River, and about 12 miles downstream from Stauffer's Big Island Refinery. The reservoir, when full, would flood out the plant, so either the reservoir would not be filled to capacity, or in addition to a $14 million dam (note that this is a pre-inflation estimate), a dike costing $3 million would have to be built. Tipton and Kalmbach recommended development of the Plains Reservoir instead; there there would be the problem of

massive evaporation. The need for this water is largely industrial, p. 15: "There is no doubt but that the mineral industry will soon supplant agriculture and livestock as the dominant element in the economy of the basin. Although the use of water for industrial purposes presently is but a small fraction of the amount of water consumed by agriculture, it is expected that by the end of the century non-agricultural uses of water, including amounts which may be exported out of the basin, will represent nearly 60 percent of the total water consumption . . . the cost of major new water developments will be such that *agriculture will be unable to compete with the mineral industry for the use of water.*" [italics mine.]

123 N. Allen Binns, *Effects of Rotenone Treatment on the Fauna of the Green River, Wyoming,* Fisheries Research Bulletin Number 1 (Cheyenne: Wyo. Game & Fish Comm., 1967), p. 24; removal of water is by the F.M.C. Corporation, a conglomerate headquartered in Chicago.

127–28 Horace Greeley, *An Overland Journey from New York to San Francisco,* ed. Charles T. Duncan (New York: Knopf, 1964), p. 194.

128 Banks *et al., The Fontenelle Green River Trout Fisheries,* pp. 50–51: "For several years the Seedskadee Refuge has been conducting a program to transfer most goose nesting from the river to the marsh habitat created on the refuge. This is being accomplished through the use, and manipulation of artificial goose nesting structures. Since inception of the program there has been a steady increase in the use of nest structures located on marsh islands. The current projection for the Seedskadee Refuge when fully developed is to produce 1000 to 1500 geese annually on the refuge marsh habitat."

8 FLAMING GORGE DAM TO THE GATES OF LODORE

Quadrangles: Green River, Firehole Basin (15-min.), McKinnon Junction (15-min.), Buckboard Crossing (15-min.), Wyoming; Manila, Flaming Gorge, Dutch John, Utah-Wyoming; Goslin Mountain, Clay Basin, Warren Draw, Utah; Swallow Canyon, Utah-Colorado; Lodore School, Canyon of Lodore North, Colorado.

Two series of river guides begin here: Laura Evans and Buzz Belknap, *Flaming Gorge, Dinosaur National Monument, Dinosaur River Guide* (Boulder City, Nevada: Westwater Books, 1973) are handsomely designed and informative. Westwater Books (P.O. Box 365, Boulder City, Nevada 89005, also publishes a good list of available river books.) Those of the Powell Society are more geologically oriented: Philip T. Hayes and Elmer S. Santos, *River Runners' Guide to the Canyons of the Green and Colorado Rivers with Emphasis on Geologic Features, Vol. 1, Flaming Gorge Dam to Ouray, Utah* (Denver: Powell Society, 1969). A U.S.D.A.–U.S.D.I. brochure, "Three Faces of the Green River," gives descriptive information, flow cycles, and rules and regulations for boating below the dam. Gay Staveley, *Broken Waters Sing* (Boston: Little, Brown, 1971), is a boatman's narration of a trip begun at Flaming Gorge Dam through the Colorado.

133 Woolley, *Green River,* described the hermit, p. 42: ". . . 71 years old and had lived in the canyon about 20 years. His house or hovel was a crude tepee of boards over a small hole in the ground. It was hardly big enough for one person but might be classed as a good-sized dog kennel. His wardrobe was as meager as the house, consisting of a piece of dirty canvas with a hole cut in the middle for his head to pass through, a ragged pair of overalls, and a unique pair of shoes with soles of large pieces of cowhide about 15 inches long with the hair on the bottom side and uppers apparently cut from old rubber boots and laced to the soles with rawhide strings." See Milt Riske,

"Dreamboat on the Green," *Denver Post* Empire Magazine, 25, no. 7 (July 7, 1974), pp. 34–35.

Flaming Gorge Dam is the only large dam on the Green. The Colorado River Storage Project provided for four large mainstream dams or "storage units" and eleven irrigation or "participating projects." Of these, the Seedskadee Project is Fontenelle Dam; none of the others have been built. William Purdy, "Mainstem of the Colorado," *Utah Hist. Quar.* 28, no. 3(1960): 250–261: "The utilization of every drop of water in the Colorado River system has long been the goal of the Bureau of Reclamation. They have surveyed the entire length of the river, mapping possible damsites, and setting up a development program for the consideration of the people and Congress. By 1946 thirty-three potential projects were outlined for use of water in the Green River division alone."

134   There are few studies of the effects of this dam. David Vanicek, "Distribution of Green River Fishes in Utah and Colorado Following Closure of Flaming Gorge Dam," *Southwest Naturalist,* 14, no. 3(1970): 297–315, p. 297: "Flaming Gorge Dam has caused a major change in the ecology of the downstream Green River by alteration of seasonal flows and water-temperature patterns as far as the mouth of the Yampa River, 65 miles below the dam. As a result, native fish populations, particularly in the first 26 miles below the dam, have largely been replaced by introduced rainbow trout (*Salmo gairdneri*). Below the Yampa River mouth, fish populations were similar to those reported during the pre-impoundment years. During years of high summer discharge from the dam with resultant lower water temperatures (1964 and 1966), no reproduction of any native fishes was found in the Green River above the mouth of the Yampa River."

136   Wallace R. Hansen, *The Geologic Story of the Uinta Mountains,* U.S.G.S. Bull. 1291 (Washington, D.C., 1969), is a comprehensive presentation, with excellent diagrams and photographs. Hansen, *Geology of the Flaming Gorge Area, Utah-Colorado-Wyoming,* U.S.G.S. Profess. Paper 490 (Washington, D.C., 1965), is a survey of Flaming Gorge canyons before inundation. See also W. H. Bradley, *Geomorphology of the North Flank of the Uinta Mountains,* U.S.G.S. Profess. Paper 185-I (Washington, D.C., 1936), and Norman C. Williams, ed., *Guidebook to the Geology of the Wasatch and Uinta Mountains* (Salt Lake City: Intermountain Association Petroleum Geologists, 1959); the latter contains pertinent articles, especially Edgar B. Heylmun, "The Ancestral Rocky Mountain System in Northern Utah," pp. 172–74

139   John Burroughs, *Where the Old West Stayed Young* (New York: William Morrow, 1962), p. 41, quotes Ewing. Charles Kelly, *The Outlaw Trail: A History of Butch Cassidy and His Wild Bunch* (New York: Bonanza Books, 1959) contains some inaccuracies that render the book unreliable; Burroughs is by far the best account.

Woolley, *Green River,* p. 44.

141   Although the name of Brown's Hole is widely assumed to commemorate Baptiste Brown, the truth may be more complex; see Janet LeCompte, "Jean-Baptiste Chalifoux," in Hafen, *Mountain Men,* 7:57–74. The elimination of the apostrophe and change from Hole to Park is generally attributed to Powell, but Ann Bassett Willis, "Queen Ann of Brown's Park," *The Colorado Magazine* 29, no. 2(1952): 95, says her mother, on entering the area, averred that "no place as lovely as this should ever have been called a 'hole.' It's more like a park. That's what it is—a tremendous park! Brown's Park!"

142   According to Charles Kelly, *Outlaw Trail,* p. 14, George Parker's "Butch"

was acquired from Matt Warner's old needle gun that Warner called "Butch." When Parker fired it, the recoil sent him sprawling and from then on he was called "Butch." Pearl Baker, *The Wild Bunch at Robbers Roost* (New York: Ballantine, 1973), pp. 171 ff., and Burroughs, *Where the Old West Stayed Young*, p. 119, suggest that the name came from a winter in Rock Springs when Parker worked as a meat cutter, a brief, notably unsuccessful experiment in legitimate employment. All agree that the name "Cassidy" came from Mike Cassidy, a cowboy whom Parker admired. Burroughs, p. 130, sums up the predicament of Browns Park residents: turning a blind eye toward illegal activity "was one condition of their continued survival. A certain amount of froternizing with the outlaws was inescapable." (For instance, Isom Dart worked on the Bassett Ranch.) "In brief, everybody in Brown's Hole was acquainted with the outlaws, was aware that they were outlaws, and let it go at that."

143   Hansen, *Geology of the Flaming Gorge Area*, p. 133, relates that old-time residents remember the now disappeared grasslands, and that there seems little doubt that gullying has contributed significantly to this; the long-term result has been a lowering of the water table, transforming meadowlands into scrub and desert.

143–45   For a character study of Charlie Crouse, see Burroughs, *Where the Old West Stayed Young*. G. E. Untermann, a marvelous story-teller and fine geologist, who has lived and written about Uintah County for many years, told me about the flour first aid.

147   Ann Willis, "Queen Ann," p. 95, described her mother.

148   Julius Stone, *Canyon Country*, p. 52, coming across Browns Park in 1909, wrote: "There is a very heavy wind which at times amounts almost to a gale, so that it requires the hardest kind of work to make any headway against it." Every estimate given us by local people was qualified by "if the wind don't blow." According to Ann Willis, p. 91, the cemetery was presented to the district by Mrs. Valentine Hoy.

150–51   The ruins of Fort Davy Crockett have never been found. Frederick Mark, "William Crain," in Hafen, *Mountain Men*, 2:99–116, made a diligent search and believed it to be at Vermilion Creek (p. 108), "because large stands of cottonwood still remain, and the area is almost completely encircled by Green River and Vermilion Creek, along which is a high rough escarpment providing a natural barrier to hold livestock in close proximity to the establishment." For an account of the horse raid, see LeRoy Hafen, "Philip F. Thompson," in Hafen, *Mounatin Men*, 3:340–47, and "Fort Crockett, Its Fur Men and Visitors," *The Colorado Magazine* 29, No. 1 (January, 1952): 17–33. Thomas Farnham was a young Vermont lawyer who came west to recover from ill health and chronicled his journey in *Travels in the Great Western Prairies, the Anahuac and Rocky Mountains, and in the Oregon Territory*, in Reuben G. Thwaites, ed., *Early Western Travels 1748–1846* (Cleveland: Arthur H. Clark, 1906), Vol. 28, p. 252. Wislizenus, *Journey*, pp. 129–30. Ann Bassett Willis, "Queen Ann," p. 84, quotes her uncle's journal.

9   THE GATES OF LODORE TO ECHO PARK

Quadrangles: Canyon of Lodore North and Canyon of Lodore South, Colorado. The name was misspelled "Ladore" for many years, but was officially corrected to "Lodore" by Congress in 1925.

155   William Darrah, "Hawkins, Hall, and Goodman," *Utah Hist. Quar.* 15 (1947):106–108. Andrew Hall was the character of the 1869 trip; at 18, he had already spent 5 years as a bullwhacker, to which he returned after the river trip. He was murdered while guarding a stagecoach 13 years later. See also Bartlett, *Great Surveys,* pp. 241, 244.

156–60   The clearest explanation of Lodore Canyon is in Hansen, *Uinta Mountains;* for terminology, see Bloom, *Surface,* pp. 91–92. S. F. Emmons, "The Origin of Green River," *Science* 6 (July–December, 1897) and C. A. Davis, "Is Green River antecedent to the Uinta Mountains?" *Science* 5 (April 23, 1887):647–48. See also G. E. and B. R. Untermann, *Geology of Dinosaur National Monument and Vicinity,* Bulletin 42, Utah-Colorado (Salt Lake City: Utah Geological and Mineralogical Survey, June, 1954).

160   John Ground to Park Superintendent Earl M. Semingsen, October 26, 1963. The original letter is in the National Park Service records at Dinosaur National Monument; a copy was made available to me through the courtesy of Dr. Richard Beidleman, who wrote an administrative history of the monument.

160–61   Gilbert, *Transportation,* first worked out the relationship between velocity and transportation power in 1914; the latter increases geometrically, so that doubling the velocity of the current quadruples its transportation ability. For lighter materials held in suspension, carrying power is even more increased by turbulence; Coker, *Streams, Lakes, Ponds,* p. 132, estimates that this may be up to a fifth or sixth power of the velocity. Stone, *Canyon Country,* p. 138.

162   Luna Leopold, "The Rapids and the Pools—Grand Canyon," U.S.G.S. Profess. Paper 669-C (Washington, D.C., 1969), pp. 13–45.

William L. Manly, *Death Valley in '49* (New York: Wallace Hebberd, 1894), p. 69. Dale L. Morgan, introduction, "The Exploration of the Colorado River and the High Plateaus of Utah by the Second Powell Expedition of 1871–72," *Utah Hist. Quar.* 16(1948): 1–9, p. 3: "The fugitive records of the fur trade yield up some hints that mountain men soon undertook an exploration of this portion of the river—spurred, no doubt, by the hope of finding a fabulous new beaver country. Thus on June 28, 1858, the San Francisco Daily Alta California picked up a story about two trappers, Luis Ambrois and Jose Jessum, the latter a half-breed Arikara, who in 1831 had descended the Green in a canoe, but had had to abandon the enterprise and climb the Colorado precipices to same themselves."

163   Donald Baars and C. M. Molenaar, 1971, *Geology of Canyonlands and Cataract Canyon* (Four Corners Geological Society, Sixth Field Conference, 1971): Baars, a geologist, writer, and himself a boatman, describes Powell's method, pp. 8–9: "The rapid was entered bow-first, with one or two oarsmen pulling hard with their backs to the rapid; the more difficult the rapid the harder they would row to get up sufficient speed for positive control by a rudder tended by a third man. Dellenbaugh's descriptions of this type of rapid running indicate that it was a bit unnerving to row backwards into the roaring rapid, not knowing where one was going, and then to be pounded by waves washing over one's head in the bucking boat as it entered the waves. . . . The boat must, of course, maintain a speed greater than the current of the river to afford maneuverability, consequently increasing the rate at which dangers were encountered."

Galloway designed a light, maneuverable boat a little over 16 feet long, 4 feet across the beam, and 16 inches deep, made of 5/8-inch white pine, weighing about 240 pounds. Ron Smith, a modern boat designer, built one much like this that is now owned by Glade Ross at Lodore Ranger Station. Stone returned to the river 30 years later, when he was 83, with his son, George, Dr. A. L. Inglesby (after whom a rapid in Split Mountain is named), Charles Kelly, and others.

O. Dock Marston describes the French kayak trip in "Fast Water," in Wallace Stegner, ed., *This Is Dinosaur* (New York: Knopf, 1955), pp. 58–70, 68. The history of these and other river expeditions has been impeccably researched by Mr. Marston; see also "River Runners, Fast Water Navigation," *Utah Hist. Quar.* 28, no 3(1960):291–308.

164　J. W. Powell, *The Exploration of the Colorado River and Its Canyons* (1895, reprint), p. 160: "Here we have three falls in close succession. At first the water is compressed into a very narrow channel against the right-hand cliff, and falls 15 feet in 10 yards. At the second we have a broad sheet of water tumbling down 20 feet over a group of rocks that thrust their dark heads through the foam. The third is a broken fall, or short, abrupt rapid, where the water makes a descent of more than 20 feet among huge fallen fragments of the cliff. We name the group Triplet Falls. We make a portage around the first, past the second and the third we let down with lines." See Leopold "The Rapids and the Pools—Grand Canyon," pp. 134–35, for waves in rapids.

167–69　Stegner, *This Is Dinosaur*, pp. 16–17, Pat Lynch was the first man to use the canyons for both livelihood and pleasure. He may have heard about this area from Powell. Castle Park, on the Yampa seems to have been his main headquarters. Ellsworth Kolb (*Through the Grand Canyon*, facing p. 84) has a marvelous portrait of Pat Lynch on horseback; he has a full white beard and tips his hat with a courtly gesture. Paul Ellis, of the National Park Service, interviewed Ralph White, Clerk of the Moffat County Court at Craig, Colorado, November 14, 1963; White met Lynch in 1912 when Lynch came into Craig to see about his Civil War pension: "He was very large in stature and he had a very deep voice which fit the stature. Not very talkative. He talked only when you asked him questions. He possessed intelligence well better intelligence, than you would expect of a man who has no education, however, he could read some and could sign documents in order to get his citizenship properly restored and to get his pension. . . . He went up into Lily Park, became sick and dies, so the[y] buried him right there." The typescript of this taped interview is at Dinosaur National Monument Headquarters; copy made available through the courtesy of Dr. Beidleman.

10　ECHO PARK THROUGH SPLIT MOUNTAIN

Quadrangles: Canyon of Lodore South, Colorado; Jones Hole. Utah-Colorado; Island Park, Split Mountain, Dinosaur Quarry, Utah. A full-color geological map of the Dinosaur National Monument, Colorado-Utah, by G. E. and B. R. Untermann, 1:62500, is published by the Dinosaur Nature Association with the Utah Geological and Mineralogical Survey, and the Utah Field House of Natural History.

169　The Green River raft was designed by Ron Smith (*pers. comm.*) as an answer to the diminishing supply of war surplus 10-man assault rafts, and to their design, with a tapered, flat stern, that was meant for use with a motor. Smith's design eliminated the taper and put a "bow" at each end and added large twart tubes and D-rings for cross-wise rigging.

One of the most controversial dams of recent years was proposed for the Echo Park–Split Mountain area. A National Park Service study of 1950 had stated that such a dam's effects upon "irreplaceable geological, wilderness, and related values of national significance would be deplorable." Secretary of the Interior Oscar Chapman nevertheless directed that the dam be built, triggering such an effective protest campaign that the whole project was eventually dropped. Jay R. Bingham, "Reclamation and the Colorado," *Utah Hist. Quar.* 28(1960):232–49, notes that the bill including the building of the dam was passed by the Senate April 20, 1955, but (p. 240) "strategists in the House advised deferring Echo Park and substituting Flaming Gorge in order to get development started. The combination of opposition from conservationists, antireclamationists, and conservation-minded congressmen, was thought to be too formidable to risk defeat or further delay." One of the most eloquent statements was that of historians, writers, and naturalists in *This Is Dinosaur,* edited by Wallace Stegner.

174   Andy Hall's remarks were recalled by fellow boatman Jack Sumner and recorded by Robert Stanton Brewster, *Colorado River Controversies,* James M. Chalfant, ed. (New York: Dodd, Mead Co., 1932), p. 175; see also p. 237.

177   Don Hatch tells me that 50 years ago undergrowth was so thick at Jones Hole that you could hardly push your way through; Stone's entry suggests the same. Tom Hansen at Dinosaur National Monument kindly sent me a copy of the unpublished manuscript of the history of Jones Hole; according to G. E. Untermann, it was written by Sue Watson, a daughter of Henry C. and May Ruple, who homesteaded Island Park. It was Henry C. Ruple who told Jones that he was not wanted for murder (Henry Ruple was Mrs. Untermann's grandfather). I am much indebted to Mr. Untermann for the loan of his inscribed copy of Julius Stone's *Canyon Country;* it is inscribed to Arthur Ruple, Henry Ruple's son, who lived at Island Park when Stone came through in 1909.

178–81   Pottery shards are from a private collection; all other artifacts are from the Department of Anthropology, University of Utah, through the great courtesy of Dr. Jesse Jennings, Donald Hague, Director of the Utah Museum of Natural History, and Gardiner Dalley, who selected examples for drawing. Drawings show only a detail of Fremont basket fragments: upper left-hand corner, 42 BO 268/FS 279–2/24346; open hole bottom, 42 BO 268/FS 166–1/24346; closed hole, 42 BO 268/FS 129–1/24346. Of the gaming pieces, the longest is 3½ inches, 42 IN 40/FS 524–17/24354; shortest is 1⅛ inches, 42 IN 40/FS 200–113/24338;/shuttle-shaped, 42 IN 40/FS 59–217/24338; single hole, 42 IN 40/FS 42–11/24338;/with many perforations, 41 IN 40/FS 300–40/24354.;/metatarsal bone punch, 42 IN 40/540–4/24354.

    The Fremont were first defined by Noel Morss, *The Ancient Culture of the Fremont River in Utah* (Cambridge: Peabody Museum of American Archaeology and Ethnology Papers, Harvard University, 12/(3), 1931). John P. Marwitt, *Median Village and Fremont Culture Regional Variation* (Salt Lake City: University of Utah Anthropological Papers, No. 95, 1970) is the most recent and authoritative paper and contains a definitive bibliography. Marwitt notes a significant continuity from the Desert Archaic Culture and feels that by about A.D. 900 the "Fremont can be shown to be a fully crystallized cultural pattern, internally well differentiated and patently distinct from Anasazi manifestations to the south . . . the Fremont emerged as a recognizable archeological entity about A.D. 500 or before, and disappeared about A.D. 1300." Of Marwitt's five regional variants, the Uinta and San Rafael Fremont lie along the Green River.

183   The Ruple Ranch was established in 1883, according to the "Historic Ranch Report," typescript in Dinosaur National Monument Headquarters. Information about Pat Lynch and Mr. Ruple, and life on an Island Park ranch, are

from G. E. Untermann. Billie Untermann was a child when Butch Cassidy came through the Ruple Ranch at Island Park; she admired his spurs and he made her a gift of them, but the next morning, the best horses on the ranch had disappeared for good. Mr. Untermann's courtesy at the Utah Field House of Natural History made it possible for me to draw from their fine collection of fossils.

185   I am indebted to Don Hatch for information on how Split Mountain's rapids were named. Dr. Arthur L. Ing'esby came to Utah in 1896 as a young dentist, and retired in the late 1930s. Edith Lamb, Executive Secretary of the Utah Museum of Natural History at the University of Utah, tells me that he was an amateur geologist and his specimens are in most major collections in the world.

11   SPLIT MOUNTAIN TO WILD HORSE BENCH

Quadrangles: Dinosaur Quarry, Jensen, Rasmussen Hollow, Vernal SE, Brennan Basin, Pelican Lake, Ouray, and Uteland Butte, Utah.
Laura Evans and Buzz Belknap, *Desolation River Guide* (Boulder City, Nevada: Westwater Books, 1974) covers the river from Split Mountain to Green River, Utah. Felix Mutschler, *River Runner's Guide, etc., Vol. IV, Desolation and Gray Canyons* (Denver: Powell Society, 1973) covers from Ouray to Green River.

191–92   See Charles B. Hunt, *Cenozoic Geology of the Colorado Plateau,* U.S.G.S. Profess. Paper 279, and Otto G. Seal, ed., *Guidebook to the Geology of the Uinta Basin* (Salt Lake City: Intermountain Assoc. Petr, Geol., 1957). The latter contains articles of interest in geomorphology, the discovery of gilsonite, archeology, oil shale and oil, and the history of the basin.

193   No biography exists of Earl Douglass; my information is from G. E. Untermann and Dr. Richard Beidleman. See also an obituary, J. W. Holland, "Earl Douglass: A Sketch in Appreciation of His Life and Work," *Annals of the Carnegie Museum* 20, nos. 3 and 4 (reprint issued June 30, 1931.) Douglass's stone house is described by Stegner, *This Is Dinosaur,* p. 13.

194   James Madsen, Assistant Research Professor, Department of Geology and Geophysics, University of Utah, gave me drawing space and selected these dinosaur teeth: right maxilla of *Camptosaurus,* UUVP 5946; *Camarasaurus,* in front and back view, UUVP 3986; finely serrated tooth of carnivorous *Allosaurus,* UUVP 5948, showing new tooth growing in from the top; left dentary of *Stegosaurus,* UUVP 5947, a vegetarian whose teeth were half the size of a little fingernail. Scale is slightly smaller than life size. Jim Howell, graduate student in the department, generously checked these and all other fossils for identification and accuracy.

193–97   Esca'ante's diary is in the Newberry Library, Chicago; it is reprinted in Herbert E. Bolton, "Pageant in the Wilderness. The Story of the Escalante Expedition to the Interior Basin, 1776, Including the Diary and Itinerary of Father Escalante, Translated and Annotated," *Utah Hist. Quar.* 18(1950). Herbert E. Auerbach, ed., "Father Escalante's Journal with Related Documents and Maps," *Utah Hist. Quar.* 11(1943), contains a minutely different Escalante journal, and Miera's handsome maps.

    Escalante's entry, Sept. 14–15: "Before noon the quadrant was set up to repeat observation by the sun, and we found ourselves no higher than 40°59' and 24". We concluded that this discrepancy might come from the declination of the needle here, and to ascertain this we left the quadrant fixed until night for the north star stands on the meridian of the needles.

As soon as the north or polar star was discovered, the quadrant being in the meridian mentioned, we observed that the needle swung to the northeast. Then we again observed the latitude by the polar star and found ourselves in the same 41° 19′ as on the previous night. In this place there are six large black cottonwoods which have grown in pairs attached to one another and they are the nearest to the river. Near them is another one standing alone, on whose trunk, on the side facing northwest, Don Joaquin Lain with an adz cleared a small space in the form of a rectangular window, and with a chisel carved on it the letters and numbers of this inscription—"the year 1776"—and lower down in different letters—"LAIN"—with two crosses at the sides, the larger one above the inscription and the smaller one below it." Several have searched for the cottonwoods Escalante describes; Crampton, *Discovery,* thought that the trees were gone when he looked in the early 1950s. Dr. Beidleman says that 150 years is the outside age for cottonwoods, and these particular trees were probably well down by 1900. No mention is made of a search on fallen logs.

Frémont's maps were drawn by Charles Preuss, published 1845 and 1848; they delineated the Great Basin and eliminated the mythical river. Gloria Cline, *Exploring the Great Basin* (Norman: University of Oklahoma Press, 1963), p. 215, states that although maps before 1840 (among them, Bonneville's) hinted at interior drainage Preuss's were the first to define it; she also presents an excellent survey of the maps of the time. Frémont's search is documented on pp. 271, 310, 315–20, 337, 368–69.

202 William C. Darrah, ed., "George Y. Bradley's Journal May 24 —August 30, 1869," *Utah Hist. Quar.* 15(1947):31–72, is one of the better accounts of Powell's first trip. Quotes, pp. 37 and 44.

208 Kelly, *Outlaw Trail,* p. 159: Cassidy rode from Robbers Roost to Ouray in 3 days, and on the 5th rode down Crouse Creek into Browns Park.

209 Denver *Post,* 25 August 1974; the Paraho process is now being tested.

210 A. C. Veatch, *Geography and Geology of a Portion of Southwestern Wyoming,* U.S.G.S. Profess. Paper 56 (Washington, D.C., 1907), and H. S. Gale, *Coal Fields of Northwestern Colorado and Northeastern Utah,* U.S.G.S. Bulletin 415 (1910), describe field methods. Gale was engaged in preliminary examination and classification of public lands, retracing old section lines, trying to establish township boundaries, etc.; p. 15: "This was done with a pocket compass, the distance being measured by pacing and checked by the corners that were found along the lines. An average of about five working days for one man was devoted to each township, and this may serve as a rough measure of the detail that could be obtained in such a review of the area."

211 There are two Wild Horse benches on the Green River, this and another some 60 miles downstream.

12 WILD HORSE BENCH TO GREEN RIVER, UTAH

Quadrangles: Uteland Butte, Utah. Following are all 15-min. series: Nutters Hole, Firewater Canyon, Flat Canyon, Range Creek, Gunnison Butte, and Green River, Utah.

217 Frank E. Williams, Paul L. Russell, and M. J. Sheridan, *Potential Applications for Nuclear Explosives in a Shale-Oil Industry* (Washington, D.C.: U.S. Department of Interior, Bureau of Mines, 1969); most of the oil companies involved in exploration have promotional pamphlets and brochures for the asking, as well as fairly expensive publications, such as Colony Develop-

ment Operation of Atlantic Richfield: *An Environmental Impact Analysis for a Shale Oil Complex at Parachute Creek, Colorado,* and *Oil Shale: A Symposium for Environmetal Leaders: The Colony Case Study.* Thoughtful reading of reports such as these can only make one agree with Gary Soucie, "Oil Shale—Pandora's New Box," *Audubon* 74(1): 106–112: "Oil shale may be the most complex and perplexing environmental and natural resource conservation problem in history, involving as it does the whole chronicle of federal land and resource policy." Deputy Under Secretary of Interior Jared C. Carter says a 100,000 barrel-per-day oil-shale plant would require 20 000 acre-feet of water annually, and others estimate one barrel of shale oil will require 3½ barrels of water (*High Country News,* 10 May 1974); see also "AEC Doubts Shale Will Fill Energy Gap," Denver *Post,* 28 April 1974.

218 Powell, *The Exploration of the Colorado River and its Canyons,* p. 119: "For scientific work, we have two sextants, four chronometers, a number of barometers, thermometers, compasses, and other instruments." On the 1869 trip they proposed taking readings every 50 miles for longitude and latitude, and barometric readings three times a day.

220 Stegner, *Beyond the Hundredth Meridian,* pp. 197–98: "Later surveys of the river had had less unnamed country to work with and less imagination to turn loose. Since 1923 the fashion has been strictly practical. As plans for reclamation dams have crept down the canyons, surveyors' instead of explorers' language has come with them. Now on the detailed maps you will find every previously unnamed gulch and wash labeled for its distance from the head of the survey. . . . Now they are Six Mile Wash and One Hundred and Thirty Mile Canyon. . . . At their very worst, Powell and Dutton did not name by transit or plane table or chain. Bright Angle Creek and Sockdolager Rapid . . . seem livelier than Hundred and Ten Mile Point or 38° 40' Spring."

228 Stone, *Canyon Country,* pp. 66–67.

230–31 LeRoy Hafen, *Old Spanish Trail* (Glendale, California: Arthur H. Clark, 1954), pp. 305–16, the actual trail crossing was about 3 or 4 miles north of the present town of Green River and about 5 miles below the mouth of Gray Canyon; facing p. 311 is a sketch of the crossing by R. H. Kern, with the Gunnison Expedition. See also Nolie Mumey, *John Williams Gunnison* (Denver: Artcraft Press, 1955).

Edwin Beckwith, *Report of Exploration for the Pacific Railroad on the Line of the Forty-first Parallel of North Latitude* (Washington, D.C., 1854), p. 62.

231–2 Bardach, *Downstream,* pp. 237–42, discusses riparian rights and problems.

232 Mancos Formation clam shells, all from Department of Geology and Geophysics, University of Utah: *Collingnoniceras* species, UUIP K–137; *C. woollgari,* UUIP K–163, from Emery County, Utah; *Inoceramus* species, UUIP K–186, and no catalogue number; all from Emery County. *Scaphites warreni,* collection of Jerry Vaninetti, found just west of Green River, Utah.

233 Dr. James Schiel, *Journey through the Rocky Mountains and the Humboldt Mountains to the Pacific Ocean,* in Mumey, *Gunnison,* pp. 86–87.

Naval Oil Reserve blocked on the Green River quadrangle goes back to pre-World War I. Boyd Guthrie, *Studies of Certain Properties of Oil Shale and Shale Oil* (U.S.D.I., Bureau of Mines, 1938), p. 3: the bureau's early study of oil shale resulted in an executive order signed by President Wilson, Dec. 6, 1916, to establish two oil-shale reserves "to be held for the exclusive use or benefit of the United States Navy . . . Naval Oil-Shale Reserve 2 is in

Utah, east of the Green River, about 50 miles north of Elgin, on the Denver & Rio Grand Western R.R." Information about the naming of Green River, Writer's Program of Works Projects Administration for the State of Utah, *Utah* (New York: Hastings House, 1941).

13 GREEN RIVER, UTAH, TO FORT BOTTOM

The only standard 7.5-min. quadrangle is that of Green River, Utah. Those from here to the confluence are in rough black and white only; James Keogh, U.S.G.S., Denver, tells me that they were printed in 1951 for uranium exploration; they have never been translated into standard quadrangle maps, nor is such mapping currently authorized. These are: Tidwell 1 NW, Tidwell 1 SW, Tidwell 1 SE, Tidwell 4 NE, Tidwell 4 SE, Moab 3 SW, Orange Cliffs 1 SE, Carlisle 2 SW, Carlisle 3 NW, Utah. There are 15-min. maps of Bowknot Bend, Upheaval Dome, and the Needles. The scale of "Canyonlands National Park and Vicinity" is 1:62500 and begins south of Green River at Bowknot Bend. River guidebooks are by Bill and Buzz Belknap, *Canyonlands River Guide* (Boulder City, Nevada: Westwater Books, 1974) and Felix E. Mutschler, *River Runners' Guide, etc. Labyrinth, Stillwater, and Cataract Canyon* (Denver: Powell Society, 1969). James A. Peterson, ed., *Geology and Economic Deposits of East Central Utah* (Salt Lake City: Intermountain Assoc. Petr, Geol., 1956) has articles of interest, including stratigraphy, mineral development on public lands, and gem collecting.

237 Robert B. Stanton, *Down the Colorado,* ed. Dwight L. Smith (Norman: University of Oklahoma Press, 1965), p. 39.

237–38 Helen J. Stiles, ed., "Down the Colorado in 1889," *The Colorado Magazine* 41, no. 3(1964):225–46. Kendrick's original journal is deposited in the Documentary Resources Department, The State Historical Society of Colorado, in Denver. Kendricks last entry on May 18 reads: "Got in Denver at 7 A.M. reported to Brown & was unable to get away until 3 P.M. He seems to be well pleased with our work. Then went home with M. G. & saw my Darlings once more. How nice it is to be at home again. I have given up going back as I think a mans place is near home & those he loves rather than far away even if he does not make so much money or gain as much glory."

For other attempts at navigating the Green, Marston, "River Runners," and Woolley, *Green River,* p. 54. The last spike of the railroad was driven March 30, 1883, a few miles west of town. See also C. Gregory Crampton, *Standing Up Country* (New York: Knopf and University of Utah Press and Amon Carter Museum of Western Art, 1965), a handsomely illustrated historical account of this area.

240 Frederick S. Dellenbaugh, *The Romance of the Colorado River* (1902, reprint Chicago: Rio Grande Press, 1965).

Stephen V. Jones, "Journal of Stephen Vandiver Jones," April 21, 1871–December 14, 1872, ed. Herbert E. Gregory, *Utah Hist. Quart.* 16(1948):19–173, pp. 73–74.

241 Powell, *The Exploration of the Colorado River and its Canyons,* p. 203. On the U.S.G.S. map *Trin Alcove* is called Three Canyons.

246 Helen L. Cannon, *Description of Indicator Plants and Methods of Botanical Prospecting for Uranium Deposits on the Colorado Plateau,* U.S.G.S. Bulletin 1030–M (Washington, D.C., 1957), pp. 339–516, and "The Effect of Uranium-Vanadium Deposits on the Vegetation of the Colorado Plateau," *Am. Jour. Sci.* 250(1952):735–70.

246 Leopold, *Water: A Primer*, pp. 86–87, and *pers. comm.*: the reason for entrenched meanders is simply not known.

251 Dale L. Morgan, introduction to "The Exploration of the Colorado River
and the High Plateaus of Utah by the Second Powell Expedition of 1871–72,"
Utah Hist. Quart. 16(1948):1–9, p. 3: ". . . it must have taken rare courage
and an obstinate belief in himself to induce the mountain man, Denis
Julien, to take his chances in the lower canyons. . . . Five inscriptions
carved by Julien, all dated 1836, and scattered from Stillwater Canyon to
Cataract Canyon, attest an exploration of the canyons. As record of Julien
is lacking after this date, the question arises whether he may have lost his
life in some tumultuous stretch of the river." See also Charles Kelly, "The
Mysterious D. Julien," *Utah Hist. Quart.* 6(1933):83–88, and O. Dock Marston,
"Denis Julien," in Hafen, *Mountain Men*, 7:177–190, p. 188: "This brief
period of Julien's career, and probably tragic end, remain shrouded in
mystery. Fo'klore accepts that he, and his Indian wife, became 'gone beaver'
in the rapids. Obscurely he lived and obscurely died."

14 FORT BOTTOM TO TURKS HEAD

260 Donald Baars, "Permian System of the Colorado Plateau," *Am. Assoc. Petr.
Geol. Bull.* 46, no. 2(1962):149–218, and Baars and W. R. Seager, "Stratigraphic Control of Petroleum in White Rim Sandstone (Permian) in and
near Canyonlands National Park, Utah," *ibid.*, 54 (1970):709–18. Dr. Baars,
pers. comm., points out that the older usage of "Cutler Formation" with three
members is prevalent in most U.S.G.S. literature as well as the *River Runners'
Guide*. The Cutler now has group status, containing four formations—White
Rim Sandstone, Organ Rock Shale, Cedar Mesa Sandstone, and Halgaito
Shale—of which the first three are exposed in Stillwater.

265–66 For Fremont in Canyonlands, see Floyd W. Sharrock, *An Archeological
Survey of Canyonlands National Park* (Salt Lake City: University of Utah,
Department of Anthropology, Number 83, miscel'aneous collected papers
11–14, November, 1966). Robert F. Burgh and Charles R. Scoggin, *The
Archaeology of Castle Park, Dinosaur National Monument* (Boulder,
Colorado: University of Colorado Studies, Series in Anthropology, 1948), p.
71: "Whatever the cliff decorations may have meant to the aboriginal artist,
for us they have little symbolic or narrative significance. It is a matter of
regret that the Indians did not use their art to inform us, but we can only
deplore their neglect." Rudolf Arnheim, *Art and Visual Perception* (Berkeley:
University of California Press, 1971), p. 295: "To assert that these are
children's or primitives' misconceptions eradicated by modern science would
mean closing our eyes to universal visual experiences which are reflected in
artistic presentations. Our image of the world is all but unchanged because
it is dictated by compelling percepetual conditions that prevail everywhere
and always."

269 Leopold, Wolman, and Miller, *Fluvial Processes*, p. 76; and Woolley, *Green
River*, p. 159. The sediment measure was made at Green River, Utah. No data
are available for lower on the Green.

15 WATER CANYON TO THE CONFLUENCE

273–74 Donald Baars, William Parker, and John Chronic, "Revised stratigraphic
nomenclature of Pennsylvanian System, Paradox Basin," *Bull. Amer. Assoc.*

Petr. Geol. 51(1967):393–403, p. 395, defines the newer nomenclature for the rock strata below the Cutler Group. Formerly called the Hermosa Formation, it is now the Hermosa Group. The Cedar Mesa Sandstone was probably a near-shore marine to coastal dune deposit, the source of which was somewhere to the northwest of Canyonlands. See also William W. Mallory, "Pennsylvanian Coarse Arkosic Redbed and Associated Mountains in Colorado," Rocky Mountains Association of Geologists, Symposium on Pennsylvania Rocks of Colorado and Adjacent Areas, *Guidebook,* 1958.

276   J. W. Powell *Explanations of the Colorado River and Its Canyons,* p. 209.

276–77 George R. Stewart, *Names on the Land* (New York: Random House, 1945), documents the history of the name change.

The inhospitality of this region is reflected in the sparsity of documents about it; most are the journals of river runners—Powell and his men, Kolb, Stone. However remote, the confluence was once thought of as a reservoir: E. C. LaRue, *Colorado River Utilization,* p. 134: "The largest known reservoir site in the area drained by the Colorado is that at the junction of Green and Grand rivers. A dam to raise the water level 270 feet, constructed on the Colorado immediately below this junction, would create a reservoir having storage capacity of 8,600,000 acre-feet. Recent investigations by the Reclamation Service throw some doubt on the feasibility of developing this site on account of the absence of satisfactory foundation for a high dam." W. L. Rusho, ed., "River Running in 1921: The Diary of E. L. Kolb," *Utah Hist. Quart.* 37(1969):269–83, records the mapping expedition of the U.S.G.S. and Southern California Edison Company. Kolb (p. 277) noted that the first suitable spot for a dam was some way downstream, "but the walls are rotten, just as they have been all through, and wide apart."

The only land journey is that of Captain J. N. Macomb, *Report on the Exploring Expedition from Santa Fe, New Mexico, to the Junction of the Grand and Green Rivers of the Great Colorado of the West* (Washington, D.C., 1876), who, in 1859, made base camp just northeast of the confluence. Professor J. S. Newbury, geologist with the expedition, described the scene as they stood some 1,300 feet above and looked down (p. 87): "Perhaps four miles below our position [Grand River] is joined by another great chasm coming in from the northwest, said by the Indians to be that of Green River. From the point where we were it was inaccessible, but we had every reason to credit their report in reference to it."

INDEX

Page numbers in *italic* refer to illustrations.

LODORE